THE ROOTS
OF PAGAN ANTI-SEMITISM
IN THE ANCIENT WORLD

SUPPLEMENTS TO
NOVUM TESTAMENTUM

VOLUME XLI

LEIDEN
E. J. BRILL
1975

THE ROOTS
OF PAGAN ANTI-SEMITISM
IN THE ANCIENT WORLD

BY

J. N. SEVENSTER

LEIDEN
E. J. BRILL
1975

Published with financial support from the Netherlands
Organization for the Advancement of Pure Research (Z.W.O.)

ISBN 90 04 04193 1

PRINTED IN BELGIUM

CONTENTS

I am greatly indebted to the Netherlands Organisation for the Advancement of Pure Research (Z.W.O.) for having provided the financial support which made possible the publication of this work.

This is the second work which Mrs. de Bruin has translated into English for me. Again I thank her sincerely for the amount of work, attention and care she has devoted to it.

I am grateful to ... and to the Netherlands Organization for the Advancement of Pure Research (Z.W.O.) for the ... which made possible the publication of this book.

INTRODUCTION

The term anti-Semitism is not old and was apparently first used by W. Marr, who began the publication of his *Zwanglose antisemitische Hefte* in 1880.[1] Obviously it expresses most inadequately what it is usually taken to mean. This holds good for the present and certainly for the ancient world. The word suggests a racial distinction which, scientifically, is highly disputable and, to say the least, doubtful. The coupling of intellectual to physical characteristics usually results in the postulation of all sorts of dilettantish contentions bereft of any scholastic foundation whatsoever and worth little or no serious consideration, were it not that they have already contributed to those explosions of destructive madness which have cost the lives of millions.

The term Semites encompasses, moreover, other peoples as well as the Jews. It is not surprising, therefore, that the grand mufti of Jerusalem once complained to Alfred Rosenberg about the use of the term anti-Semitism, because he considered it derogatory towards some Semites. Naturally the objection to the use of this term applies equally to the ancient world. Babylonians and Arabs are just as Semitic as the Jews.

It has long been realised that there are objections to the term anti-Semitism, and therefore an endeavour has been made to find a word which better interprets the meaning intended. Already in 1936 Bolkestein, for example, wrote an article on *Het "antisemietisme" in de oudheid* (Anti-Semitism in the ancient world) in which the word was placed between quotation marks and a preference was expressed for the term hatred of the Jews.[2] But this term does not do full justice to the diversity of feelings towards the Jews in the ancient world, not even when of a hostile nature. The contempt, even the venomous irony, of various Roman authors was often really a symptom of hatred of the Jews and Judaism, but the feelings enter-

---

[1] Cf. I. Heinemann, Art. Antisemitismus in *Paulys Real-Encyclopädie der classischen Altertumswissenschaft*, Supplementband V, 1931, p. 3; F. Lovsky, *Antisémitisme et mystère d'Israël*, 1955, p. 9; H. Bolkestein, Het "anti-semietisme" in de oudheid, *De socialistische gids*, 1936, p. 155; Art. Anti-Semitism in *Encyclopaedia Juduica*, 3, 1971, p. 87.

[2] Bolkestein, *op. cit.*, pp. 152ff.

tained for them would be too circumscribed if classified under this heading.

Nowadays the term anti-Judaism is often preferred. It certainly expresses better than anti-Semitism the fact that it concerns the attitude to the Jews and avoids any suggestion of racial distinction, which was not, or hardly, a factor of any significance in ancient times. For this reason Leipoldt preferred to speak of anti-Judaism when writing his *Antisemitismus in der alten Welt* (1933).[3] Bonsirven also preferred this word to anti-Semitism, "mot moderne qui implique une théorie des races".[4]

Nevertheless, there are objections to the use of this word, the most important being that the word Judaism has long been used to indicate specifically certain trends in certain periods of Jewish religion and, in this respect, to characterise certain trends of thought in other periods. To Judaise always means to conform to Jewish customs (ἰουδαΐζειν). In *Esther* many of the people of the land are said to have been circumcised and to have become Jews "for the fear of the Jews fell upon them" (πολλοὶ τῶν ἐθνῶν περιετέμοντο καὶ ἰουδάϊζον διὰ τὸν φόβον τῶν Ἰουδαίων, *Esther* 8.17). Josephus relates how the commander Metilius, sole survivor of a Roman garrison that had been attacked and annihilated, saved his life by pleading and by promising to become a Jew and even to allow himself to be circumcised (—μέχρι περιτομῆς ἰουδαΐσειν ὑποσχόμενον *B.J.* I I.454). Further on in the same book he says that the Syrians believed that they had dealt once and for all with the Jews in their midst, but that every city had its Judaisers who were bound to arouse suspicion (—ἕκαστοι τοὺς ἰουδαΐζοντας εἶχον ἐν ὑποψίᾳ *B.J.* II.463).

Judaism thus became a certain way of life, thought and belief. It was in this sense that Paul used the words Ἰουδαϊσμός and ἰουδαΐζειν (Gal. 1.13ff., 2.14). Ignatius categorically rejects such Judaising, such Judaism, and pronounces it incompatible with Christianity (Magn. 8.1; 10.3). In later times "Judaising" was also repeatedly used in this sense.[5]

Does this necessarily imply that wherever such Judaising, such Judaism was condemned and combatted there was anti-Semitism?

---

[3] J. Leipoldt, *Antisemitismus in der alten Welt*, 1933, p. 7; cf. B. Lazare, *L'Antisémitisme. Son histoire et ses causes*, 1894, p. 2.

[4] J. Bonsirven S.J., *Le judaisme palestinien au temps de Jésus-Christ*, I, 1935, p. 3.

[5] Cf. e.g. J.E. Seaver, *Persecution of the Jews in the Roman Empire (300-438)*, 1952, pp. 34f.

Some deny this categorically and consider this lack of clear distinction between anti-Semitism and anti-Judaism a serious matter. Lovsky, for example, highly praises the work of Juster, *Les Juifs dans l'empire romain*, but considers the author's failure to distinguish between these two concepts a drawback.[6] On this point he wishes to make a clear distinction : "anti-Judaism is a given theological choice, which often implies a condemnation of certain thoughts within Jewry, of a certain Jewish way of living". Little wonder, then, that some groups within Christendom were reproached by others within that same Christendom with Judaising. Lovsky gives a few striking examples of this.[7] Hence it is quite clear that the terms Judaism and Judaise can be used in theological discussion without referring personally to Jews. In this sense he can therefore say : "l'Évangile chrétien doit être considéré comme un anti-judaïsme résolu". According to him the Gospel is anti-Judaistic, but not anti-Semitic. The same applies, for example, to the Apostolicum : "*Le Symbole des Apôtres*, pleinement antijudaïque, n'est nullement antisémite". If Judaism obstinately rejects the trinitarian dogma, is not Berdjajev correct in saying : "Là gît l'abîme qui sépare la conscience chrétienne de la conscience israélite" ? Lovsky believes so, but for him this is in no way an expression of anti-Semitism. One must simply accept the fact that Christianity and Judaism differ. On this point for example, a Christian is anti-Judaistic and a Jew anti-Christian.[8]

Isaac admits that the term anti-Semitism is ambiguous, but objects to the term anti-Judaism as used by Lovsky. Does it not give rise to regrettable confusion, because it implies a certain definition of Judaism that ought to be formulated more precisely ? Is it certain that the Gospel should be considered to be positively anti-Judaistic, or is it only so in the eyes of a Christian reared according to a given theological teaching ?[9] Simon likewise thinks Lovsky's distinction rather unfortunate. He prefers the use of anti-Judaism as a preciser and more fitting synonym for anti-Semitism, and for what Lovsky calls anti-Judaism he prefers the term anti-Jewish polemic. But whichever term is used, there is undoubtedly a great difference. At times the anti-Jewish polemic can, indeed, be anti-Semitic in

---

[6] Lovsky, *op. cit.*, p. 174.

[7] Ib., p. 13f.

[8] Ib., p. 16f.

[9] J. Isaac, *Genèse de l'antisémitisme*, 1956, p. 26.

form and manner of argumentation in the sense usually attached to this term, but not so with respect to principle and essence.[10]

This distinction must be maintained. Lovsky is right in arguing again and again that what he calls anti-Judaism does not necessarily have to lead to anti-Semitism in the usual sense of that word. One need not go so far as to agree with his thesis that the Gospel must be considered a definite anti-Judaism; one might at least, like Isaac, append a question mark when that thesis is formulated in such general terms. Still one must admit the possibility of an anti-Jewish polemic on certain points—a discussion on Jewish thought and life that is sometimes carried on critically—without any question of anti-Semitism in the usual sense of that word. Admittedly such polemic can at times easily tend towards anti-Semitism, and anti-Semites can at times make all too ready use of it. Lovsky does not deny this. He knows there can be an "avilissement d'un antijudaïsme en anti-sémitisme", but believes that the disguises of the hatred so characteristic of anti-Semitism are easily recognized.[11] Here, I believe, he tends to underestimate the wiliness of anti-Semitism and to lose sight of those subtle gradations between the two conceptions which cannot always be easily fathomed. Still it would be wrong to cease all anti-Jewish polemic and to avoid critical pronouncements for fear of the dangers lurking here, for the fact remains that anti-Judaism in that sense and anti-Semitism are not identical. Isaac's thesis goes too far in the opposite direction: "L'antijudaïsme mène le plus souvent à l'antisémitisme, et tous deux sont très étroitement entremêlés".[12]

All this demonstrates clearly that the use of the term anti-Judaism is also beset with problems. Perhaps, after all, it is better to go on using the word anti-Semitism no matter how susceptible it is of misunderstandings and of suggesting to the modern mind a racial distinction that was scarcely, or not at all, a factor in the ancient world. The simple fact is that it has become the current term for a "grundsätzlich unfreundliche Gesinnung und Haltung gegen Juden",[13] a "sentiment ou préjugé antijuif",[14] the essence of which Simon has very aptly described as "une attitude fondamentalement et systématiquement hostile aux Juifs, fondée par surcroît sur des mauvaises

---

[10] M. Simon, *Verus Israel*, ²1964, p. 493.

[11] Lovsky, *op. cit.*, pp. 20f.

[12] Isaac, *op. cit.*, pp. 26f.

[13] Heinemann, *op. cit.*, p. 3.

[14] Isaac, *op. cit.*, p. 26.

raisons, sur des calomnies, sur une image incomplète, partiale ou fausse de la réalité".[15] This description applies to the ancient as well as the modern world. One can go further and ask what ultimately forms the basis of that systematic hostility towards the Jews. Is anti-Semitism a deliberate or blind revolt of the peoples against the God who chose Israel ? Is it really always the same human rebellion against the Sovereign of the world ? Does it not, in fact, always hate that sovereignty of God of which Israel is the witness ?[16] Hatred of the Jews, even in antiquity, undoubtedly springs from a more or less conscious vexation with the exclusiveness, the distinctive behaviour of the Jews proceeding from their way of living and thinking in accordance with the Torah. We shall encounter again and again this vexation, sometimes explicit, sometimes tacit, but present nonetheless. The obvious interpretation of such vexation is a theological one, but there are dangers involved in placing an historical inquiry within such a framework. From the very beginning the inclination will then be to assume there was such a revolt among all pagan peoples against the revelation of God's sovereignty, manifested in their attitude toward Israel. Chances are, then, that the historical facts would be twisted, deliberately or not, to fit into such a framework of a theological or other nature. It is a common thought that in the ancient world, too, anti-Semitism was as old as Israel itself and that it occurred in every age and everywhere among all the ancient peoples in whose midst Israel lived. Perhaps there is no author who has illustrated with so many examples "le thème de l'éternel antisémitisme" and thereafter combatted it so vigorously as Isaac.[17] Indeed, it is remarkable how often this theme recurs in diverse forms of modern literature, and it would not be difficult to add many more examples to those given by Isaac. For example, a Jewish writer says of anti-Semitism : "Sous sa forme actuelle, il est apparu à la naissance du judaïsme, au moment du pacte sacré que l'Éternel scella avec Abraham".[18] And Lovsky, who cites him, evidently agrees with him for he writes : "La source de l'antisémitisme, aussi durable que le genre humain, jaillit de l'élection d'Israel". This postulation recurs repeatedly in a non-theological form as well. With reference to the ancient world,

---

[15] Simon, *op. cit.*, p. 488.

[16] Lovsky, *op. cit.*, p. 19; cf. M. Barth, *Jesus, Paulus und die Juden*, 1967, pp. 20, 52ff.

[17] Isaac, *op. cit.*, pp. 29ff.

[18] Moïse Engelson, quoted by Lovsky, *op. cit.*, p. 18.

the famous German scholar Mommsen writes: "Der Judenhass und die Judenhetzen sind so alt wie die Diaspora selbst". But in his following words he gives a very prosaic reason: "diese privilegirten und autonomen orientalischen Gemeinden innerhalb der hellenischen mussten sie so nothwendig entwicklen wie der Sumpf die böse Luft".[19] Heinemann emphatically repudiates this representation of the matter: "Vor 88 v.Chr. hat es in der Diaspora aller Wahrscheinlichkeit nach überhaupt keine Judenhetze gegeben, und auch später nur da, wo man vor allem an der Macht der jüdischen Siedelungen Anstoss nimmt".[20]

Now that is what Isaac and a few other writers are always contending: if we adhere to the historical facts, our conclusion must be that manifest attestations of anti-Semitism in the ancient world are discernible only in the first century B.C., whereas the Diaspora is much older. Prior to that time, there were various Greek writers who made no mention whatever of the Jews which could warrant the conclusion that Greek travellers, who were often inquisitive enough, sometimes found nothing about this people strange enough to merit attention or to appeal to their imagination. Other ancient writers do mention the Jews and their cult, but in terms of praise. Isaac and those who think along the same lines emphasize the fact that whenever anti-Semitism very unmistakably occurs in the ancient world, there are few references to it in the texts, and they therefore conclude that the "Jewish question" was of secondary importance only for the people of those days. After citing the testimonials about the Jews to be found in the Roman writers, Isaac concludes that they are really very few in number: "simples broutilles au total, gouttes d'eau perdues dans la mer d'une vaste production littéraire".[21] And Poliakov does not consider it necessary to devote more than 10 pages to ancient pagan anti-Semitism in the first volume of his history of anti-Semitism.[22]

It is on the very question of the belittling of ancient pagan anti-Semitism as revealed in the above-mentioned quotations that Isaac has been criticised. Such anti-Semitic pronouncements as are found in the diverse ancient writers may not be treated as insignificant trivialities. According to Lovsky, Tacitus and Martial were read by

---

[19] Th. Mommsen, *Römische Geschichte*, V, [4]1894, p. 519.

[20] Heinemann, *op. cit.*, p. 19.

[21] Isaac, *op. cit.*, p. 116.

[22] L. Poliakov, *Histoire de l'antisémitisme*, I, 1955, pp. 19-29.

more people and over a longer period than the Church Fathers, whose readers' circle was very limited.[23] Prompted by Isaac's statement, Simon also believes that the role of ancient pagan anti-Semitism must definitely not be qualified as insignificant, even when seen from the viewpoint of later centuries.[24] Sometimes Isaac gives the impression of representing that ancient pagan anti-Semitism as unimportant as possible, so that he can let the blame for the later anti-Semitism fall with full force on the Christian church. That is understandable as reaction to various efforts to minimise and condone that blame, but it is possible that letting the historical facts speak for themselves and abandoning the traditional constructions urged repeatedly by Isaac could prove him wrong at times.

The upshot of all this is that due account must be taken of the nature and the dating of the sources when evaluating the significance of anti-Semitism in the ancient world. If, in describing that phenomenon, only those data which testify to hostility towards the Jews are cited, and if, moreover, they are cited arbitrarily out of their chronological order, an impressive image could be drawn of an "eternal anti-Semitism", but it would be a grossly exaggerated one that failed to conform with the historical reality. Isaac has rightly condemned this sort of treatment of the subject by many writers and has pointed out that, to do justice to the data, they must be placed in their proper chronological order and in their proper position within the framework of historical reality.[25] This having been done, the inevitable conclusion is that for certain regions and periods the data needed to describe anti-Semitism are very scarce and often entirely lacking. Even in the case of the vicissitudes of the Jews of Alexandria, about which we are reasonably well informed for certain periods, the truth of the matter is to be found in the comment of an author who is an expert on the history of that city : "Unsere Quellen für die Geschichte der jüdischen Gemeinde im alten Alexandria sind leider zufällig und fragmentarisch : für gewisse Zeiträume verhältnismässig reich, für andere spärlich oder gar nicht vorhanden".[26]

On the other hand, it is questionable whether the numerous testimonials of ancient writers about anti-Semitism may be treated lightly

---

[23] Lovsky, *op. cit.*, p. 75[1].

[24] Simon, *op. cit.*, p. 491.

[25] Isaac, *op. cit.*, p. 111.

[26] H.I. Bell, *Juden und Griechen im römischen Alexandreia*, [2]1927, Vorwort.

as drops of water lost in the sea of a vast literary production.[27] In
view of the divergent periods and places of those pronouncements,
they must, indeed, be said to be very scarce. But it should be remembered that the lack of testimonials from other periods and regions
naturally does not prove that there were no outbreaks of anti-Semitism
then and there, nor any occurrences of anti-Semitism in writing, in
words or in deeds. After all, our entire picture of the ancient world
rests on a relatively fortuitous selection of extant data, and that
is especially true of the present subject. It is an established fact
that in long periods Jews lived in practically all parts of the Roman
empire. Juster, already, compiled an imposing list of the regions
and places where, according to all sorts of data, there were Jewish
settlements, and those data have been greatly augmented since the
year in which his classic work appeared.[28] In all those regions and
places the Jews lived together with their non-Jewish fellow citizens.
No doubt they often lived in harmony and had peaceful relations
with each other, but it goes without saying that there was also
friction, sometimes culminating in more or less violent outbreaks,
such as those better known to us by chance from certain periods
and places. Besides, there were probably more writers who expressed
anti-Semitic sentiments than just those we happen to know of.[29]

Here and there are indications, that the relatively few testimonials
of anti-Semitism in the ancient world which have been handed down
to us may not be looked upon as scattered, stray remarks of little
significance. Certain anti-Semitic themes recur again and again. And
one often wonders along which hidden ways they have been handed
down to us, and whether all sorts of literary links, now lost to us,
nevertheless once existed. One of these themes is, for example, the
contention that the Jews worship the ass and that this is why there
was an ass's head in their temple. The earliest witness to this fable
known to us is Mnaseas, who probably lived in the second century B.C.
In different versions this story recurs in Apollonius Molon, who

---

[27] Isaac, *op. cit.*, p. 116.

[28] J. Juster, *Les Juifs dans l'empire romain*, I, 1914, pp. 179-212; cf. Th. Hopfner,
Die Judenfrage bei Griechen und Römern, 1943, pp. 71-84; J.N. Sevenster, *Do you
know Greek*, 1968, pp. 77ff.

[29] A summary of the Greek and Roman writers on this subject is given in the still
important, though no longer complete work of Th Reinach, *Textes d'auteurs grecs
et romains relatifs au judaïsme*, 1895 (reprint 1963) The same applies to the description
of the sources for our knowledge of this subject in Juster, *op. cit.*, pp. 1-39, 119-158.

was the first to write a pamphlet directed entirely against the Jews, in Posidonius, Damocritus, Apion, Plutarch and Tacitus.[30] If the *Histories* of the last-named is placed at the beginning of the second century A.D., this story can then be traced throughout three centuries, in very divergent places. In three different ways the origins of the ass-worship are explained by these writers, but the ass-cult of the Jews was apparently a wide-spread motif.[31] A much-discussed point is where this story of the Jewish ass-cult came from. Even now the solutions given greatly vary, and not one of them can be said to be supported by absolutely convincing evidence.[32] In any case the fact that this story keeps on cropping up in the course of several centuries would seem to support the hypothesis that certain connections must have existed through a legend we can no longer trace in its entirety. The different versions of the story must have had their own sources, too. In a subordinate clause Plutarch, for example, states that the Jews worship the ass which helped them discover a water-spring (τὸν ὄνον ἀναφήναντα πηγήν αὐτοῖς ὕδατος τιμῶσιν).[33] Tacitus describes this motif in much more detail. When the Jews departed from Egypt, they set out on their journey in utter ignorance, but trusting to chance. Nothing caused them so much distress as scarcity of water, and in fact they had already fallen exhausted over the plain nigh unto death, when a herd of wild asses moved from their pasturage to a rock that was shaded by a grove of trees. Moses followed them, and, conjecturing the truth from the grassy ground discovered abundant streams of water. This relieved them. Further on Tacitus refers to this story in the words: to establish his influence over this people for all time, Moses introduced new religious practices, quite opposed to those of all other religions. The Jews regard as profane all that we hold sacred; on the other hand,

---

[30] Reinach, *op. cit.*, pp. 50, 58, 121, 131, 139, 305.

[31] Heinemann, *op. cit.*, pp. 20f., 28ff.; cf. A.M.A. Hospers-Jansen, *Tacitus over de Joden*, 1949, pp. 122ff.; J. Bergmann, *Jüdische Apologetik im neutestamentlichen Zeitalter*, 1908, pp. 152-154.

[32] Cf. A. Jacoby, Der angebliche Eselskult der Juden und Christen, *Archiv für Religionswissenschaft*, 25 (1927), pp. 265ff.; E. Bickermann, Ritualmord und Eselskult, *Monatsschrift für Geschichte und Wissenschaft des Judentums*, 71 (1927), pp. 171ff., 255ff.; Hospers-Jansen, *op. cit.*, pp. 122ff.; Heinemann, *op. cit.*, pp. 28ff.; V.A. Tcheri-kover, *Hellenistic Civilization and the Jews*, 1961, pp. 365f.; F.M.Th. Böhl, Die Juden im Urteil der griechischen und römischen Schriftsteller, *Theologisch Tijdschrift*, 48 (1914), pp. 484-488.

[33] Reinach, *op. cit.*, p. 139: Plutarch, *Quaest. Conv.* IV. 5.

they permit all that we abhor. They dedicated, in a shrine, a statue
of that creature whose guidance enabled them to put an end to their
wandering and thirst, sacrificing a ram, apparently in derision of
Ammon. They likewise offered the ox, because the Egyptians worship
Apis.[34] Which writer was Tacitus' source here? A lost writing of
Pliny the Elder? An Alexandrian writer influenced by Egyptian
traditions? I believe this cannot easily be ascertained.[35]

Tacitus probably did not himself think up the story about the
ass-cult, but borrowed it from another author, since, strangely enough,
he contradicts himself on this point. Shortly after the passage quoted
above he says the Jews, in fact, did not worship any image whatsoever. The Egyptians worship many animals and monstrous images;
the Jews conceive of one God only, and that with the mind alone :
they regard as impious those who make from perishable materials
representations of gods in man's image; that supreme and eternal
being is to them incapable of representation and without end. Therefore
they set up no statues in their cities, still less in their temples; this
flattery is not paid their kings, nor this honour given to the Caesars.[36]
Though this statement disagrees with his aforesaid contention that
the Jews consecrated an image of an ass in a shrine, the contradiction
becomes even more concrete when, in one of the following chapters,
he states : the first Roman to subdue the Jews and set foot in their
temple by right of conquest was Gnaeus Pompey : thereafter it was
a matter of common knowledge that there were no representations
of the gods within, but that the place was empty and the secret
shrine contained nothing.[37]

Tertullian remarked on this contradiction between the different
statements of Tacitus. He disputes the fantastic suggestion that
an ass's head is the god of the Christians and says it is Tacitus who
started such a rumour. Then he cites what Tacitus wrote about
the herd of wild asses who led the Jews to the water. Yet this same
Cornelius Tacitus—no, not Tacit, he, but a first class chatterbox
when it comes to lies (*sane ille mendaciorum loquacissimus*, a pun
on the "*tacere*" in the name Tacitus)—in the same History tells how

---

[34] Tacitus, *Hist*. V. 3,4.

[35] Cf. Hospers-Jansen, *op. cit*., pp. 126f.; on Tacitus' sources in the *Historiae* :
R. Syme, *Tacitus*, 1958, Vol. I, pp. 176-190, on Tacitus' source for Jewish antiquities
and history, p. 78, n. 3; D.R. Dudley, *The World of Tacitus*, 1968, pp. 29ff., 194.

[36] *Hist*. V.5.

[37] *Hist*. V.9.

Gnaeus Pompey, on taking Jerusalem, visited the temple to look into the mysteries of Jewish religion, and found no image there.[38] Tertullian therefore makes grateful use of Tacitus' mendacity and hence of the shaky basis of this fable of ass-worship—a piece of fantasy first imputed to the Jews, but now to the Christians as well— "as being affiliated to the Jewish religion" (*ut Judaicae religionis propinquos*). Naturally this discrepancy has been remarked by modern writers, but it has not led them to accuse Tacitus of deliberate mendacity. In that second part of *Histories* V.5, in which Tacitus says that the Jews permit no images in their cities, let alone their temples, Isaac believes a sudden change of tone can be discerned "comme si un repentir était venu à Tacite". Yet he, too, considers the discrepancy about the worship of images really irreconcilable : "Quel Tacite croirons-nous; lequel des deux—celui pour qui les Juifs ne sont pas idolâtres, ou celui qui les veut idolâtres de l'âne" ?[39] Did Tacitus suddenly realize he was being too severe in his vituperation against the Jews and regret it ? I doubt that and think it more likely that he used different sources. As a result he twice contradicted, in V.5 and 9, what he took unverified from anti-Jewish sources in V.4, and perhaps on both occasions he was not aware of this.[40] In any case the discrepancy shows how greatly Tacitus depended on his sources. It is well worth while to compare the statement about Pompey's experience on entering the temple in Jerusalem with the statements made by Livy, Cicero and Josephus. Even though Tacitus then appears to agree most with Livy, he gives such a personal account of this happening that one wonders whether he used other sources as well, ones unknown to us. We have already seen above (p. 10) that his source for the story about the herd of asses cannot be traced. All this goes to show that anti-Semitic literary works were more numerous than is suggested by the fragments that have been preserved.

More indications of this nature can be given. For example, in his *Legatio ad Gaium* Philo states that Sejanus, the well-known prefect of the Praetorian Guard under Tiberius, once planned a large-scale attack on the Jews. From other sources it is also known that Sejanus' power and influence had been steadily increasing over

---

[38] Tertull., *Apologeticum*, XVI, 1-3.
[39] Isaac, *op. cit.*, pp. 118f.
[40] Hospers-Jansen, *op. cit.*, p. 157.

a long period, until he even began plotting against the principate. This was betrayed to Tiberius by Antonia, widow of Drusus, the emperor's brother. He was then arrested, led before the Senate and put to death in 31 A.D. Of him Philo says he wanted to destroy that race completely (τὸ ἔθνος ἀναρπάσαι θέλοντος) because he knew that, should the Emperor be in danger of being betrayed, it would offer in his defence the only, or the keenest, resistance to treacherous schemes and actions. It is not quite clear whether Philo assumes that Sejanus' attack on the Jews was actually carried out, or never got beyond the stage of a plan. According to Philo in any case, Tiberius realised immediately after Sejanus' death that the accusations made against the Jews were based on completely unfounded calumnies invented by Sejanus. He issued instructions to the governors in office throughout the empire to reassure the members of the Jewish race and to change nothing already sanctioned by custom, but to regard as a sacred trust both the Jews themselves, since they were of peaceful disposition, and their Laws, since they were conducive to public order.[41]

In one other passage, at the beginning of his *In Flaccum*, Philo mentions Sejanus' anti-Jewish mentality. The first sentence of this book relates that the policy of attacking the Jews begun by Sejanus was taken over by Flaccus Avillius. He differed from his predecessor only in that he had not the power to ill-treat outright the whole nation, for he had less opportunities of doing so.[42] This is all Philo has to say about the anti-Jewish machinations of Sejanus. He is the only one of ancient times to mention Sejanus' anti-Semitism. There are probably no grounds whatsoever for doubting the accuracy of his comments on this subject, at least with respect to the main issues. His description of Tiberius' attitude is perhaps rather tendentious, as we hope to demonstrate below. Sources for comparison are available to verify this, but not Philo's comments on Sejanus.

Was this all Philo had to say about Sejanus? The opening words of *In Flaccum* (Δεύτερος μετὰ Σηιανὸν) seem to suggest that from the book handed down to us at least one passage is missing in which Philo mentions Sejanus again. It has even been suggested that he devoted a separate and much more detailed work to this anti-Semite.

---

[41] *Leg.* 159-161.
[42] *In Flaccum* 1.

This assumption is based on diverse comments by Eusebius, especially about the five books in which, according to this Church Father,
Philo relates what befell the Jews under Gaius and also about the
second treatise entitled *"On the virtues"*.[43] It is plainly evident that
Eusebius knew data from the books of Philo which have been handed
down to us. But do the two aforesaid comments infer that he knew
of other works by Philo, or does the statement about the five books
merely refer to the subdivision of *Legatio ad Gaium* known to Eusebius
in the form known to us? Very divergent answers have been given
to these questions. From a careful comparison of Eusebius' remark
and the contents of the works of Philo known to us, some deduce
that a great many of his historical works, as well as part of the
beginning of *In Flaccum*, have been lost, whereas others deduce
that what Eusebius says refers exclusively, or almost exclusively,
to the extant writings of Philo.[44] In any case, my opinion is that
the opening words of *In Flaccum* show that Philo wrote more about
Sejanus than appears from what has been preserved of his works.

If, on the whole, Philo's statement about Sejanus is correct, it
then appears that even in ancient days certain occupants of very
high posts could be extremely dangerous to the Jews because of
their anti-Semitism. An example of such among the caesars is Caligula.
There were undoubtedly other potentates in the ancient world who
were hostile to the Jews, who, according to Philo's expression, differed
from the two named only in that they had fewer opportunities of
doing harm to the Jews, though enough to express their anti-Semitic
sentiments in actual deeds. Moreover it is possible that, in the ancient
world, a certain connection existed between such personages. It
has sometimes been suspected, for example, that Pilate's provocation
of the Jews in Palestine was partly inspired by Sejanus' anti-Semitic
policy. Sejanus had probably great influence in the appointment
of Pilate as prefect of Judaea in 26 A.D., and sometimes the fate
of Sejanus is thought to be reflected in Pilate's line of action. According
to Josephus, the latter aroused the rage of the Jewish people on
various occasions. He introduced into Jerusalem the busts of the

---

[43] Eusebius, *Hist. Eccl.* ii. 5, 6.

[44] An excellent resumé of this discussion, in which inter alia Schürer, Massebieau,
Cohn and Colson participated, is given in E. Mary Smallwood, *Philonis Alexandrini
Legatio ad Gaium*, 1961, pp. 36-42, with as concluding commentary: "The problem
of the structure of Philo's historical works and his 'five books' is one for which a certain
solution is probably unattainable".

emperor that were attached to the military standards when he brought
his army from Caesarea and removed it to winter quarters in Jerusalem;
he used money belonging to the temple for the construction of an
aquaduct (*Ant.* XVIII:55-62; *B.J.* ii. 169-177). Philo says that Pilate
set up guilded shields in Herod's palace in the Holy City. They bore
no figure and nothing else that was forbidden, but only the briefest
possible inscription—the name of the dedicator and that of the person
in whose honour the dedication was made. This in particular roused
a storm of indignation among the Jews. Pilate was in a serious dilemma,
for he had neither the courage to remove what he had once set up,
nor the desire to do anything which would please his subjects, but
at the same time he was well aware of Tiberius' firmness on these
matters. When the Jewish officials saw this, and realized that Pilate
was regretting what he had done, although he did not wish to show
it, they wrote a letter to Tiberius pleading their case as forcibly
as they could to remove the shields at once. (*Leg. ad G.* 299-305).
In my opinion it is indeed possible that Pilate's withdrawal in the
last instance under pressure from Tiberius places this event chronologi-
cally in the later years of Pilate's stay in Judaea and after the fall
of Sejanus, the man who had influenced Pilate's provocative attitude
in the first two incidents.[45]

Certain remarks in the literary sources hint that actions against
the Jews were undertaken in diverse places, though no further information is given about the nature of these events. But they, too, help
us remember that our knowledge of anti-Semitism in the ancient
world is one-sided, and completely coincidental. One example of
this from Cicero's *Pro Flacco*. L. Valerius Flaccus, propraetor of the
province of Asia in 62 B.C., had seized large sums of money which
the Jews of Asia Minor wanted to send to Jerusalem. For this the
Jews had received special permission from the authorities, since as
a rule gold could not be exported. Flaccus ignored this privilege
of the Jews and in consequence landed in trouble. Cicero undertook
his defence. To prove there was no question of common theft in
Flaccus' case, Cicero pointed out that the seizure of the Jews' gold

---

[45] Cf. E. Mary Smallwood, Some Notes on the Jews under Tiberius, *Latomus* XV
(1956), pp. 322ff.; Smallwood, *op. cit.*, pp. 244f.; cf. also P.L. Maier, Sejanus, Pilate
and the Date of the Crucifixion, *Church History*, 37 (1968), pp. 3-13; Bo Reicke,
Neutestamentliche Zeitgeschichte, 1965, pp. 175f.; S. Safrai and M. Stern, *The Jewish
People in the First Century*, 1974, pp. 18, 164, 314, 318, 349ff., 352; M. Grant, *The
Jews in the Roman World*, 1973, pp. 93f., 99.

was openly proposed and published, and the facts show it was administered by excellent men (*viri primarii*). Then Cicero cites a number
of cities where that had happened : in Apamea a little less than a
hundred pounds of gold was seized and weighed before the seat of
the praetor in the forum through the agency of Sextus Caesius, a
Roman knight, an upright and honourable man (*castissimus homo
atque integerrimus*). Something similar had happened in Laodicea,
in Adramyttium, in Pergamum.[46]

Here in the course of counsel's defence a glimpse is given of the
violent clashes which must have occurred in 62 B.C. in certain towns
of Asia Minor, mentioned by name above. If Cicero's speech for
the defence had not been preserved, we would have known nothing
of them. Now we can surmise the sort of scenes that took place in
these towns.

The literary sources having, by now, been examined thoroughly
for pronouncements about the Jews, it need hardly be said that
archeology has enriched our knowledge on a number of points and
is still furnishing new information. Now and then a completely new
light is thrown on events which were already more or less well-known.
For a long time Philo's writings formed the prime sources for describing events and relationships in Alexandria. The first of the so-called
Acts of the Alexandrian Martyrs were published between 1892 and
1898. Some of the names of these Alexandrians were known from
Philo, but here their deeds and words are illuminated from quite
a different angle. Here they are represented as men who fearlessly
dared to speak the truth to the Roman emperor, to reproach him
sharply and sarcastically for being a friend of the Jews and thus
to demonstrate their contempt. Obliquely emerges just how violently
anti-Semitic the writers of the Acts were. Are these writings part
of a literary genre of political pamphlets in which the words and
deeds of these brave martyrs from a Greek polis are completely
imaginary, or do they present, however prejudiced, a description
of actual events and conversations ? No matter what answer is given
to this question, they are still most remarkable testimonials of the
relationships in Alexandria seen from the non-Jewish, anti-Semitic
angle.[47]

---

[46] Reinach, *op. cit.*, pp. 237-241 : *Pro Flacco* XXVIII. 68, 69.
[47] See Victor A. Tcherikover and Alexander Fuchs, *Corpus Papyrorum Judaicarum*
(*CPJ*), II, 1960, pp. 55ff.

In a completely different way a papyrus, first published in 1924 and one of the most important documents in the field of papyrology in general, provides information about the position of the Jews in Alexandria. It is the letter sent by Emperor Claudius to the Alexandrians in reply to their felicitations and the complaints of a Greek embassy on the occasion of his accession in 41 A.D. It also contains a passage about the position of the Jews in Alexandria, which reveals Claudius' opinion about the relationship between the Greek citizens of Alexandria and their Jewish fellow-burghers. He reprimands both groups in words that are not always understandable, though sufficiently so to provide completely new information about the position of the Jews in the civic life of Alexandria. Some scholars are even of the opinion that this letter necessitates a radical revision of the image of the character and personality of Claudius formed prior to the publication of the papyrus. In any case this papyrus is a striking example of how archeological documents can cast an entirely new light on the field of our subject.[48] At the end of the last century our information on the events in Alexandria was almost exclusively derived from Jewish sources, but now a rather clear picture has been obtained of what the Greek citizens of that city and a Roman emperor thought about them, and of just how intensely "the Jewish problem" occupied the minds in many circles of society of that time. Establishing the fact that, in certain periods and places, anti-Semitism caused a greater disturbance of mind among many in all strata of society than was revealed by the sources up to recently, does not necessarily involve ignoring Isaac's warning that our information concerns certain periods and certain places and cannot be used indiscriminately as testimony of *the* anti-Semitism in *the* ancient world.

The third and last example of how papyrus finds have enriched our knowledge concerns the revolt of the Jews under Trajan. It lasted for three years, from 115 to 117 A.D. No precise description of those events is given in the literary sources, though several authors did write about it, of whom Eusebius in greatest detail.[49] He relates how the revolt broke out in the eighteenth year of Trajan (115 A.D.). The combat began between the Jews of Alexandria, Egypt and Cyrene, "as if shaken by a strong and rebellious spirit", and their Greek neighbours. In the following year the revolt became a war.

---

[48] *CPJ* II, pp. 36-55.
[49] *Hist. Eccl.* IV. 2.

At first the Jews had the upper hand, but the Greeks fled to Alexandria, seized the Jews in that city and put them to death. Although the Jews of Cyrene now lacked their support in battle, they continued to plunder the countryside of Egypt and ravage the estates under the command of Loukuas. Then the emperor sent a special commander Marcius Turbo, against them with infantry, navy and cavalry. Only after many battles and some considerable time did he manage to defeat the Jews. He put to death a great number of Jews, not only from Cyrene, but also many who had come from Egypt to assist their king Loukuas. Fearing that this revolt might spread to Mesopotamia, Trajan sent Lucius Quietus to that province to rid it of Jews. There, too, many were killed.

So, according to this story of Eusebius, a conflict between Jews and their Greek fellow-citizens escalated into one of the greatest and most dangerous revolts against the Romans. The war was waged with ruthless cruelty by both sides. This is testified not only by Eusebius, but also by Appianus of Alexandria, who relates how Trajan exterminated the Jews in Egypt.[50] Dio Cassius gives horrible details about the ferocity of the Jews : they massacred Romans and Greeks, they ate the flesh of their victims, made belts of their intestines, they smeared themselves with their blood; they hew many bodies in two, others were thrown to the wild animals or were forced to fight each other as gladiators. In this way they slaughtered 220,000 opponents in Greece and 240,000 in Cyprus.[51]

The papyri which directly or indirectly have to do with these events were discovered during the past decades. Apart from letters from a family archive, they are not inter-related and date from different phases of the revolt. Some deal with events in Alexandria, others with the events in rural areas of Egypt, and frequently they also describe the repercussions of those events on the day-to-day life. Sometimes these papyri confirm what we already knew from the writers, but sometimes they contain data hitherto entirely unknown. With respect to the former, these papyri make it quite clear that the fortunes of war frequently changed. They confirm the cruelty of this war. Again and again evidence is given of the fear of the rural population for enemy action. In a fragment of a letter from Eudaimonis

---

[50] Reinach, *op. cit.*, p. 153 : Appian of Alexandria, *De bellis civilibus* II.90; cf. *CPJ* I, p. 92[86].

[51] Reinach, *op. cit.*, pp. 196f. : Xiphil., *Epitome* LXVIII.32; cf. L. Fuchs, *Die Juden Aegyptens in ptolomäischer und römischer Zeit*, 1924, pp. 26ff.

to Apollonius, this mother writes to her son : with the goodwill of
the gods, above all Hermes the invincible, they may not roast you.[52]

The same passage also contains valuable, new data. Certain chronological statements establish the precise date of some events. The
mention by name of various places and districts proves that the battle
was also waged over the entire countryside of Egypt. It is clearly
evident that there the Egyptian farmers participated in the war
against the Jews. In a papyrus from the second half of 116 A.D.
it is said of the events in the Hermoupolis district : The one hope
and expectation that was left was the push of the massed villagers
from our district against the impious Jews; but now the opposite
has happened. For on the 20th our forces fought and were beaten
and many of them were killed ... now, however, we have received
the news from men coming from ... that another legion of Rutilius
arrived at Memphis on the 22nd and is expected.[53] What emerges
from the papyrus is that the Romans and Egyptian country folk
fought together against the Jews in a furious combat and that, at
times, they were hard put to hold their ground. All available fighting
forces had to be engaged in action. This might also be deduced from
the fact that Apollonius, about whom much is revealed in the family
archive, was in reality a civil servant, but served in the army. So
Greeks, Egyptians and Romans fought side by side in this bitter war
against the Jews. And 80 years later the ultimate victory over the
Jews was celebrated in the Oxyrhynchus district. The inhabitants
of that district are praised for the goodwill, faithfulness and friendship
to the Romans which they exhibited in the war against the Jews,
giving aid then, and even now keeping the day of victory as a festival
every year.[54]

Thus new facts still come to light which sometimes throw a surprising light on the position of the Jews in ancient society and on
the attitude to them of non-Jews.

---

[52] *CPJ* II, pp. 235f.

[53] *CPJ* II, p. 238.

[54] *CPJ* II, pp. 258ff.; cf. *CPJ* I, pp. 86-93, II, pp. 225-260; E.M. Smallwood,
Documents illustrating the principates of Nerva Trajan and Hadrian, 1966, nrs. 55-60,
517; S. Applebaum, Cyrenensia Judaica, *The Journal of Jewish Studies*, 13 (1962),
pp. 31-43; J. Neusner, *A History of the Jews in Babylonia. The Parthian Period*, 1965,
pp. 70-73; H.A. Musurillo, *The Acts of the Pagan Martyrs*, 1954, pp. 182f.; S.W. Baron,
A social and religious history of the Jews, II, [4]1962, pp. 94f.

When endeavouring to construct a picture of anti-Semitism in the ancient world from the literary and archeological data, it must naturally be kept in mind that the information is seldom neutral. Furthermore it is often difficult to distinguish between the truth and fabrication or exaggeration. Objective criteria for making such a distinction are not easily come by. "Manchmal muss man eigentlich auf Gewissheit verzichten, denn von mehreren möglichen Vermutungen verdient keine den unbedingten Vorzug".[55]

Josephus, whose writings constitute one of the main sources for our subject, attaches importance to letting the facts speak for themselves. "My first thought is one of intense astonishment at the current opinion that, in the study of primeval history, the Greeks alone deserve serious attention, that the truth should be sought from them, and that neither we nor any others in the world are to be trusted. In my view the very reverse of this is the case, if, that is to say, we are not to take idle prejudice as our guide, but to extract the truth from the facts themselves (—μὴ ταῖς ματαίαις δόξαις ἐπακολουθεῖν, ἀλλ'ἐξ αὐτῶν τὸ δίκαιον τῶν πραγμάτων λαμβάνειν)".[56] Whether he always adhered to this rule himself is more or less doubted by many, not merely because he makes mistakes in figures and sometimes deliberately exaggerates them, but also because he describes ideas and events according to his own, very particular choice. For example, he evidently feels sympathy for the upper classes of Jewish society. Understandably this is accompanied by a thorough dislike of all sorts of fanatical Jewish revolutionaries.[57] At times these

---

[55] Bell, *op. cit.*, Vorwort.

[56] Jos., *Ap.* i. 6; cf. Clemens Thoma, Die Weltanschauung des Josephus, *Kairos*, *Neue Folge* 11 (1969), p. 51 : "An keiner Stelle seines Bellum Judaicum lässt Josephus den radicalen Aufstandsgruppen, etwa durch Hinweise auf ihre geistig-religiösen Voraussetzungen, Gerechtigkeit widerfahren". According to Thoma this indicates "eine allgemein heilsgeschichtlich-theologisierende Tendenz des Josephus", cf. p. 41 where he says of Jos. that he was "keineswegs ein Geschichtsschreiber 'sine ira et studio' " and reproaches him for "seine weitgehende Verständnislosigkeit der inneren Dramatik, Dynamik und Krisis der damaligen jüdischen Gruppen"; cf. J. Parkes, *The Foundations of Judaism and Christianity*, 1960, p. 240[18]; about Josephus' judgment on Herod see A. Schalit, *König Herodes. Der Mann und sein Werk*, 1969, pp. 646ff.; cf. also F.J. Foakes Jackson, *Josephus and the Jews*, 1930, pp. 257f.; A. Schalit, *Zur Josephus-Forschung*, 1973, pp. viii, 70ff., 104ff. (from R. Laqueur, *Der judäische Historiker Flavius Josephus*, 1920); Safrai-Stern, *op. cit.*, pp. 20ff.

[57] A very unfavourable criticism on Josephus as historiographer is given by H. Drexler, Untersuchungen zu Josephus und zur Geschichte des jüdischen Aufstandes, *Klio*

tendencies will have been strengthened by the knowledge that the Romans would also read his works and by his desire to toady up to them through his historical accounts. Still, one gets the impression that he need not have made a special effort in this matter, since he also expressed his own aversion.

These prejudices must certainly have coloured Josephus' description of what happened in Alexandria. Even there he does not dissemble his antipathy for the Jewish revolutionaries. True, they were provoked. When the Alexandrians were holding a public meeting on the subject of an embassy which they proposed to send to Nero, a large number of Jews flocked into the amphitheatre, where the Greeks greeted them with shouts of "enemies" and "spies". The majority of the Jews took flight, but three of them were caught and dragged off to be burnt alive. Thereupon the whole Jewish colony rose to the rescue; first they hurled stones at the Greeks, and then snatching up torches rushed to the amphitheatre, threatening to consume the assembled citizens in the flames to the last man. And this they would actually have done, had not Tiberius Alexander, the governor of the city, curbed their fury. He first, however, attempted to recall them to reason without recourse to arms, quietly sending the principal citizens to them and entreating them to desist and not to provoke the Roman army to take action. But the rioters only ridiculed this exhortation and used abusive language of Tiberius.[58]

It is obvious who has Josephus' sympathy—Tiberius Alexander. This is all the more remarkable, though on closer reflection comprehensible, since the provocation in this instance came from the Alexandrian Greeks rather than the Jews, and Tiberius Alexander could not really be called an attractive personage. But whenever Josephus describes certain Jewish groups as rebels ($\sigma\tau\alpha\sigma\iota\acute{\omega}\delta\epsilon\iota\varsigma$), this usually means they could no longer count on his sympathy. On the other hand, eminent Jews who had achieved much in the world always had the advantage with Josephus. Now Tiberius Alexander was definitely one of this group. He was the son of Alexander the alabarch, Philo's brother, one of the richest bankers of Alexandria.

19 (1925), pp. 277-312 : "unglaublich lückenhaft und oberfächlich (p. 284), unklar und anstössig (p. 287), Nebelhaftigkeit (p. 292), vollkommen hintergrundslos und irreal (p. 303), Josephus verschont uns nicht mit belanglosem Geschwätz, für das Wesentliche lässt er uns elend im Stich... (p. 312)".

58 *B*. ii. 490-493.

The son had an illustrious career. He had filled numerous civil and military posts.[59] The latter involved a military oath and could therefore never be aspired to by Jews who remained faithful to their creed. But Tiberius Alexander was not so. Elsewhere Josephus says of him that he did not stand by the practices of his people.[60] Nevertheless he champions here this apostate, who was then not only governor of Alexandria, but also prefect of Egypt. The reason why Josephus let him play an admirable role in the riots in Alexandria in 66 A.D.— though he does not conceal the fact that he ruthlessly struck down the revolt of the Jews of Alexandria when his attempt at reconciliation failed—could be connected with Tiberius Alexander's former office as procurator of Judaea (46-48 A.D.) and his position as one of the highest and most important counsellors of Titus during his military campaigns in Judaea.[61]

Such a concrete example shows that Josephus did not always and exclusively aim at extracting the truth from the facts themselves, but that, in his own way, he selected, arranged and interpreted the facts. Of course much laborious work is needed to discover where and in what way he did this. Where other literature is not available for comparison, the best that can sometimes be achieved is hypothesis.

Philo, the other Jewish writer whose works are of such great importance for our subject, has less need to suggest that his aim is a neutral description of persons and events. When, at the beginning of his work *In Flaccum*, he praises the satrap as a man who at first gave to all appearance a multitude of proofs of high excellence, he expects the protest: "My dear sir, after deciding to accuse a man you have stated no charge, but come out with a long string of praises. Are you out of your senses and gone quite mad? No, my friend, says Philo, I praise Flaccus not because I thought it right to laud an enemy, but to show his villainy in a clearer light".[62] It may truly be said of this remark of Philo that "it shows a temper remote indeed from that of the historian".[63]

---

[59] A summary is to be found in *CPJ*, II, pp. 188-190, in the introduction to a group of papyri in which his name is also mentioned.

[60] *A*. XX. 100.

[61] *CPJ* I, pp. 78ff.; Philo probably had a very different opinion about his nephew's career. Perhaps he even expresses it in insinuations, "in code", in his writings, cf. E.R. Goodenough, *The Politics of Philo Judaeus*, 1967, pp. 30ff., 65f.

[62] *Flacc*. 2, 6, 7.

[63] H.I. Bell, *Jews and Christians in Egypt*, 1924, p. 16; cf. V.A. Tcherikover, The

In the rest of the writing aimed against Flaccus, this temperament does not belie itself. The early, good qualities of Flaccus are enumerated merely to give greater relief to his later wickedness and to establish with all the greater satisfaction how the terrible ultimate fate of this villain proves that no wretch can escape the clutches of divine justice. With obvious pleasure, Philo describes at the end of this work how Flaccus was stabbed in all parts of his body by a disorderly gang of brutes, till he lay carved like a sacrificed victim. In Philo's mind there was no doubt that it was the will of justice that the butcheries she wrought on his single body should be as numerous as the number of the Jews whom he unlawfully put to death. And almost triumphantly the last sentence of his work declaims : such was the fate of Flaccus, who thereby became an indubitable proof that the help which God can give was not withdrawn from the nation of the Jews.[64]

Throughout all his compositions, Philo frequently uses black-white contrasts. The enemies of the Jews are almost always arrant knaves. For some instances we have material for comparison deriving from the enemies. Philo prefixed the names of a group of leading Alexandrians with original adjectives : a popularity-hunting Dionysius, a paper-poring Lampo, Isidorus, faction leader, busy intriguer, mischief contriver and state embroiler.[65] It is quite possible, that the Dionysius mentioned here by Philo is one and the same as the Gaius Julius Dionysius and the Dionysius, son of Theon, mentioned in a letter from Claudius to the Alexandrians.[66] If they may, indeed, be identified, then it appears from Claudius' letter that Dionysius was one of the leading Greek Alexandrians and that, as one of their representatives, he strongly and at length advocated the interests of his group. In the *Acts of the Alexandrian martyrs*, the names mentioned by Philo also appear, naturally in an entirely different light. "In this literature the archrogues and villains have become the true patriots who withstand the pernicious influence of the Jews and the tyranny of Rome".[67]

Decline of the Jewish Diaspora in Egypt in the Roman Period, *The Journal of Jewish Studies* 16 (1963), p. 17 : "Philo was not in duty bound to report everything : nor was it always in his interest to tell the truth and nothing but the truth. We have to read between the lines to discover the true situation".

[64] *Flacc.* 189-191.

[65] *Flacc.* 20.

[66] *CPJ* II, pp. 39 and 41 (lines 17 and 76); cf. H.I. Bell, *Jews and Christians in Egypt*, pp. 29f., 36.

[67] F.H. Colson, *Philo* IX, p. 532.

No matter how widely the descriptions of persons here vary, nor how strongly Philo paints the darker tints,[68] it is still obvious what was going on in Alexandria in the period described by him. In word and deed the leaders of the Greek segment of the population of Alexandria fiercely defended the interests of this group against the Romans and the Jews and in all sorts of ways endeavoured to win over their fellow citizens to their side. It is probably true that they were δημοκόποι, demagogues. But for Philo that was just about the worst thing that could be said of leaders of the people. Isidorus is such a ἄνθρωπος ὀχλικός, a mob courtier, popularity hunter, practised in producing disturbance and confusion, a foe to peace and tranquillity, an adept at creating factions and tumults where they do not exist and organising and fostering them when made, ever at pains to keep in contact with him an irregular and unstable horde of promiscious, ill-assorted people, divided up into sections, or what might be called syndicates.[69] Philo has a profound contempt for that rabble, and what vexes him is that such people are set in action against the Jews by those contemptible demagogues.

A strong contributing factor to this judgment undoubtedly was the fact that Philo belonged to a certain social class. As noted above, he was the brother of one of the richest bankers of Alexandria. He belonged to a stratum of society that abhorred all social unrest. He was convinced that it definitely was not impossible to live in peace with either the Roman or the Greek sections of the population, he therefore put it to his fellow Jewish citizens that nothing could be gained by violence. He was prepared to leave his quiet study to participate in an embassy sent to defend once more the Jewish standpoint before the emperor. This he did, however, as a member of the rich and eminent upper class of Jews in Alexandria, who wished to maintain as long as at all possible their communication and intercourse with Romans and Greeks, and considered this very possible as long as the differences were not pushed to extremes, and violence was not resorted to. On the other hand it is clear enough that there were many among the other layers of the Jewish population in and outside Alexandria who wished to have nothing to do with such a peace-loving, reconciliatory course of action, expected nothing

---

[68] *CPJ* II, p. 69 : Philo's character-drawing is, of course, biased and cannot be trusted in every detail.

[69] *Flacc.* 135.

to come of it, and advocated a much fiercer opposition, with violence
if necessary. As will appear, there are indications of prejudice on
this point in Philo's description of the state of affairs in Alexandria.

Seen against this background, it is understandable that Philo
could not paint the role of the rabble black enough. In his *In Flaccum*
and *Legatio ad Gaium* he has an arsenal of adjectives to express
his contempt of that riff-raff. It is the lazy and unoccupied mob
in the city, a multitude well practised in idle talk, who devote their
leisure to slandering and evil speaking;[70] it is that undisciplined
mob,[71] not the peaceful, public-spirited crowd, but the crowd which
regularly fills everything with confusion and turmoil, that pursues
a worthless life,[72] that, once it has broken loose, commits in a wild
pogrom against the Jews every crime imaginable.[73] When such a
promiscuous and unruly Alexandrian mob unmasks the hatred which
has long been smouldering, everything is thrown into chaos and
confusion.[74] Flaccus must be seriously blamed for not having immediately put an end to this mob-rule (ὀχλοκρατία).[75]

Now it must be admitted that Philo was not alone in his particularly
adverse opinion about the Alexandrian mob. Also Seneca—and he
was in a position to know from experience—says of all Egypt that
it was a province gossipy and ingenious in devising insults for its
rulers, one in which even those who shunned wrongdoing did not
escape ill fame—where all sorts of persons take pleasure in even
dangerous witticisms.[76] Examples of those dangerous witticisms
(*periculosi sales*) can be read in the works of various other writers.[77]
And so it is definitely not exceptional when, in celebration of the
Jewish king, the Alexandrians stage a farcical performance in his
honour.[78] The rabble of Alexandria apparently had a bad reputation
in the ancient world.

Philo's descriptions of persons and events are often supported by
accounts from elsewhere, but sometimes there are grounds for doubting

---

[70] *Flacc.* 33.

[71] *Flacc.* 35.

[72] *Flacc.* 41.

[73] *Flacc.* 62ff.

[74] *Leg.* 120 : ὁ 'Αλεξανδρέων μιγὰς καὶ πεφορημένος ὄχλος, cf. *Ebr.* 113, 198.

[75] *Leg.* 132 ; cf. Goodenough, *op. cit.*, p. 52.

[76] *Helv.* XIX. 6 : *loquax et in contumelias praefectorum ingeniosa provincia.*

[77] Smallwood, *op. cit.*, pp. 213f.; Mommsen, *op. cit.*, pp. 582f.

[78] *Flacc.* 36ff.

the neutrality of his communications. Very occasionally the reason
for his version of the matter can be traced. On p. 12 was noted
that Philo describes Tiberius as one of the emperors who were well-
disposed towards the Jews. When Sejanus planned a large-scale
attack on the Jews, Tiberius immediately took counter-measures.[79]
But several authors say that Tiberius himself once drove the Jews
out of Rome.[80] These statements by Josephus, Tacitus, Suetonius
and Dio Cassius agree mutually on the main issues. There are differences
in details, and they disagree somewhat about the dating of this deed
of Tiberius. Tacitus gives the exact year, 19 A.D. The only one who
differs on this is Josephus, who says this event occurred during Pilate's
procuratorship of Judaea.[81] As a rule, however, Tacitus' dating is
assumed to be correct. If so, Tiberius' expulsion of the Jews cannot
be the same event as Sejanus' attack on the Jews as described by
Philo, so Philo must have kept silent about the measure taken by
Tiberius against the Jews. There is a very plausible reason for this.
Philo was particularly concerned to demonstrate that, with the
exception of the villain Caligula, all Claudius' predecessors were
favourably inclined towards the Jews.

There are also three versions of the tensions and outbreaks in
Judaea in the last year of emperor Caligula, though they vary greatly
in scope. Philo and Josephus, understandably, devote considerable
attention to Caligula's plans for erecting a large statue in the temple.
Tacitus devotes not one line to them.[82] There are rather large dis-
crepancies between the statements of Philo and Josephus concerning
various matters, but on this they both agree, no mention is made
by either of any armed resistance by the Jews to the imminent and
atrocious desecration of the temple. From Josephus' account it would
rather seem that the Jews were quite prepared to offer passive resistance to the limit, but that they were not prepared to start a war.
When the Roman governor of Syria visited Tiberias, according to
Josephus, many tens of thousands faced Petronius who besought

---

[79] *Leg.* 159-161 .

[80] Jos., *A.* XVIII. 81-85; Tac., *Ann.* ii. 85; Suet., *Tib.* XXXVI. 1, Dio Cassius
LVII. 18.

[81] Jos., *A.* XVIII. 65 : ὑπὸ τοὺς αὐτοὺς χρόνους; cf. Hospers-Jansen, *op. cit.*, pp. 105f.;
Smallwood, *op. cit.*, pp. 243f.; E.M. Smallwood, Some Notes on the Jews under Tiberius,
Latomus 15 (1956), pp. 314-329; L.H. Feldman, *Josephus*, IX, pp. 60f.; Syme, *op. cit.*,
II, p. 468 : Dudley, *op. cit.*, pp. 194f.

[82] *Leg.* 184-348; *A.* XVIII. 261-310; *B.* ii. 184-203; *Hist.* V.9.

him by no means to put them under constraint nor to pollute the
city by setting up the statue. "Will you then go to war", said Petronius", regardless of his resources and of your weakness?". "On no
account would we fight", they said, "but we will die sooner than
violate our laws". And falling on their faces and baring their throats,
they declared that they were ready to be slain. They continued to
make these supplications for forty days. Furthermore, they neglected
their fields, and that, too, though it was time to sow the seed. For
they showed a stubborn determination and readiness to die rather
than to see the image erected.[83]

Philo also records this incident, but places it in the harvest, not
sowing season. He states explicitly that Petronius was afraid that
the Jews, despairing of their traditions and despising life, would
either ravage their fields or set fire to their cornlands in the hills
and on the plains. Petronius wanted to secure, by military intervention
if necessary, the safe gathering in of the harvests—the harvest from
the fruit-trees as well as that from the fields.[84]

Philo therefore places this incident in a different season of the
year than Josephus, but both assume, Josephus more emphatically
than Philo, that the Jews had no intention of offering armed resistance,
but passive resistance to the very limit. In a few words Tacitus says
of this incident: "Under Tiberius all was quiet. Then, when Caligula
ordered the Jews to set up his statue in their temple, they chose
rather to resort to arms, but the emperor's death put an end to their
uprising".[85] The last part is mentioned by Philo and Josephus, too,
but only Tacitus says the Jews resorted to arms (*arma potius sumpsere*)
on this occasion.

Which statements on this subject are correct, those of Philo and
Josephus, or that of Tacitus? A remarkable point is that, in his
description of the tumult in Alexandria, Philo also repeatedly emphasises the innocence of the Jews and, as proof, points out that they
carried no weapons whatsoever. The Roman soldiers were ordered
to search the houses of the Jews. When the latter heard they were
ordered to do so because enormous stocks of arms were expected
to be found, they felt pleased in one way, being perfectly sure nothing
would be found, but in another way deeply pained that such grave

---

[83] *A.* XVIII. 271, cf. 274.
[84] *Leg.* 249.
[85] *Hist.* V.9.

slanders were so readily believed. What was found during the search ?
Enormous stocks of arms ? Why ! absolutely nothing, not even the
knives which suffice the cooks for their daily use.[86] Did the idea
of armed action never occur to the Jews in Alexandria ? Did they
allow themselves to be slaughtered without resisting during the
clashes of 38 A.D. ? Were they once more unarmed during the events
of 41 A.D. ? When the Alexandrian Greeks penetrated their temples
and placed statues of Caligula there, did they stand aside passively ?
Some scholars think this highly improbable and consider it at least
probable that the Jews, wiser after their experience of 38, certainly
did not watch their synagogues being desecrated without offering
armed resistance. Box thinks this a "necessary deduction" which
must be made from Philo's account. He points out that Philo also
says that Flaccus was out to fan the flame of insurrection as much
as lay in his power and to cause a civil war between the population
groups throughout the world.[87] Bell thinks it an established fact
that the Jews offered armed resistance : Ohne Frage leisteten die
Juden Widerstand, und in dem folgenden Kampfe litten die Synagogen
schwer.[88] In my view this cannot be stated so positively. One naturally
assumes that the reason for Philo's triumphant declaration was that
the Jews had no arms in their homes : they were in no way to blame
for the riot, the other side was completely to blame. Was this also
the reason why neither Philo nor Josephus said anything about
the violent resistance of the Jews in Judaea during the tumults
caused by Caligula's threat to desecrate the temple ? In his brief
comment on this, does Tacitus give a correct picture of what really
happened ? It might be noted that, at times, Josephus does not
hesitate to admit that the Jews also reacted very fiercely on occasion
and certainly did not allow themselves to be slaughtered without
offering resistance. He says, for instance, that on the death of Gaius,
the Jews, who had been humiliated under his rule and grievously
abused by the Alexandrians, took heart again and at once armed
themselves.[89] Josephus therefore declares here that the Jews, having
become wiser through the experience of the preceding years and
embittered about what had been done to them, now really did prepare

---

[86] *Flacc.* 86-91.
[87] H. Box, *Philonis Alexandrini In Flaccum*, 1939, pp. LIX f.
[88] Bell, *Juden und Griechen...*, p. 20 ; cf. *CPJ* I, p. 68[42], II, p. 52 ; Grant, *op. cit.*, p. 131.
[89] *A.* XIX. 278.

for armed combat. Consequently some have seen a connection between this and those obscure passages in Claudius' letter to the Alexandrians about two embassies to Rome and presume both consisted of Jews, one of "moderates" under Philo's leadership, the other of "radicals" who had called in the assistance of their fellow people from Egypt and Syria during their armed conflict in Alexandria.[90] Similarly Josephus' description of the events in Alexandria in 66 A.D., the only one we have of them, clearly hints that the Jews carried out severe attacks on their opponents at that time.[91] But here we must discount again Josephus's antipathy towards Jewish revolutionaries. And as for Tacitus' brief statement about events in Judaea under Caligula, it must not be forgotten that when he wrote his *Histories*, the cruel Jewish war of 66-70 A.D. under the Romans was well enough known and that, unwittingly, he could have presumed for an earlier period the behaviour of the Jews in those years.

It is glaringly evident that it is often very difficult to determine with any certainty when either party is guilty of bias. An objective criterion for discerning exaggeration cannot readily be found. An established fact is that non-Jewish writers sometimes invented all sort of horrible stories about the Jews and did not draw the line at deliberate libel. Does this imply that they always lied when they told evil things about the behaviour of Jews in certain situations and times? Sometimes this cannot be said for certain. A statement by Dio Cassius about atrocities committed by the Jews during the revolt under Trajan is quoted above (p. 17). Is such a statement based on pure imagination? Bell thinks such a statement need not be taken seriously: "Nach Dio Cassius verzehrten die Juden sogar das Fleisch ihrer Opfer bei kannibalischen Orgien. Seine Behauptungen darf man nicht zu ernst nehmen, da in solchen Zeiten, wie im vergangenen Kriege, die menschliche Einbildungskraft Schauerliches erzeugt". He adds almost immediately, however: "aber es liegt auf der Hand, dass der aufgesparte Hass und Groll fast eines halben Jahrhunderts sich in zügelloser Wildheit entlud".[92] And Tcherikover says much the same about this story of Dio Cassius: "its exaggerations (especially as regards numbers) are too evident for it to be taken

---

[90] *CPJ* II, p. 41, lines 90, 91 and pp. 50ff.; Bell, *Jews and Christians in Egypt*, 1924, pp. 17f.

[91] *B.* ii. 487ff.; cf. *CPJ* I, pp. 78ff.

[92] Bell, *Juden und Griechen...*, p. 38.

seriously; yet the fierce character of the struggle is attested by other sources and is not to be doubted".[93]

True, the numbers of victims mentioned by Dio Cassius are very high, 220,000 in Cyrene and 240,000 on Cyprus. But does he exaggerate on this point only, or does he also paint a very one-sided picture of the savageries committed by the Jews on that occasion? Both Bell and Tcherikover appear to presume that Dio Cassius' statement must contain a modicum of truth, considering the intensity of the conflict.

It has also appeared (pp. 17f.) that this statement now is authenticated to a certain extent by the letter of Eudaimonis cited in a papyrus. This lady may justifiably be said to have been an "irascible old lady", who resolutely declares she will throw over the gods if her son is not returned to her safe and sound, who is rather quick to say that presently, in the winter season, she will have nothing to wear. Indeed "the old lady is inclined to rather strong language".[94] Her anxiety for her son's life and for the cruelties accompanying his death should he fall in the hands of his enemy need not have been unfounded. Several of these papyri breathe a fear for all sorts of threats which, perhaps, may not be disposed of simply as war-psychosis.[95] In that respect these papyri could provide indirect confirmation of Dio Cassius' statement, or at least of its purport.

Distinguishing between partialities and biases will always be difficult. Despite the conviction that not a single writer of the ancient world was entirely free of prejudice, especially on this tender point, our picture of the history of that age is based largely on their attestations. Often, when other sources provide material for comparison, the historical events can be described with a little more certainty. Sometimes, too, the reasons why those events are misinterpreted are so obvious that it is possible to determine which statements are influenced by those motives. Nevertheless in spite of the clear realisation that the writers in question were anything but unprejudiced, they continue to be consulted on certain points, because often they are our only witnesses for events and relationships in certain periods. It is a generally recognised fact that Tacitus was not always an impartial historiographer, and certainly not when writing about the Jews.[96] As we

---

[93] *CPJ* I, p. 86.

[94] *CPJ* II, pp. 236, 245f.; cf. *CPJ* I, p. 89.

[95] *CPJ* II, p. 236.

[96] Thiaucourt's opinion is: "Le triste fragment du cinquième livre des Histoires

have seen, however, a certain ambivalence can be discerned even in his statements about the Jews, and they were not all unfavourable to them. So these data must also be examined for their own worth.

Josephus and Philo definitely do not write impartial history. That is now evident. Whether the latter may justly be called "ein Geschicht-schreiber von Zufalls Gnaden und keineswegs ein guter", remains to be seen, but Bell, who says this of him, seems to be convinced that both Philo and Josephus "wie parteiisch sie auch die Ereignisse darstellen mochten, darüber doch wenigstens besser berichtet waren als irgend ein moderner Forscher und dass wir ihre Behauptungen nicht einfach darum verwerfen dürfen, weil sie den Juden günstig sind". But Bell does not claim that he always made the right choice when evaluating their testimonials as objectively as possible.[97]

It would seem a most natural and logical tenet that statements may not be rejected simply because they favour the Jews. Perhaps Bell is here referring to those scholars who are a priori suspicious of anything good said about the Jews. When he says that the ancient testimonials are biased, he adds immediately : "ein Fehler, der übrigens auch einigen modernen Werken über die Juden anhaftet".[98] Bell wrote this in 1927. At that time already, some authors were finding it difficult to write objectively about the subject. Even then there were those who were bent on collecting for modern ends anti-Semitic material dating from the ancient days, and whenever it was open to varying interpretations, the one unfavourable to the Jews was always chosen. A stream of anti-Semitic prejudications, calumnious imputations, distortions of the truth and also of the historical truth has poured over the world since then, making it all the more difficult for both Jewish and non-Jewish authors to write objectively on this subject. How difficult it often is, now that the overt, crude anti-Semitism seems to have subsided, to uncover the latent anti-Semitism,

---

de Tacite, conservé pour son malheur comme le reste est perdu pour le nôtre, est un monument éternellement honteux de l'historiographie ancienne", C. Thiaucourt, ce que Tacite dit des Juifs, *Revue des études juives*, 19 (1889), p. 56; Reinach speaks of "son injustice passionée envers le judaïsme", *op. cit.*, p. IX; Bousset: "Seine Polemik gegen das Judentum gehört zu dem Bittersten und Fulminantesten, das er je geschrieben" W. Bousset, *Die Religion des Judentums im neutestamentlichen Zeitalter*, ²1906, p. 88; Lovsky: "Aucun écrivain latin n'a calomnié les Juifs aussi complaisamment, aussi durablement que l'historien Tacite", *op. cit.*, p. 75; Grant, *op. cit.*, p. 233 : "—this strangely ill-informed account—".

[97] Bell, *Juden und Griechen...*, p. 15 and Vorwort.
[98] Bell, *J.u.G.*, Vorwort.

the secret arrogance of the non-Jew who sometimes assumes the garment of sympathetic philo-Semitism. Many will now be inclined to interpret the material used by ardent anti-Semites in their campaign against the Jews as favourably as possible for the Jews. Objective historiography, not to take idle prejudices as our guide, but to extract the truth from the facts themselves, as Josephus says,[99] has become more difficult than ever before.

Sometimes it is at once obvious that a writer has not gone to any trouble on this point. One of the books on anti-Semitism in ancient days begins with these two sentences: "Niemand kann sich im Blick auf die moderne Judenfrage dem verschliessen—vollends nicht im gegenwärtigen Schicksalskampf Europas—dass von allen ihren Hintergründen derjenige eines über die Welt hin ausgebreiteten und allenthalben seine Machtpositionen haltenden und von ihnen her das politische, wirtschaftliche und geistige Leben der Völker durchsetzenden *Weltjudentums* der drohendste ist. Unter den vielen Fragen, die das Judentum als merkwürdige Erscheinung der Völkergeschichte aufgibt und die in ihrer Gesamtheit die Judenfrage ausmachen, ist die Tatsache eines Weltjudentums und seiner Auswirkungen die für die nicht-jüdische Menschheit weitaus unheimlichste". Add to this the fact that the book appeared in Germany in 1943 as one of the "Schriften des Reichsinstituts für Geschichte des neuen Deutschlands", as Volume 7 of a series of "Forschungen zur Judenfrage", with the title "Das antike Weltjudentum", and the result is extremely little faith in the objectivity of this work.[100] Nevertheless it claims to be a highly scholarly work. It is "die Frucht einer echten Gemeinschaftsarbeit zwischen Geisteswissenschaft und Naturwissenschaft". The former, it must be admitted to the scandal of this branch of learning, is here represented by the New Testament scholar Gerhard Kittel, and the second by a specialist in the study of races to whom we are indebted for a "rassenkundliche Prüfung von achtzig Mummienportraits" and a "rassenkundliche Prüfung der antiken Judenkarikaturen", with a series of portraits showing ancient alongside of modern Jews.[101]

Isaac has described this work as follows: "la documentation en est riche, l'interprétation très contestable".[102] One might almost say

---

[99] *Ap.* i. 6.

[100] Eugen Fischer/Gerhard Kittel, *Das antike Weltjudentum*, 1943.

[101] Pp. 109-163, 172-174.

[102] Isaac, *op. cit.*, p. 34; an excellent and very critical discussion of the whole series

that, unfortunately, the first part of this characterisation of the book is also true. It contains a very compendious collection of ancient texts relevant to the Jews and translated in German. Sources are carefully recorded. A short introduction is followed by a series of hundreds of such texts, with relatively brief comments, sometimes without any further elucidation, and arranged in larger or smaller groups. Every educated German layman was thus able to read the translated texts for himself, if he had the time for it "im gegenwärtigen Schichsalskampf Europas". In any event the constructive character of this work was enhanced for him when he read above certain groups and texts such comprehensive titles as : "Der Geschäftsjude; Steuer-, Münz- und Geldjuden; Spitzbuben".[103] These were titles which were so familiar to him midst the dramatic war of destiny of his own day.

Since it is patently anti-Semitic, this book undoubtedly may be classified with those modern works which, according to the English scholar Bell, share their extreme one-sidedness with many ancient works. However, there are other works which definitely are not impregnated with explicit anti-Semitism, but in which latent anti-Semitism sometimes emerges in a more or less subtle form. It is even questionable whether Bell's own work is entirely free of it. At the beginning of his description of the clashes between Greeks and Jews in Alexandria, he gives a short character sketch of both groups. Of the Greek Alexandrians he mentions their love of intrigue, their talent for making malicious statements and goes on to say : "Die Juden des Altertums ihrerseits waren anerkanntermassen Ruhe-störer, und zu keiner Zeit hat sich diese Rasse durch taktvolles Benehmen im Wohlstand hervor getan".[104] The first part, could be held to be an establishment of historical fact, although the generalisa-

---

is given in the article by F. Werner, Das Judentumsbild der Spätjudentumsforschung im Dritten Reich, Dargestellt anhand der "Forschungen zur Judenfrage", Bd. I-VIII in *Kairos, Neue Folge*, 13, 1971, pp. 161-194, on Fischer-Kittel pp. 180ff. Even such a book as that of Th. Hopfner, *Die Judenfrage bei Griechen und Römern* is suspect of partiality simply because it was published in 1943 and in the series *Abhandlungen der deutschen Akademie der Wissenschaften in Prag*. The contention that in their "Prose-lytenmacherei" the Jews had a powerful means "ihre Wirtsvölker—auch rassisch zu schwächen" (p. 26) clearly indicates from which quarter the wind blows here. Quite properly L.H. Feldman also designates articles by H. Gogner and G. Bertram from the period 1937-1942 as "clearly anti-Semitic", *Studies in Judaica, Scholarship on Philo and Josephus (1937-1962)*, n.d., pp. 19, 49.

[103] Pp. 53, 55, 59.

[104] Bell, *J.u.G.*, p. 15.

tion here is noticeable—*the* Jews of *the* ancient world, who are qualified as trouble-makers. Even so, such a generalising hypothesis should be backed by evidence. But yet another judgment is passed which suddenly is declared valid for all times and for the entire race. Suddenly the word "race" occurs, certainly not suggested to the author by his lecture of the works of the ancients, but a word whose frequent use in this context springs mainly from modern anti-Semitism, and from the latter derives the arrogant presumption with which it is expressed. Moreover, one wonders what historical-statistical data enabled Bell to make such a comment, and what material was available to him to demonstrate that in all ages non-Jews outshone "diese Rasse durch taktvolles Benehmen im Wohlstand".

Still, Bell shows elsewhere that he has a keen eye for the exaggerations of anti-Semites, including the modern ones. In his treatment of the *Acts of the Alexandrian martyrs*, he quotes the furious outburst of one of them against the emperor : "Your Council is filled with impious Jews". Bell's comment is : "die Behauptung der Beirat sei voller Juden war ebenso gegenstandlos wie die Versicherung heutiger Antisemiten, diese oder jene Regierung oder gar Europa im Ganzen stehe unter jüdischer Aufsicht".[105] How can anyone who recognises and resolutely rejects such unfounded assertions of anti-Semites propagate, himself, such a dangerous, generalising hypothesis, which is scarcely better founded ?

Sometimes a modern writer's choice of a given interpretation of data about the Jews is undoubtedly determined by his anti-Semitism, often right down to details. Let one example suffice. In ancient times Jews lent money, sometimes to fellow Jews, sometimes to Gentiles. Reference is made to the latter in a papyrus that has become famous for one sentence. In a letter dated 41 A.D., the merchant Serapion writes to his friend Heracleides, perhaps also his representative in Alexandria. Evidently the latter has become involved in financial difficulties and is seeking in vain to find a way out of them. His friend tells him of a man who might be able to help him, if he is approached with humble petitions, daily if necessary, until he takes pity on him. If not, Serapion says to Heracleides, like everyone else, do you too beware of the Jews : 'Ἐὰν μή, ὡς ἄν πάντες καὶ σὺ βλέπε σατὸν ἀπὸ τῶν Ἰουδαίων.[106]

---

[105] Bell, *J.u.G.*, pp. 35f.; *CPJ* II, pp. 83, 84.
[106] *CPJ* II, p. 34.

Wilcken says that in these words "der geschäftliche Antisemitismus den wir bisher nur ahnen konnten" finds "einen geradezu klassischen Ausdruck".[107] He takes it for granted that this warning also encompasses an accusation that the Jews imposed exorbitant rates of interest, but at the same time he points out that the date of this letter must be borne in mind. In 41 A.D., immediately upon the death of Caligula, the Jews had unleashed "eine Griechenhetze" (Jos. *Ant.* XIX.278ff.). It should therefore be remembered that this letter was written during a period of extreme political tension.[108] Nowadays many hold this to be the most important, if not only reason for the warning against the Jews and reject the presumption that the reference is to the excessive rates of interest demanded by them. It is pointed out that the Jews could certainly raise the rates of interest, but not arbitrarily, and in any case held no monopoly. Besides there is no indication that the Jews were ever attacked on this point. And it cannot be said for sure of this statement that it is all the more remarkable since "bisher in der gesamten antisemitischen Literatur des Altertums, von der freilich nur geringe Reste uns erhalten sind, der Vorwurf des Wuchers nicht begegnet".[109] It could indeed be due to the paucity of information that we hear nothing of this reproach, but the lack of any mention of it must also automatically imply a reminder not to read the taking of usurious interest in a letter in which it is not stated in so many words. Nor does Philo, who wrote at length about the law against usury, give the slightest hint of acquaintance with such a reproach against the Jews. At most one might suspect that it was for this reason that he wrote so indignantly about exorbitant usury and the loan of food on interest to the poor, because he had in mind such practices in the Jewish community in Alexandria.[110]

---

[107] U. Wilcken, Zum Alexandrinischen Antisemitismus, in the XXVII. Bd. of the *Abhandlungen der philologisch-historischen Klasse der königl. Sächsischen Gesellschaft der Wissenschaften*, No. XXIII, 1909, p. 792; cf. Tcherikover, *op. cit.*, p. 520[29], where he quotes another comment made by Wilcken : "Der Brief ist somit das älteste Zeugnis eines geschäftlichen Antisemitismus"; L. Fuchs, *op. cit.*, p. 60 says exactly the same.

[108] Wilcken, *op. cit.*, pp. 790f.; cf. Bolkestein, *op. cit.*, pp. 162f.; J. Parkes, *The Conflict of the Church and the Synagogue*, 1934, p. 13 : "—the letter dates from a time of violent political feeling—"; Safrai-Stern, *op. cit.*, p. 130 : "The tense conditions prevailing in Alexandria at that time are reflected...".

[109] Wilcken, *op. cit.*, p. 790; cf. A.N. Sherwin-White, *Racial Prejudice in Imperial Rome*, 1967, p. 93 : "The sources are entirely silent about economic rivalry of any sort"; Baron, *op. cit.*, I, p. 194 : "Nowhere are the Jews accused of usury".

[110] *Spec. Leg.* ii. 74ff., cf. *Virt.* 82ff.; Heinemann, *op. cit.*, pp. 40f.; *CPJ* I, p. 49.

One thing is in any case certain, here there is no warning against the Jews because they exacted high rates of interest. The context does make clear, however, that there were Jewish moneylenders in Alexandria who had transactions with non-Jews as well, a fact verified by other sources. It is quite possible that Heracleides was warned, simply because it could have been fatally dangerous to seek contact with Jews in a period of great political tension. Merely to enter those quarters of the city where Jews lived could have cost him his life.

At the very least it is uncertain whether these words can be interpreted as referring to dubious financial trade practices on the part of the Jews. One reason why this is sometimes done as a matter of course could be connected with what Tcherikover says of this letter in his introduction: "Modern anti-Semites were glad to find in it evidence for Jewish dishonesty in business".[111] It is very significant that, for example, Kittel appends just one sentence to the reproduction of the German translation of the warning against the Jews in this letter: "Das kann nur als Warnung vor den Geldjuden verstanden werden: Hüte Dich, von ihnen Geld zu leihen und ihrem Wucher anheimzufallen". In these few words the German national-socialist heard once more the familiar anti-Semitic jargon. We shall often encounter this "arbitrary interpretation of several papyri which have won the particular affection of modern anti-Semites".[112] All the more reason to persist in the endeavour to avoid all that is one-sided and biased in the treatment of our subject.

---

[111] *CPJ* II, p. 33.
[112] Tcherikover, *op. cit.*, pp. 369f.

CHAPTER ONE

RACE ?

Nowadays, the consensus of opinion is that racial theories, in the modern sense of the word, played little or no role in the anti-Semitism of the ancient world. Leipoldt, who wrote a short work on *Antisemitismus in der alten Welt* in 1933 in Germany—note time and place—says of anti-Semitism at the beginning of his discussion of "Die Gründe" : "Der Mensch der Gegenwart ist geneigt, den Antisemitismus vor allem auf Rassengegensätze zurückzuführen. Für die alte Welt hatte dieser Gesichtspunkt freilich nur begrenzte Gültigkeit".[1] This is an understatement. Actually racial distinctions were never used in ancient days, at least not in the form of special external or cultural characteristics being ascribed to the Jewish race as such to prove its inferiority to other races. Various modern writers therefore use stronger terms for this than Leipoldt. Lovsky writes : "D'Apion à Tacite, d'Épiphane à Celse, l'antisémitisme antique n'est pas raciste".[2] And Simon says of Graeco-Roman anti-Semitism : "L'aspect ethnique en est totalement absent. La notion de race, en effet, telle que l'ont popularisée, en l'appliquant en particulier aux relations entre Juifs et "aryens", les théories pseudo-scientifiques du racisme contemporain, est absolument étrangère à la mentalité antique".[3]

Although it is now practically a general assumption that the modern concept of race did not exist in ancient days, this does not preclude the repeated use of the word "race" in the translation of ancient literary passages relating to the Jews, nor the occurrence of the concept "race" in all sorts of discussions on anti-Semitism. With regard to the former, no matter what one thinks of such trans-

---

[1] Leipoldt, *op. cit.*, p. 7.

[2] Lovsky, *op. cit.*, p. 80.

[3] Simon, *op. cit.*, p. 239; cf. S.L. Guterman, *Religious Toleration and Persecution in Ancient Rome*, 1951, p. 95 : —of antisemitism in the sense of a movement based on race or nationality Rome was ignorant; after noting that the Latin antisemitism adopts most of the themes of the Alexandrian antisemitism, Isaac goes on to say : "Pas plus que celui-ci, il ne fait grief aux Juifs de leurs richesses ou de leur race", *op. cit.*, p. 128.

lations, if one does translate in this way, one must at least avoid any suggestion of racial differences. In view of this, it is better not to use the word "race" too often, especially when other words can readily be used to interpret the meaning. Clearly illustrative of this are the varying interpretations of the same word by different translators. Somewhere Josephus mentions Strabo's remark about the widespread dispersion of the Jews throughout the entire known world of that time. He states that the population of Cyrenaica consisted of various groups, one of which was the Jews, and goes on to say of the latter: Αὕτη δ'εἰς πᾶσαν πόλιν ἤδη παρελήλυθε καὶ τόπον οὐκ ἔστι ῥᾳδίως εὑρεῖν τῆς οἰκουμένης, ὃς οὐ παραδέδεκται τοῦτο τὸ φῦλον, μηδ'ἐπικρατεῖται ὑπ'αὐτοῦ. Reinach's rendering of this text is: "Ces derniers (les Juifs) ont pénétré dans tous les États et il n'est pas facile de trouver, dans le monde entier, un seul endroit qui n'ait pas fait acceuil à cette race et où elle ne soit devenue maîtresse".[4] The translation of φῦλον given in this passage is also to be found in Juster[5] and Bonsirven,[6] who probably borrowed it from Reinach. Isaac, however, uses the term "ce peuple" and in a note remarks—and this is very important in connection with the sound of this term: "Strabon emploie l'expression *touto to phulon* qui ne paraît pas nécessairement péjorative".[7] In his translation of Jos. *Ant.* XIV.115, where this statement of Strabo is quoted, Marcus uses the term "this nation".[8] Kittel speaks of "dieses Volk".[9] In itself, no objection need be made to the use of the word "race" in this quotation from Strabo's work. Liddell and Scott give "race", "tribe" or "class" as prime meanings of φῦλον. But especially when one reads "this race", association with the jargon of the 20th century anti-Semitism suggests in such a translation a very unfavourable opinion about the Jews, emanating from bitter hostility and contempt. And then what one hears in Strabo's statement is an opinion about the Jews which is absolutely alien to this particular writer. He is noted, above all, for what Isaac says of him: "—les nombreux passages relatifs à la Judée, à ses habitants, à son histoire, sont d'un ton neutre et objectif, sans nulle trace d'antisémitisme".[10]

---

4 *A.* XIV. 115; Reinach, *op. cit.*, p. 92.
5 Juster, *op. cit.* I, p. 180.
6 Bonsirven, *op. cit.* I, p. 6.
7 Isaac, *op. cit.*, p. 90.
8 Loeb-ed. VII, p. 509.
9 Fischer-Kittel, *op. cit.*, p. 16.
10 Isaac, *op. cit.*, p. 90.

Suchlike variations in the translation are repeatedly encountered. The word γένος is often translated as "race".[11] No objection need be made to this. As prime meaning of this word, Liddell and Scott give "race, stock, kin". But inevitably this translation evokes modern racial notions when the expression in Posidonius of Apamea τὸ γένος ἄρδην ἀνελεῖν τῶν Ἰουδαίων is translated by Reinach as "anéantir complètement la race juive", or by Walton as "to wipe out completely the race of Jews".[12]

The word ἔθνος is often translated as "nation".[13] Sometimes, however, different words are used in the translation, even on occasion "race". At the end of his work *In Flaccum*, Philo once more emphatically establishes that the fate of Flaccus is an indubitable proof that the help which God can give was not withdrawn from the Jews τὸ Ἰουδαίων ἔθνος.[14] Colson's translation is "the nation of the Jews".[15] Delaunay speaks of "le peuple juif",[16] but Goudenough of "the race of the Jews".[17] And when Reinach translates τοῦτο τὸ ἔθνος in a fragment of Strabo as "(l'antique aversion pour) cette race",[18] or Smallwood uses "that race" (Sejanus, who wanted to destroy that race completely), where there is only τὸ ἔθνος and not τοῦτο τὸ ἔθνος,[19] one hears, willy-nilly, a modern pejorative tone echoing in these translations.

The Latin word 'gens' is also sometimes translated as "race" and quite often precisely where this could give rise to misunderstanding. Often the interpretation given is "nation".[20] Considerable differences occur in the various translations of Pliny the Elder's famous expression *gens contumelia numinum insignis*. Reinach's translation is "nation célèbre par son mépris des divinités",[21] Isaac's is "ce peuple se dis-

---

[11] E.g. Jos. B VII. 43, 359 (Loeb-ed. III, pp. 517, 607), Ap. i. 1, ii. 296. (Loeb-ed. I, pp. 163, 411).

[12] Reinach, op. cit., p. 56: Diod. Sic. XXXIV, Fragments 1, Vol. XII, p. 53; cf. Isaac, op. cit., p. 77: la race de Judéens; Philo, Heres 203 (Loeb-ed. IV, p. 385).

[13] E.g. Ap. i. 5, ii. 282 (Loeb-ed. I, p. 165, 407); A. XIV. 117 (Loeb-ed. VII, p. 509); Reinach: nation pp. 56, 92, race p. 57.

[14] Flacc. 191.

[15] Loeb-ed. IX, p. 403.

[16] F. Delaunay, Philon d'Alexandrie. Écrits historiques, 1867, p. 269.

[17] Goodenough, op. cit., p. 10.

[18] Reinach, op. cit., p. 57.

[19] Smallwood, op. cit., pp. 94, 243.

[20] E.g. Reinach, op. cit., pp. 263 (cf. Isaac, op. cit., p. 114), 321.

[21] Reinach, op. cit., p. 281.

tingue par son dédain des divinités",[22] but Radin's is "a race famous for its insults to the gods".[23] *"Obscura gens"* in Rutilius Namatianus is translated as "son ignoble race" by Reinach,[24] and as "race obscène" by Isaac.[25] And the erroneously modern connotation of the word "race" is, perhaps, most liable to be heard in the translation of Tacitus' expression *taeterrima gens* : in Radin "that disgusting race".[26]

Certain translations may erroneously suggest racial differences in the modern sense, but expressions are also frequently encountered in the discussions on anti-Semitism in the ancient world which could give rise to misunderstanding. Bell, for instance, writes that racial hatred was probably intensified by the continuing demands of the Jews of Alexandria for more privileges,[27] and in one passage he calls the revolt under Trajan of the Jews of Egypt, Cyrenaica and Cyprus "a race war".[28] Sherwin-White published a series of papers he delivered in Cambridge under the title *Racial Prejudice in Imperial Rome.*[29] There he gives numerous examples of this racial prejudice. It is questionable however, whether these examples are indeed illustrations of it. Sometimes the author evidently doubts this himself, as when he points out that the prejudices often concern not the race, but the nation and especially the culture of other peoples.[30] In conclusion he discusses the attitude of the Romans to the Jews and says of Juvenal and Tacitus that their attitude was anti-Semitic, "because it is a dislike of Jews based on their way of life". Later he adds : "I have called this antagonism racial for convenience. But this is misleading. Though Greeks and Latins refer to the Jews as an ἔθνος or a *natio* or a *gens*, i.e. a folk or tribe, there is no genuinely racial or racist connotation. The distinction is political, social and religious, national rather than genetic. The large mass of converts among other peoples prevented the racial idea from developing."[31] This holds good not only for the attitude of the Romans to the Jews,

---

[22] Isaac, *op. cit.*, p. 116².

[23] M. Radin, *The Jews among the Greeks and Romans*, 1915, p. 196.

[24] Reinach, *op. cit.*, p. 359.

[25] Isaac, *op. cit.*, p. 122.

[26] Radin, *op. cit.*, p. 307; cf. Hospers-Jansen, *op. cit.*, p. 21; J. W. Meyer, *Publius Cornelius Tacitus, Historiën*, 1958, p. 270 : people.

[27] Bell, *J.u.G.*, p. 30.

[28] *Ibid.*, p. 36.

[29] A.N. Sherwin-White, *Racial Prejudice in Imperial Rome*, 1967.

[30] E.g. pp. 74, 76 : cultural and national prejudice.

[31] Sherwin-White, *op. cit.*, p. 99.

but almost always for their opinion about other peoples as well. Criticism is expressed about their way of life, their barbarous morals, their social and cultural backwardness, the primitive conditions in which they must live, but seldom about the peculiarities of a race or about their lineage.

The opinion of Roman writers about alien peoples was dictated by a strong sense of superiority based not on racial consciousness, but on pride in their own power and especially their own culture. Tacitus may be said to provide a typical example of this in his work on the Teutons. In his *Germania* the viewpoint is based on the situation of the Roman Empire. He takes it for granted that everything that can be said about the Teutons must be judged accordingly as it is favourable to the maintenance and the power of the Roman Empire. When describing the drinking habits of the Teutons, he says it is fortunate they cannot moderate their thirst : if you humour their drunkenness by supplying as much as they crave, they will be vanquished through their vices as easily as on the battlefield.[32] How fortunate for the Roman Empire, especially when fate's threat is dire, that the Teutons are so divided among themselves. Long may it last, I pray, and persist among the nations, this—if not love for us—at least hatred for each other—Fortune can guarantee us nothing better than discord among our foes.[33]

At times, too, he uses his description of the Teutons' way of life to criticise tacitly but unmistakably the Roman society. He lauds the well-protected chastity of the Teuton women, who are not corrupted by the seductions of plays nor by the provocations of the dinner tables. For prostituted chastity there is no pardon; beauty nor youth nor wealth will find her a husband. No one laughs at vice there; no one calls seduction, suffered or wrought, the spirit of the age. Good habits have more force with them than good laws elsewhere.[34] One need hardly ask where Tacitus thinks all these signs of moral depravity are to be found. In Rome Augustus had promulgated in 18 B.C. and 9 A.D. laws intended to improve marital morality, but they had little or no effect.

---

[32] *Germ.* XXIII. 2.

[33] *Germ.* XXXIII. 2.

[34] *Germ.* XIX. 1, 2, 3, 5; what is certainly applicable here is Scramuzza's description of the *Germania* : An ethnographic study of a little-civilised people serves the author as a foil to set off the degeneracy of his own countrymen, V.M. Scramuzza, *The Emperor Claudius*, 1940, p. 19.

Tacitus thus holds up the Teutons as example to the Romans in certain respects. Sometimes he also praises them in general, for example for their great hospitality.[35] At other times he says much good of a particular tribe. The Chauci, for instance, most eminent tribe of the Teutons, prefer to protect their vast domain by justice alone : they are neither grasping nor lawless; in peaceful seclusion they provoke no wars and dispatch no raiders on marauding forays; the special proof of their startling strength is, indeed, just this, that they do not depend for their superior position on injustice; yet they are ready with arms, and, if circumstances should require, with armies, men and horses in abundance; so, even though they keep the peace, their reputation does not suffer.[36] Latent in these words of praise lies, perhaps, a tacit reproach aimed at those Romans who have to use force to maintain their empire, who have spent the past 210 years conquering the Teutons, as Tacitus bitterly remarks, who have celebrated many triumphs right up to recent times, but who have never gained a decisive victory over Germania.[37]

In addition to praise, however, Tacitus also passes severe judgment on the Teutons. Sometimes concerning their morals, as in his description of their exceptionally reckless gambling, in which they stake everything. Contemptuously he then says : such is their persistence in a wicked practice, or their good faith, as they themselves style it.[38] But it is in their culture that the Teutons lag so far behind the Romans. Where they live must be a terrible place. Who, to say nothing about the perils of an awful and unknown sea, would have left Asia or Africa or Italy to look for Germania ? With its wild scenery and harsh climate it is pleasant neither to live in nor to look upon unless it be one's fatherland.[39] Those Teutons live amidst bristling forests and unhealthy marshes, with much rain and wind.[40] Those who live in such a climate cannot but be wild barbarians who only attain a higher level of culture if they come into contact with the

---

[35] *Germ.* XXI. 2.

[36] *Germ.* XXXV. 2, 3, 4; Syme's characterisation of the *Germania* can be applied here, but, in my opinion, it in no way applies to all of this work by Tacitus : "...the *Germania* with its idealized, conventional, and nostalgic portrayal of virtue and integrity among the strong and untainted", R. Syme, *Tacitus*, Vol. II, 1958, pp. 530f.

[37] *Germ.* XXXVII. 2, 6.

[38] *Germ.* XXIV. 4.

[39] *Germ.* ii. 2.

[40] *Germ.* V. 1.

Romans and allow themselves to be led by them. These are no people
who can patiently cultivate their fields and wait for the year's
returns.[41] They do not realise what can be got out of well-kept lands.
It does not enter their minds that they could then lay out orchards,
water-meadows, vegetable gardens and could harvest much more
than by adhering to their primitive agricultural habits.[42] They build
their villages in a most remarkable way, quite different from the
way the Romans do. They lay out their villages not with buildings
contiguous and connected; everyone keeps a clear space round his
house, whether it be a precaution against the chances of fire, or
just ignorance of building.[43] What Tacitus also thinks strange—
though what else could be expected of barbarians—is the lack of
any desire to investigate things more deeply. They let amber lie
among the flotsam and jetsam of the sea until Roman luxury gave
it fame. But even then they showed no desire whatsoever to learn
what substance or process produces it.[44] The phrase reveals the
usual scoff of the superior man, says Sherwin-White when quoting
this passage.[45]

Such judgment of alien peoples recurs ever and again in the works
of Greek and Roman writers. If it is to be termed racial prejudice,
attention must be paid to the distinction rightly drawn by Radin
between the concept "race" formed on the grounds of a biological
theory and the term "race" used to designate a totality of national
and social characteristics. The first connotation of the concept "race"
goes no further back than the last century and was certainly not
known in the ancient world.[46] In describing the opinion of Greek
and Roman writers about other peoples, the use of the word "race",
without further definition of meaning, can indeed be misleading.
The irrevocable establishment of the inferiority of people on racial
grounds is patently absent in the work of Tacitus, and in that respect
he can certainly be accounted representative of many Greek and
Roman writers. The Teutons still have a low level of civilization,
but when certain tribes come into closer contact with the Romans
it appears perfectly possible to make good such a cultural backlog.

---

[41] *Germ.* XIV. 4.
[42] *Germ.* XXVI. 2.
[43] *Germ.* XVI. 2.
[44] *Germ.* XLV. 5.
[45] Sherwin-White, *op. cit.*, p. 37.
[46] Radin, *op. cit.*, pp. 48ff.

All *homines feri ac barbari*, as Caesar repeatedly calls them, can be civilized, and then an unfavourable judgment of them can be commuted to a favourable one.

Roman writers did, of course, remark on the external characteristics of certain peoples. Tacitus, for instance, mentions with a degree of surprise that Teutons grow up amid nakedness and squalor into that girth of limb and frame which is to our people a marvel.[47] They have piercing blue eyes, red hair, tall frames, powerful only spasmodically.[48] The last qualification reveals one of the reasons why the Romans were so fascinated by the outward appearance of the Teutons. They often stood in awe of these colossal Teutons when facing them in battle. It appears that often the Roman soldiers had to conquer a natural fear of these outwardly and ostensibly so powerful antagonists and had to be reminded that their own superior weapons and strategy could enable them to vanquish the enemy. In the practice of warfare, even Caesar had to contend with the enormous size of the Teutons' bodies, *ingens magnitudo corporum*[49] and with the contempt of the Gauls, who were also large by nature, for the *brevitas*, the short posture of the Romans.[50]

All such outward characteristics, however, are mentioned by these authors as interesting pieces of information, or because for one reason or another they were important in their intercourse with these peoples, but not as peculiarities of a race that for this reason must always be hated or despised. In his *Germania* Tacitus says that one peculiarity of the Teutons is the value they attach to blood-relationship. The Treveri and Nervii claim a German origin and value this highly, for they believe that this illustrious ancestry delivers them from any affinity with the indolent Gauls.[51] He says that the Semnones congregate in a sacred wood, then all tribes of the same name and blood, *omnes eiusdem sanguinis populi*, send delegations and after publicly offering up a human life, they celebrate the grim "initiation" of their barbarous worship.[52]

In this same work, Tacitus says he is of the opinion that the Teutons have not intermingled with other peoples. According to

---

[47] *Germ.* XX. 1.
[48] *Germ.* IV. 2.
[49] Caesar, *B.G.* i. 39.
[50] *B.G.* ii. 30.
[51] *Germ.* XXVIII. 4.
[52] *Germ.* XXXIX. 2.

him they are indigenous and very slightly blended with new arrivals
from other races or alliances (*minimeque aliarum gentium adventibus
et hospitiis mixtos*). In my opinion, to translate *"mixtos"* as "rassisch
verfälscht" is to limit this intermingling too much.[53] Elsewhere in
the same work he says he associates himself with the opinions of
those who hold that in the peoples of Germania there has been given
to the world a race unmixed by intermarriage with other races, a
peculiar people and pure, like no one but themselves. In this pronouncement too much emphasis is placed on race if *propria et sincera et
tantum sui similis gens* is translated as : "ein eigenwüchsiges, rasse-
reines Volk von unvergleichlicher Eigenart",[54] and in a comment
on these two passages, moreover, mention is made of the "Reinblütig-
keit" and the "Rassenmerkmale" of the Teutons.[55] Inevitably the
emphasis then falls on the wrong place. Besides, it must be borne
in mind that in the latter passage Tacitus describes the non-inter-
mingling of the Teutons with other peoples primarily from the viewpoint of the Teutons, as he describes it in both passages mentioned
above. In any case, this description is also intended to be a neutral
statement from Tacitus' point of view, in which he neither glorifies
nor condemns the Teutons. Here, again, racial characteristics are
not used as criteria for judging a people. Time and again it is apparent
that, when it mattered, the Romans never allowed themselves to
be persuaded into accepting racial characteristics as definitive for
correlationship with other peoples. In the *Annals* Tacitus relates
that the leading citizens of Gallia Comata were claiming the privilege
of holding magistracies in the capital. Some objected violently to
this request. They argued that the members of the Senate should
be recruited only from the original inhabitants of Italy, the Roman-
born (*indigenae*) and nations whose blood was akin to their own
(*consanguineis populis*). That was how it had always been and that
had always been good enough. Claudius strongly opposed this argument.
Had not history long demonstrated that intermingling of races often
had a very favourable effect ? Did not the Lacedaemonians and
Athenians, despite their strength of arms, suffer defeat because
they held the conquered aloof as alien-born ? And was not Romulus

---

[53] *Germ.* ii. 1; A. Mauersberger, *Tacitus, Germania*, n.d., p. 3; cf. J.G.C. Anderson,
Cornelii Taciti de origine et situ Germanorum, 1938, p. 37 : free from any (subsequent)
admixture of foreign blood by immigration and friendly intercourse.

[54] *Germ.* IV. 1; Mauersberger, *op. cit.*, p. 9.

[55] Mauersberger, *op. cit.*, pp. 112, 114; cf. Anderson, *op. cit.*, pp. 53f.

so wise that he fought and naturalised a people in the course of the same day? That was even more applicable now, since the Gauls had always blended so much with Romans as regards customs, culture and the ties of marriage.[56] It is doubtful whether *consanguineus* should be rendered as blood-relation. But even if the group which used that word in this case wished thus to emphasise a connectedness by blood, it is all too clear from the emperor's reply that, in determining his attitude towards the request of the Gauls, no value whatsoever would be ascribed to this argument.[57] So here again no trace can be found of hostility towards certain peoples because of race in its modern sense. Therefore I believe widely divergent motives are rated equivalent when it is said that in the various works of Tacitus can be found "the traditional dislike and mistrust of the barbarians or of certain of their characteristics, which is the kernel of what we now call race hatred".[58]

A somewhat longer treatment of Tacitus' opinion about other peoples is to my mind warranted, since, rather than being exceptional among Roman writers in this respect, he proves the rule. Besides, of them all, he wrote at greatest length about the Jews. In doing so he was activated by a strong sense of superiority and deep contempt. He wrote many derogatory things about them, but not based on any established racial differences. And not another Roman writer uses the outward traits of the Jews as a means of ridiculing them as a race or of characterising them as an inferior sort of people. One of the very few texts in which reference is made to certain physical traits of a Jew is to be found in the *Acts of Paul*, in which a description is given of the impression made by Paul on a man who saw him for the first time. "He saw Paul coming, a man little of stature, thin-haired upon the head, crooked in the legs, of good state of body, with eyebrows joining and nose somewhat hooked, full of grace; for sometimes he appeared like a man, and sometimes he had the face of an angel".[59] The context in which this passage stands makes it immediately manifest, however, that this description is definitely not prompted by racial hatred. On the contrary, it indicates the

---

[56] *Ann.* XI. 23, 24.

[57] Cf. Sherwin-White, *op. cit.*, pp. 59f.

[58] Sherwin-White, *op. cit.*, p. 51.

[59] *Acts of Paul* 3, M.R. James, *The Apocryphal New Testament*, 1924, p. 273; cf. E. Hennecke-W. Schneemelcher, *Neutestamentliche Apokryphen in deutscher Übersetzung*, II. Band, ³1964, p. 243.

mystery that was revealed in this unsightly, undistinguished figure, this quite exceptional apostle among the people.

A remark about Marcus Aurelius is to be found in the work of Ammianus Marcellinus, fourth century A.D. When travelling to Egypt, via Palestine, this emperor, filled with disgust at the evil-smelling and vociferous Jews, is said to have exclaimed : "O Marco-manni, O Quadi, O Sarmatae, at last I have found people who are of still lower rank than thee".[60] Here is therefore reference to that *faetor judaicus* which was so often proclaimed to be an established fact in the Middle Ages. Still it is evident that an endeavour to collect data on the racial characteristic of the Jews from the writings of ancient writers yields, with difficulty, but a few.

The same applies to archeological data. The work of Fischer-Kittel tends to suggest that such material flows in abundance when this source is tapped. The three volumes of their work are devoted to firstly the literary data, secondly the earliest Jewish portraits and thirdly the earliest caricatures of world Jewry. The text of the last two volumes is profusely illustrated with reproductions. A careful perusal of the text, however, reveals that it cannot be demonstrated conclusively that the accompanying reproductions are of Jews, and certainly not exclusively Jews.[61] As for the mummy portraits, it is absolutely not certain whether, or even if, they depict Jewish faces. The caricatures of all sorts of figures portrayed in terra-cotta, dating from the third and fourth centuries A.D. and deposited in the *Rheinische Landesmuseum* in Trier, are associated with Jews, because several have hooked noses and some are believed to embody a patent and recognisable representation of circumcision. Fischer's argumentation concerning the mummy portraits is not very convincing. At the conclusion of his discussion the author betrays considerable hesitation and admits that no one could be more convinced than himself of the difficulties and resultant deficiencies of his research.[62] Nor does his argumentation concerning the terra-cotta's seem to

---

[60] Reinach, *op. cit.*, p. 353 : *Judaei faetentes*; cf. Martial, *Epigr.* IV. 4, Reinach, *op. cit.*, p. 287; Hopfner, *op. cit.*, p. 47.

[61] Fischer-Kittel, *op. cit.*, pp. 95-108, 167-174.

[62] Fischer-Kittel, *op. cit.*, p. 163; Leipoldt, *op. cit.*, p. 18 believes that certainly seven of the 94 mummy portraits may be classified out of hand as Jewish; Bolkestein, *op. cit.*, p. 161 refutes this and believes that this would be tantamount to adopting the erroneous hypothesis "that nowadays everyone in every region of the globe is capable of identifying a person as a Jew"; cf. Hopfner, *op. cit.*, pp. 45f.

me to be very conclusive. Nothing whatsoever is said to indicate that these caricatures are of Jews. Even the representation of a hooked nose or of circumcision—even if firmly established as such—could hardly be termed absolutely convincing and certainly does not prove that the aim was to ridicule only the Jews. It is quite possible that the Semites, people from the Orient in general, were the target.[63]

Frequently it appears that sharp, hostile comments about the Jews are also directed, almost as a matter of course, against other oriental peoples. Again and again, for example, the Jews are mentioned in one breath with the Syrians. Even Herodotus probably meant the Jews when he mentions in various passages the Syrians of Palestine, e.g. where he states that the Phoenicians and the Syrians admit the Egyptians taught them circumcision.[64] Theophrastus apparently assumes that the Jews belonged to the larger group of the Syrians.[65] Josephus quotes Apion as having said that the Jews came from Syria.[66] Similarly the Roman writers sometimes link up the Syrians with the Jews. Cicero mentions them together.[67] Ovid speaks both of a *Judaeus Syrus* and a *Palaestinus Syrus* in the same passage.[68] Juvenal repeatedly gives vent to his contempt for the Syrians. He does not identify them directly with the Jews. Still, it is certainly not mere accident that, after pouring forth his contempt of the miserable fortune-teller who was one of those Jews who sell their customers all the dreams they want for the minutest of coins, he goes on to mention Armenians and Syrians, who are also prepared to foretell what everyone yearns to hear.[69]

The repeated coupling of Syria and Palestine, of Syrians and Jews, is strong proof that the Jews were not looked upon as a separate

---

[63] Cf. Simon, *op. cit.*, p. 240.

[64] Opinions on this point are divided, however. Reinach, *op. cit.*, p. 2 believes reference is made here to Philistines; Schürer, *op. cit.*, I, p. 675 and Isaac, *op. cit.*, p. 52, believe the reference is to the Jews; Juster, *op. cit.* I, p. 172 does not take sides; Radin, *op. cit.* p. 80 believes, that here Herodotus was evidently using second-hand information for his statements, and therefore we cannot be sure whether or not he refers to Jews. Josephus, who quotes Herodotus ii. 104 takes it for granted that the reference here is to Jews, *Ap.* i. 169, *A.* VIII. 262.

[65] Καίτοι Σύρων μὲν᾿Ιουδαῖοι ... Reinach, *op. cit.*, p. 7: "Parmi les Syriens, les Juifs..."; Radin, *op. cit.*, p. 82: "...the Jews, those Syrians, who...".

[66] *Ap.* ii. 33.

[67] Reinach, *op. cit.*, p. 241: *De prov. cons.* V. 10.

[68] Reinach, *op. cit.*, p. 248: *Ars amat.* I. 75, 415·

[69] *Sat.* VI. 542ff.; He also mentions Syrians *Sat.* III. 63f., VI. 352, VIII. 159.

race, but as part of a larger whole. Moreover the appellation Syrian
was not used to indicate certain racial characteristics, but rather
people of questionable character from the Orient, of whom the Syrians
were best known as slaves, as merchants, as players of all sorts of
music instruments whose reputation in Roman society was not too
good. In his long and bitter philippic against the Greeks, Juvenal
aims a few sentences against the Orient in general : the Syrian Orontes
has long since poured into the Tiber, bringing with it its lingo and
its manners, its flutes and its slanting harpstrings; bringing too
the timbrels of the breed, and the trulls who are bidden ply their
trade at the circus.[70] The use of the name Syrians almost automatically
implied a certain degree of contempt. When the Jews are vaguely
identified, or mentioned in one breath with that eastern people,
as does Cicero when he calls them both "races, themselves born to
be slaves (*nationes natae servituti*)", then they inevitably share in
the contempt felt for the Syrians.[71]

This contempt of the Syrians could at times be a concretising
of an opinion about the Semites, orientals, or even aliens in general.
Some writers attribute the origins of pagan anti-Semitism in the
ancient world to a xenophobia that began mainly in Egypt.There
from time immemorial prevailed a fear of invaders from the east
and a hatred of those Asians, those pludering nomads who had their
eyes on the riches of Egypt. Accordingly, then, anti-Semitism was
absolutely not limited originally to the Jews, but encompassed all
the Semites of Asia. At any moment it could flare up. Thus the later
anti-Semitism of the Greeks in Alexandria could be referred back
to old local traditions.[72] Some scholars have remarked on the striking
similarity between the terminology of later anti-Semitism and the
traditional names for alien invaders, such as the Hyksos in Egypt.
Several versions of a "history of the unclean" occur in Hecataeus,
Manetho, Lysimachus and Chaeremon, but in spite of all their differences there emerges a certain type of story which derives from Egyptian
literature. After analysing the various versions, Yoyotte's conclusion
is : "complété par un examen de quelques thèmes qui apparaissent,
çà et là chez d'autres auteurs, cette étude pousse à se demander
si l'ensemble de la thématique anti-judaïque ne dérive pas d'une

---

[70] *Sat.* iii. 62-66.

[71] Cf. Radin, *op. cit.*, pp. 76ff., 81ff., 215ff.

[72] Cf. Isaac, *op. cit.*, pp. 43ff., 49, 62f., 72, 125.

image, cohérente à sa manière que la philosophie théologico-rituelle du sacerdoce égyptien dressait de l'ennemi étranger".[73] On this point he believes it would be worth while to compare pharaonic leitmotifs with expressions used in the Roman world to define the Jews, e.g. godless, enemies of the gods, enemies of the human race.[74]

The construction of a relationship between Egyptian xenophobia and later anti-Semitism seen as hatred of the Jews is rather loose here and there.[75] The texts adduced to prove this relationship are neither particularly numerous nor always clear. Moreover it is not likely that subsequent to the invasion of the Hyksos and their temporary sovereignty over Egypt, the Egyptians looked upon all conquerors from the east as Asian invaders without distinguishing the various nationalities. They knew they were dealing with different peoples, and they undoubtedly recognised the Jews as a distinct nation. In my view that is demonstrated conclusively by the contents of the papyri of Elephantine. Therein mention is made of Jews who loyally supported the Persian rulers of Egypt in the fifth century B.C. In 410, during the absence of the Persian satrap, the Egyptian priests incited their fellow countrymen to destroy the temple of the Jews. This surely is proof positive that the Egyptians of that region were fully aware of the presence in their midst of the cult of a very special, alien people who honoured their own private God. There is some uncertainty as to whether anti-Semitism was involved in this happening. The religious fanaticism appears to have been directed primarily against the sanctuary. When the Jews sent in their bitter protests about the ravaging of their temple, they did not say unequivocally that the fanaticism was aimed against them personally. Obviously, however, such religious hatred of an alien cult, which for various reasons must have irritated beyond measure the adherents of the national cult, could easily find its outlet in anti-Semitic outbursts. Therefore I should like to reverse Isaac's statement that, if necessary,

---

[73] J. Yoyotte, L'Égypte ancienne et les origines de l'antijudaïsme, *Bulletin de la société Ernest Renan*, in: *Revue de l'histoire des religions*, 1963, pp. 133-143, quotation pp. 135f.; cf. Lazare, *op. cit.*, p. 23.

[74] Yoyotte, *op. cit.*, p. 141; Isaac is also of the opinion that the traditional anti-semitism—in the true sense—later assumed the form of anti-Judaism. "*Lépreux, pestiférés*, n'étaient-ils pas les termes traditionels de mépris appliqués aux Hyksôs?", *op. cit.*, p. 62; according to Yoyotte the later charges of ritual murder and ass-worship made against the Jews indicate this connection, pp. 141f.

[75] Isaac recognises this as regards part of his argumentation on this point, *op. cit.*, p. 62.

what happened in Elephantine could be explained as an anti-Jewish anti-Semitism, but that it could equally well, or even better, be explained otherwise.[76]

Still, it is precisely what happened in Elephantine which once more clearly demonstrates that the Jews were not hated for their racial characteristics, but for the unusual place they always and everywhere occupied in ancient society because of their own choice and their peculiar beliefs.

The Jews were one of those peoples of the ancient world who were attacked by all sorts of writers. Several Roman authors who expressed their opinions about the Jews in one way or another did the same about other peoples at the same time, sometimes in the same work and with no less contempt and animosity. This is particularly true of Tacitus. Cicero passes severe judgment on the Jews in his defence of Flaccus, who was accused of having misappropriated large sums of "Jewish gold" in 62 A.D. while propraetor of Asia. He says in his defence plea that he will speak in a low voice (*summissa voce*), so that only the jurors may hear. He knew that the case would be tried at a place where the Jews could congregate in large numbers, and it was well known how they stick together, how influential they are in informal assemblies. Those are not wanting who would incite them against him and against every respectable man. He shall not help them to do this more easily. Cicero says in praise of Flaccus that "to resist this barbaric superstition was an act of firmness, to defy the crowd of Jews when sometimes in our assemblies they were hot with passion, for the welfare of the state was an act of the greatest seriousness". To the prosecutor Cicero emphatically says: "each state, Laelius, has its own religious scruples, we have ours. Even when Jerusalem was standing and the Jews were at peace with us, the practice of their sacred rites was at variance with the glory of our empire, the dignity of our name, the customs of our ancestors". But now, Cicero adds, "how dear that nation was to the immortal gods is shown by the fact that it has been conquered, let out for taxes, made a slave".[77]

Here Cicero brings all his rhetoric art into play to defame the Jews. He enumerates their bad qualities, knowing this will appeal to a particular section of his audience. He wields the weapons of

---

[76] Isaac, *op. cit.*, p. 50; Lovsky, *op. cit.*, pp. 48f.; Bonsirven, *op. cit.* I, pp. 3f.

[77] Reinach, *op. cit.*, pp. 237-241 : *Pro Flacco* XXVIII. 66, 67 ,69, see above pp. 14f.

irony and sarcasm skilfully. All this, naturally, fitted in well with
his line of defence, for the issue was the gold which that despicable
people, who always stick together and so always form a pressure
group, annually sent to Jerusalem to support the centre of that
barbara superstitio which evidently had not endeared them so very
much to the gods after all. So we see Cicero pouring forth his contempt
over the Jews, but Jews as a nation, people who are always closely
linked together and have their own particular superstition. What he
does not do is to speak of them as a distinctive race with destinctive
external or internal characteristics. He would certainly have done so
in this instance, if these had formed contributing factors to the contempt and scorn of the Jews.

May the things Cicero said about the Jews in his plea on behalf
of Flaccus be termed manifest evidence of his anti-Semitic feelings?
This way of construing his words has often been made little of, since
the passage was just a piece of rhetoric in a plea aimed at making
his client look as noble and his opponent as black as possible. "Mais
quoi", exclaims Isaac, "malmener, discréditer l'adversaire, le traîner
dans la boue, n'est-ce pas, au barreau, la règle de tous le temps"?[78]
And Radin, who believes that "the abuse arises from the necessities
of the case", even goes so far as to assume that Cicero was prepared
to say exactly the opposite if it would have helped his case: we may
be sure if Cicero were prosecuting Flaccus, a few eloquent periods
would extol the characteristics of those ancient allies and firm friends
of Rome, the Jews.[79] I have doubts about the latter. For Cicero,
who had been taught by Posidonius of Apamea and Apollonius
Molon, such an attack on the Jews would not merely have been
the rhetorical tricks of a defence advocate. It is Radin's belief that,
if he had been influenced by these two teachers, he would have
adopted more of their methods.[80] I would not be surprised if Cicero
knew perfectly well that rhetorical restraint is more, and an abundance
of material less effective. What he says closely accords on many
points with what his teachers had said before him. Cicero does not
literally quote his teacher Posidonius, who called the Jews the only
people to reject all social contact with other peoples as being enemies,
who considered them godless and hated by the gods, who accused

---

[78] Isaac, *op. cit.*, p. 112.

[79] Radin, *op. cit.*, pp. 231f.

[80] Radin, *op. cit.*, pp. 232f.; cf. Reinach, *op. cit.*, p. 241[1].

them of misanthropy and said they would never sit at table with
another nation nor display any goodwill towards him; nevertheless
these do echo very clearly in Cicero's extremely original sarcasm
the anti-Semitic themes of Posidonius. The same applies to Apollonius
Molon, where he says of the Jews that they were godless and haters
of men and reproaches them for not receiving in their midst people
who held different opinions about the godhead and for not having
any intercourse with those who adopted a different way of life than
they.[81]

Consequently Cicero's pronouncements cannot be set aside as
merely the tricks of trade of a lawyer which have little validity as
evidence of anti-Semitism in ancient days. He must definitely be
seen within this framework and, as will appear below, he fits in there
exceptionally well. It has rightly been pointed out that the Jews
were far from being the only target for attack in Cicero's court
pleadings. Cicero directed his attacks against diverse nations, depen-
ding on how it suited his defence pleas. In the case of Flaccus, he
aimed his rhetorical weapons at the Jews, in his defence of Fonteius
at the Celts.[82] In another lawsuit the Sardinians were the opponents,
whom he called a tribe so utterly worthless that they imagine that
freedom is to be distinguished from slavery only by the licence which
it gives for the telling of lies.[83]

Evidence can be found in the works of other Roman authors to
show that the Jews shared with other peoples the hatred, contempt
and ridicule of the Romans. Ovid really not only mentions the Jewish
synagogue as a place fit for carrying on the *ars amatoria*, but for
this purpose he also advises a walk in the Porticus of Pompey, on
the Campus Martius, or the place where Venus bemourns Adonis,
or the Egyptian Isis temple, or the place where the Appian water
pipe splashes into view near the marble temple of Venus, or the
theatres.[84] The Jewish Sabbath is not the only suitable day for such

---

[81] Posidonius of Apamea, Reinach, *op. cit.*, pp. 56-59, Apollonius Molon, *ibid.*,
pp. 60-64.

[82] *Pro Fonteio* XIV. 30.

[83] *Pro Scauro* XVII. 38; cf. Radin, *op. cit.*, p. 196 and what he says about the
"pretty lies", which Cicero also defends, *De officiis* ii. 14, *op. cit.*, pp. 173f.; Isaac,
op. cit., p. 112[2]: "Cicéron n'hésite pas à malmener de même les Gaulois, les Alexandrins,
les Asiatiques quand les besoins de la cause l'exigent"; Art. Anti-Semitism in *Encyclopaedia Judaica*, 3, 1971, p. 95.

[84] *Ars amatoria* i. 55ff.

activity; the day of the defeat near the Allia is also a good one for
starting courting.[85]

Juvenal fulminates against others as well as the Jews in his satires,
and often more fiercely and at greater length. He detested the Greeks
intensely, since they intruded into many circles of Roman society
and with their fine talk managed to brush aside the true Romans.
They are masters of flattery, ferret out the secrets of the house,
play up to all the female members of the household, even the grand-
mother if necessary. They oust their rivals with a drop of their
national poison. No matter whether the Romans have served their
master long and faithfully, they have to go. The Greeks are greatly
in fashion in Rome; ladies of high society say and do everything
in Greek. They are cunning men, those Greeks, for whom Juvenal
expresses his deepest contempt in the diminutive : *omnia novit Graecu-
lus esuriens*, III.77f. He cannot bear to see how all of Rome is Graecised
by those beings, the race which is most dear to our rich men (*gens
divitibus nostris acceptissima*, III.58), but which he avoids like the
plague.[86]

Juvenal's philippic against the Greeks was obviously prompted by
jealousy. The way those clever foreigners worked their way into
every profession distressed him. He says this in so many words :
"There is no room for any Roman here, where some Protogenes,
or Diphilus, or Hermarchus rules the roast".[87] However, there is
more to it than just personal rancour and envy. It annoyed him
to see Rome gradually being inundated by an alien people with
their alien manners, customs, language, way of thinking and beliefs.
In the end nothing would remain of the real Roman way of life and
thinking. This vexation is probably at the back of his mind when,
in his 15th satire, he speaks with possibly even more contempt of
the Egyptians than the Greeks, At length he fulminates against
their monstrous idolatry, which he had learned of during a stay
in Egypt and probably therefore could describe in detail. No word
is vehement enough to scourge those absurd superstitions, that lunatic
adoration of crocodile, ibis and ape, the criminal acts of cruelty

---

[85] *Ibid.*, i. 413ff.

[86] *Sat.* iii. 58-125; cf. *Sat.* VI. 187-193, 295ff.; Radin, *op. cit.*, pp. 323ff.; Sherwin-
White, *op. cit.*, pp. 71ff.

[87] *Sat.* iii. 119, 120.

perpetrated in the name of superstition.[88] If something is known
of all those atrocities in Egypt, how is it possible that even the slightest
vestige of the Egyptian culture is tolerated, indeed welcomed with
enthusiasm in Rome.

Now it was the very same fear of Rome being invaded by alien
peoples with their alien customs and ideas which Juvenal harboured
against the Jews. Everywhere one comes across members of that
miserable people. Old or sacred places are desecrated by their presence.
One meets them as beggars and fortune-tellers. But worst of all,
these people are also gaining ground in Rome. If the father was
inclined towards Judaism, the children succumb to it completely.
Though the father was a man who observed the Sabbath, the son
will worship nothing but the clouds and the divinity of the heavens
and see no difference between eating swine's flesh, from which their
father abstained, and that of man; and in time they take the circumcision. Having been wont to flout the laws of Rome, they learn and
practice and revere the Jewish law, and all that Moses committed
to his secret tome.[89]

The basic, recurring motif in Juvenal is thus the threat that the
ways of life and thought of alien people will supplant those of Rome.
Other writers also show concern for the proselytising of the Jews.
Reference has already been made above (p. 37) in a different context
to Strabo's remark, as recorded by Josephus, about that people
who are to be found everywhere throughout the world and who
have made their power felt.[90]

Seneca is of the opinion that the practice of that damned people
has become so prevalent that it has already been adopted in all
lands. The conquered have given laws to their conquerors.[91] In
suchlike words Rutilius Namatianus concludes a few sarcastic remarks
about the Jews after having been treated unpleasantly by a Jewish
innkeeper, who spoiled a beautiful day for him : that plague, which
seemed to have been eradicated so thoroughly by the arms of Pompey

---

[88] Isaac, *op. cit.*, p. 115[3] : Juvénal s'en prend aux Égyptiens plus violemment qu'aux
Judéens.

[89] *Sat.* iii. 10ff., VI. 542ff., XIV. 96ff.; Reinach, *op. cit.*, pp. 290-292.

[90] Marcus translates μηδ'ἐπικρατεῖται ὑπ'αὐτοῦ as "(in which) it has not made its
power felt", but he also admits the possibility of translating the passage as "(in which)
it has not become dominant" or "(which) has not been occupied by it" (*A*. XIV. 115,
Loeb-ed. VII, p. 509c).

[91] Reinach, *op. cit.*, pp. 262f. : Augustinus, *De civ. Dei* VI. 11.

and Titus, has spread its pollution even further. The conquered people oppress the conquerors.[92] It is a continual source of vexation that all sorts of cults, and especially the Jewish, win adherents in Rome and that therefore the innate character of Roman society is in constant danger. It is clear that this vexation was not really confined to the Jews, that they were not hated because of their race. Besides, it is precisely the hostility directed against the proselytes belonging to completely different nations which proves that the motif of racial prejudice did not play a role.[93]

It need cause no surprise, therefore, that all sorts of other accusations made about the Jews were often directed against other peoples as well and consequently were expressed without any ulterior thoughts about race or lineage. Tacitus, for example, frequently speaks of the *superstitio* of the Jews, but this *taeterrima gens* is certainly not the only one he accuses. According to him, even Antiochus had endeavoured to abolish Jewish superstition and to introduce Greek civilization; the war with the Parthians, however, prevented his improving this basest of peoples.[94] Elsewhere he speaks of the Jews as a people which, though prone to superstition, is opposed to all propitiatory rites.[95] But he uses this same term for the Teutons, for example the Semnones, whose superstition is linked up with a sacred grove,[96] for the Naharvali,[97] for the Aestii, of whom he says they worship the mother of the gods : "as an emblem of that superstition they wear the figures of wild boars".[98] Tacitus knows of an ancient Germanic custom, which regards many women as endowed with prophetic powers and, as the superstition grows (*augescente supersitione*) attributes divinity to them.[99]

Similarly in Britain are to be found the Gallic ceremonies and Gallic religious beliefs (*superstitionum persuasiones*).[100] After the Roman conquests, the groves consecrated to the savage cults of the Druids (*saevis superstitionibus sacri*) were cut down.[101]

---

[92] Reinach, *op. cit.*, pp. 359f. : *De reditu suo* I. 395ff.
[93] Cf. Sherwin-White, *op. cit.*, p. 99; see above pp. 39f.
[94] *Hist.* V. 8.
[95] *Hist.* V. 13 : *gens superstitioni obnoxia...*
[96] *Germ.* XXXIX. 4.
[97] *Germ.* XLIII. 4.
[98] *Germ.* XLV. 2, 3.
[99] *Hist.* IV. 61.
[100] *Agric.* XI. 3; here the text is not certain.
[101] *Ann.* XIV. 30.

In his brief, trenchant delineation of the province Egypt occur these words : "given to civil strife and sudden disturbances because of the fanaticism and superstition of its inhabitants".[102]

So we see that in Tacitus there is fundamentally little difference between the charge of *superstitio* against the Jews and that against other peoples. Occasionally he mentions the Jews in the same breath as others regarding this matter. Under Tiberius both the Egyptian and Jewish cults were banished simultaneaously from Rome. By decree of the senate, 4000 people of the class of *libertini* who were tainted with that superstition (*ea superstitione infecta*) were exiled to Sardinia. In his comment on this event, Suetonius also mentions both the Egyptian and the Jewish rites. That Tacitus is not here referring to the Jewish race, not even to the Jews as a people, would be even more manifest if he used the term *libertini generis* to refer not merely to the emancipated Jews and the term *superstitione infecta* to indicate that he had proselytes in mind, as Radin believes.[103] Whatever the case may be, the fact that here Tacitus and Suetonius bundle both the Jewish and the Egyptian cults, as a matter of course, under *superstitio*, is indeed proof that the Jews were judged not as a race, but as a people, as a given community of faith and morals, in the same way as any other peoples. It is well-known that both these writers used the same expression when mentioning the Christians.[104]

Thus not a single indication is to be found in ancient literature that anti-Semitism in the ancient world used the theory of race as weapon of attack.

---

[102] *Hist.* I. 11 : *superstitione ac lascivia discordem et mobilem.*

[103] *Ann.* ii. 85; cf. Suet., *Tib.* XXXVI. 1. In this connection he, too, speaks of the *Aegyptii Judaicique ritus* and of those, *qui superstitione ea tenebantur.* Dio Cassius LVII. 18 also mentions this happening; it is also described, with different details, by Josephus, *A.* XVIII. 81-85 (cf. Loeb-ed. IX, pp. 59ff.) Seneca probably also hints at it, *Ep.* CVIII. 22. Regarding the text and its translation cf. A. Beltrami, *L. Annaei Senecae ad Lucilium Epistulae Morales* II, 1949, p. 179; Loeb-ed. of the *Ep. Mor.* III, 1953, p. 243; E. Phillips Barker, *Seneca's Letters to Lucilius* II, 1932, p. 227; Radin, *op. cit.*, p. 310; Hospers-Jansen, *op. cit.*, p. 105.

[104] Tacitus, *Ann.* XV. 44 : *exitiabilis superstitio*; Suet. *Nero* XVI. 3 : *superstitio nova et malefica*; Pliny the Younger, *Ep.* X. 96 : *superstitio prava, immodica.*

CHAPTER TWO

SOCIAL STATUS?

There have always been divergent answers to the question as to
how far anti-Semitism in ancient days was due to the economic
position of the Jews in the community. Many scholars have ascribed
great significance to it, believing that the important role of the Jews
in commerce and banking was responsible to a large extent for fostering
hostility towards them. Herzfeld feels obliged to explain and, in
a certain sense, to excuse the commercial spirit imputed to the Jews
of the ancient world. His opinion is that the Jews in the Diaspora
in particular applied themselves to commerce. Economic conditions
often drove them to leave Palestine voluntarily and to settle down
in more westerly countries, especially in the large towns that were
trading centres in the Hellenistic period. They were unable to purchase
land and engage in agriculture, so they turned to commerce and
in it often acquired great riches. This was one of the main reasons
for the hatred and envy they evoked around them; but their commercial acumen was practically forced upon them by the historical
situation.[1] The theme of Jewish predominance in the economy of
the ancient world being one of the most important roots of anti-
Semitism can be heard in diverse variations in the literature relevant
to our subject, though, it must be admitted, more often in the older
than the newer. Certainly, too, in the strongly or lightly anti-Semitic-
tinted literature, though not exclusively. Evidence of this is provided
by the book of Levi Herzfeld, a rabbi of Brunswick.

It was the normal thing at the beginning of this century to ascribe
to the lucrative commercial transactions of the Jews a great influence
on the inception and intensification of anti-Semitism. Striking examples
of this are the works of Stähelin and Bludau.[2] The latter, for example,
writes: "Der Reichtum der Juden, selbst wenn er durch Fleiss,
Treue und Gewandtheit in ehrlicher Weise erworben war, erregte

---

[1] L. Herzfeld, *Handelsgeschichte der Juden des Altertums*, 1879, ²1894.

[2] F. Stähelin, *Der Antisemitismus des Altertums*, 1905; A. Bludau, *Juden und Judenverfolgungen im alten Alexandria*, 1906.

schon den Neid und die Missgunst der heidnischen Städter, erst recht
die in rücksichtloser Weise, vielleicht durch wucherischen Geldhandel
erzielten geschäftlichen Erfolge".[3] Sometimes one gets the impression
that writers borrowed such pronouncements from each other without
personally verifying them, for not long after Bludau another wrote :
"Als Geschäftsleute und Bankiere gelangten viele zu grossem Reichtum, der selbst dann, wenn sie ihn auf redliche Weise, durch Fleiss
und Klugheit, erworben hatten, den Neid und den Hass der Volks-
menge auf sie lenkte, um so mehr noch, wenn sie ihn rücksichtlos
durch Betrug und Wucher zu vermehren trachteten".[4] Another
writer did not deem it necessary to check the following statement
against the sources, or even to motivate it by quoting from other
works : "Sein Reichtum, die Überlegenheit und Skrupellosigkeit im
Handel, die der Jude als Orientale mitbrachte, seine Fähigkeit, die
Gunst der Umstände zu benutzen, die anschwellende Volkskraft des
Judentums erregten den Hass und die wilde Leidenschaft des Pöbels".[5]
Later, too, various authors who cannot be suspected of anti-Semitism
commented on the important role the Jews were supposed to have
played in the economic sphere in certain periods and countries.[6]

There are also a few writers who do not deny completely the influence
of economic factors on the rise of anti-Semitism in the ancient world,
but ascribe only secondary significance to them.[7]

In the long run, however, the majority of the writers have come
to believe that the economic factors were of little or no importance.
On this point they accuse their opponents of having projected the
relationships that developed in the Middle Ages and afterwards back
into the ancient world.[8] Naturally these writers do not deny there

---

[3] Bludau, op. cit., pp. 45f.

[4] P. Heinisch, Griechentum und Judentum im letzten Jahrhundert vor Christus, 1908,
p. 22.

[5] W. Bousset, Die Religion des Judentums im neutestamentlichen Zeitalter, [2]1906,
p. 87; cf. Wilcken, op. cit., pp. 788f.

[6] L. Fuchs, op. cit., p. 4 : "Die Juden müssen Alexander durch ihre über die ganze
Welt verbreiteten Handelsbeziehungen ...zu wertvollen Freunden geworden sein";
J.B. Frey, Corpus Inscriptionum Judaicarum I, 1936, p. LXIV : "La diaspora occidentale
est née de l'esprit d'affaires".

[7] Bell, Jews and Christians in Egypt, 1924, p. 11 : "Economic factors were not
without influence..."; Leipoldt, op. cit., p. 34 : "Neben den religiösen und politischen
Gründen des Judenhasses spielen wirtschaftliche eine geringe Rolle".

[8] Noted already by Juster, op. cit. II, p. 314[1] : "on a transporté à l'antiquité des
idées qu'on avait acquises par l'étude du moyen-âge"; cf. Bolkestein, op. cit., p. 16;
Tcherikover, op. cit., pp. 343, 369; CPJ I, p. 11; Heinemann, op. cit., p. 40.

were certainly many Jews in ancient times who engaged in commerce and financial transactions and that some of them acquired riches. But they dispute the contention that, more than any other peoples, the Jews practised such professions primarily or exclusively. Their opinion, based on the sources, is that the Jews of the ancient world had very divergent professions and were not different from any other nation in this respect. They term it a misconception that the Jews of the Diaspora lived exclusively or mainly in the towns and, moreover, point out that in those days a large area of land surrounding the cities was accounted urban territory. According to them there were undoubtedly Jews who became very wealthy in certain professions, but they were the exceptions and definitely did not constitute the great majority.[9] In any case, they say, the sources contain no evidence that the Jews were hated for their wealth or commercial practices. Not one single writer of antiquity mentions such when pouring forth his hatred and contempt of the Jews. If allusions to such things have been found in certain papyri, then usually this could only have happened afterwards, when unconsciously the interpretation of the passages was influenced by later anti-Semitism. Moreover there are various data, literary and archeological, which testify to a contempt and scorn of the dire poverty of the Jews. "Im ganzen hat als typisch jüdisch nicht der Reichtum, sondern seit der Kaiserzeit eher die Armut gegolten".[10] "The usual reason for despising the Jews was their poverty, not their wealth".[11]

Hence many writers categorically deny the significance of economic factors as a reason for the anti-Semitism of the ancient world. Understandably their numbers have increased in the course of time, for the papyri often give a different picture of the social position of the Jews than the one formed prior to their discovery. The opinion that the economic situation played at most a minor role can thus be said to have gained a great many supporters, excepting, of course, those writers who use historiography to defend modern anti-Semitism.[12]

---

[9] Tcherikover, *op. cit.*, p. 343; L. Fuchs, *op. cit.*, pp. 46-50.

[10] Heinemann, *op. cit.*, p. 41.

[11] *CPJ* I, p. 11.

[12] Examples of the repudiation of the importance of the economic factor : E.R. Bevan, *A History of Egypt under the Ptolemaic Dynasty*, 1927, pp. 8, 111 : "We think of the Jews today as pre-eminently financiers and traders. But in those days they had not yet any special reputation in that line"; Simon, *op. cit.*, p. 240 : "S'il n'offre aucun caractère ethnique, l'antisémitisme des anciens n'a pas davantage de fondement économi-

Regarding this point, opinions appear to differ rather widely. It is not easy, indeed sometimes impossible, to attain absolute certainty. In the first place there is a relative paucity of data illustrative of the economic situation of the Jews. In the course of time archeological excavations have increased their number, but not sufficiently to warrant definitie conclusions. All too often we have to make do with statements that have been preserved more or less by chance and that originally were not really intended to impart information about the economic position of the Jews. For instance, some knowledge of the variety of professions of the Jews of Alexandria in the first half of the first century A.D. has been gained from Philo's comment on the ruinous consequences for the economy of Alexandria of a progrom held in that city. Jewish activity in all sorts of sectors in which they worked came to a standstill, and as a result many other groups lost their employment. Such a comment is inevitably one-sided, since Philo naturally would mention especially those professions which were most significant for economic affairs.[13]

In the second place it must always be remembered that the data are largely determined by time and locale. Regarding Egypt, the situation in Alexandria was already fairly well known for some time from literary sources, especially the writings of Philo and Josephus. Now that many papyri from that country are also known, the economic picture of the Egyptian rural areas has become clearer, and certain conclusions drawn from the literary data must be revised. Papyri and inscriptions from other parts of the world of that time have cast a new light on the economic relationships. Proportionally, however, they are scarce, and we know nothing on this point about many places, regions, countries and periods. Conclusions must therefore not be drawn too hastily from these scarce and incidental data. For example, the fact that some Jewish professions are mentioned a few times more often than others does not necessarily signify that they were special to them. Nor may the silence of the sources about other professions lead to the conclusion that the Jews were not engaged in them.

---

que. Il n'est jamais question d'une mainmise d'Israël sur l'activité commerciale ou industrielle"; Sherwin-White, *op. cit.*, p. 93: "The sources are entirely silent about economic rivalry of any sort"; B. Jacob, Art. Antisemitismus in *Encyclopaedia Judaica* II, 1928, p. 966: "Dem Antisemitismus im Altertum lagen keinesfalls wirtschaftliche Motive zugrunde"; cf. Bolkestein, *op. cit.*, pp. 161ff.; Heinemann, *op. cit.*, pp. 39ff.; Hospers-Jansen, *op. cit.*, p. 36; *CPJ* I, pp. 10f.; Tcherikover, *op. cit.*, pp. 333f., 343, 369f.

[13] *Flacc.* 57.

Different periods often require different evaluations of the situation of the Jews. With respect to professions in Egypt, for instance, a wide distinction must be made between the age of the Ptolemies and that of the Romans. The Romans disbanded the entire army as it existed under the Ptolemies. Jews had occupied various ranks in that army. The system of collecting taxes in that country was also altered radically by the Romans. Native tax collectors were replaced by government officials. The former had included Jews. If the conclusion drawn from sources dating from the period of Roman supremacy in Egypt is that Jews were never soldiers and never had anything to do with the collecting of taxes, then that obtains for the period of Roman occupation, not for the preceding centuries. This change in the status of the Jews in Egypt was due exclusively to a change in the policy of the ruling powers.

In the third place account must always be taken of the viewpoint behind the treatment of economic relationships. As appeared above, Josephus' sympathy was clearly for the upper classes, and eminent Jews had an advantage in his eyes, even when, like Tiberius Alexander, they had renounced their Jewish faith.[14] Similarly, the fact that Philo belonged to a given social class strongly influenced his historiography.[15] One consequence is, for example, that "Philo had no interest in poor people".[16] And the general rule is, of course, that the lower classes received little attention from authors who were only interested in describing the history they considered important. In it people from the lowest ranks of society played no part at all, except as a dark background formed by an impersonal, anonymous rabble. Even then the authors felt no compulsion to say what place those people occupied in society. Hence it is highly probable that the percentage of eminent Jews, of the "higher" professions among them, is rated too high if based solely on data from literary sources. Only when writers deliberately aim at ridiculing the Jews for their abject poverty, as Juvenal does, it is possible that the bias in the news reported inclines in the opposite direction.

All in all, therefore, it is not a simple matter to determine the degree to which economic factors influenced the attitude towards the Jews in the ancient world. There are practically no unequivocal

---

[14] Above pp. 19f.

[15] Above pp. 23f.

[16] *CPJ* I, p. 50.

indications that they had a significant influence. Those who rate highly the importance of the economic factors admit this frankly, though at times almost ostensibly with some reluctance. Bludau, mentioned above, admits : "Merkwürdig bleibt, dass die Anklage des Wuchers oder der geschäftlichen Unredlichkeit von den Judenfeinden des Altertums nie gegen die Juden direkt erhoben worden ist". But he goes on to say : "Freilich in Unredlichkeit und geschäftlicher Geriebenheit konnten ja auch Griechen und Syrer nicht überboten werden, und die Römer gaben diesen nicht viel nach".[17] Still, it is remarkable that this charge was never clearly made directly against the Jews in ancient times. Nevertheless it is frequently assumed that there were many such charges, an assumption based on conclusions drawn from the facts, not on the facts themselves. According to Wilcken, for example, it is "wohl zweifellos" that the enormous and progressive expansion of the Jewish Diaspora must inevitably have activated friction in the community and social life, particularly since, ar the papyri testify, the Jews were operating in the most divergent spheres, "vor allem wohl im Handel". But to this comment on the share of the Jews in commerce, he has to add a footnote admitting : Urkundliche Belege gibt es bisher wohl wenige. To compensate this weak point in his hypothesis he puts forward the supposition : "Im übrigen ist es wohl nicht zweifelhaft, dass der grosse Reichtum, der zu Beginn der Kaiserzeit in einzelnen jüdischen Familien in Alexandrien herrschte, in erster Reihe durch Handel und Geschäfte erworben ist".[18] Obviously, if the sources contain not a single indication concerning this point, the accuracy of such a conclusion is open to doubt. More or less credible surmises are all that can be expected.

Such an inclination to combinations which cannot be based directly on data becomes all the more questionable when it also engenders "an arbitrary interpretation of several papyri which have won the particular affection of modern anti-Semites".[19] A sample of such an interpretation has been given above (pp. 33ff.). Two more follow, and then the stock of data capable of being used to illustrate the discreditable dealings of the Jews is about exhausted. Within the context of this chapter it is therefore all the more important to demonstrate how, in the interpretation of these two papyri, probabilities are sometimes assumed to be certainties.

---

[17] Bludau, *op. cit.*, p. 33; cf. above p. 34 : Wilcken, *op. cit.*, p. 790.

[18] Wilcken, *op. cit.*, pp. 788f.

[19] Tcherikover, *op. cit.*, pp. 369f.

The first of the two papyri concerns the charge made by a woman
from the Egyptian village Alexandrou-Nesos against a certain Dorotheos, who is accused of stealing her cloak and making off with it.
He took it to a synagogue. Lezelmis, a wealthy Thracian landowner
who had 100 arourai of land, came up to help, apparently put an
end to the argument and handed the cloak over to Nikomachos,
verger of the synagogue. The woman summoned Dorotheos and Nikomachos before the court in order to retrieve her cloak, or its worth
in money.

Bludau comments on this papyrus as follows : "der Spitzbube
Dorotheos, ein Jude in Alexandronesos, welcher einer Frau, während
sie in einem Bade oder in einer Leinwandfabrik weilte, ihren Mantel
entwendete, und sein Helfershelfer Nikomachus, der Synagogendiener
des Ortes, der den Mantel in Verwahrsam nahm werden nicht die
einzigen Schurken ihrer Art gewesen sein".[20] This *could* have been
how it happened, but it is not certain, and not even likely in one
respect. In the first place it is not said in the papyrus that the accused
culprit was a Jew. That is sometimes added. The point is that only
the right-hand half of the papyrus has been preserved, and therefore
the supplementations of the left-hand half are based on more or
less feasible surmises.[21] One such follows "Dorotheos" at the beginning
of the letter : "(a Jew who lives in) the same village". The assumption
that he was a Jew is based, not entirely unjustly, on the fact that
he fled with his loot into a synagogue. That could mean that, as
Jew, he could expect to find there fellow Jews willing to help him
hide the cloak. Another possibility is, however, that as thief—not
necessarily as Jewish thief—he sought refuge in a sanctuary where
he could temporarily take advantage of the right of asylum. That
also a synagogue was sometimes used as such a sanctuary is known
from a few sources.

As νακόρος of the synagogue, Nikomachos was of course a
Jew.[22] But there is absolutely no proof that he was a "Helfershelfer"
of the thief, even though Wilcken assumes that the thief had concealed
the cloak "bei einem offenbar mit ihm unter einer Deckes steckenden
Hazzan der jüdischen Synagoge".[23] This document contains an

---

[20] Bludau, *op. cit.*, p. 45.
[21] Cf. *CPJ* I, pp. 239ff.
[22] For his function see *CPJ* I, p. 241, line 7.
[23] Wilcken, *op. cit.*, p. 789.

expression which argues the contrary. It is said that Nikomachos
will retain the custody of the cloak ἕως κρίσεως (till the case
was tried). This sounds more as if the synagogue official acted as
the person who could safely be entrusted with the stolen goods for
the time being. The mention of the important man in the village,
the landowner who had a large say in matters concerning the villagers,
could likewise point in the same direction : "he put an end to the
argument by mediating, for the moment, between the two parties".

Hence it cannot be concluded definitely from this papyrus that
two Jews acted wrongly, not even that the thief was a Jew, though
very likely he was. If so, it simply shows that there were also thieves
among the Jews. Another papyrus confirms this in a report of the
superintendant of an estate, in which it is stated that three Jews
raided a vineyard, stripped the grapes from the vine, and, when
the guard ran out against them, they maltreated him and struck
him on any part of the body that offered; and they carried off a
vine-dresser's pruning-hook. The reporter estimated the grapes
gathered as enough to make 6 metretai of wine.[24] This papyrus
contains conclusive proof that the ancient Jews sometimes stole.
But this they had undoubtedly in common with all non-Jews, regardless of nationality. Many papyri from the land where these incidents
took place mention theft, deceit, evil practices of all kinds committed
by Hellenes and Egyptians. So it is not at all surprising that there
is nothing to show that Jews in particular were reproached with
such practices.

Similarly the second papyrus, which so often has won the particular
affection of modern anti-Semites, contains less certain grounds for
such than is often thought. It is a letter from Menon to his brother
Hermokrates. It appears that Hermokrates had told Menon he would
send him a mare that would be brought by a Jew, whose name he
did not know. He states in the letter that he did not give the mare,
nor the carriage which went with it, πορεία αὐτῆς. The meaning
of the last expression is obscure. It is sometimes translated as "cost
of transport", sometimes it is taken to be a slip of the pen for τὸ
πορεῖον and is then translated as "wagon".[25] This is not the only
obscurity which renders the interpretation of the papyrus uncertain.
The two verbs, which are of such importance for the interpretation

[24] *CPJ* I, pp. 157f.
[25] *CPJ* I, pp. 249ff.

and which are rendered as "to send" and "to be brought", are missing in the Greek. The lacunae at those places in the papyrus are filled in differently, but on this depends, however, whether or not this papyrus contains any mention of discreditable commercial practices of a Jew. The latter is assumed as a matter of course by Wilcken, for example, who says that the letter speaks "von einem Juden, der bei einem Pferdehandel seinen Verpflichtungen nicht nachgekommen ist",[26] and who calls this Jew in a later work "ein betrügerischer jüdischer Pferdehändler".[27] Bludau uses such an interpretation of this papyrus to draw up a far-reaching conclusion: "Als Händler werden viele (Juden) im Lande ihr Brot erworben haben, nicht immer vielleicht in ehrlicher Weise, wie z.B. jener jüdische Pferdehändler". Elsewhere in his work he refers again to this papyrus: "Die Beschwerde über die Betrügereien des jüdischen Pferdehändlers Daniel ist ein interessantes Indizium dafür dass die Juden nicht ausschliesslich durch ihre religiösen Eigentümlichkeiten das Missfallen ihrer Nachbarn erregten".[28] So we see on what slight and, moreover, unsound grounds is constructed the picture of the Jews in ancient times as dealers with evil practices and of the hostile reactions to them of the non-Jews, whereas in this instance, if one confines oneself to the direct, manifest testimony of the papyrus, one must simply say: "A private letter from Menon to his brother Hermokrates. The latter authorised a Jew to hand over a mare to Menon, but the Jew did not carry out the order. This is the only clear knowledge we can get from the papyrus. All other suggestions are mere guess-work".[29] Nowhere in this papyrus is it stated clearly that the man was a Jewish horse-dealer. Hence it is quite possible that Hermokrates wanted to give his brother a horse (together with something else), that the Jew was supposed to deliver the mare, but that so far he had not done so. The delay could have been caused by any number of things. Menon was evidently worried and probably suspicious too, but in no case can it be definitely concluded that Menon referred to the deceptive machinations of a Jewish horse-dealer. It is important to establish this point, for only by interpreting the papyri in question in a certain manner can they be used as evidence

---

[26] Wilcken, *op. cit.*, p. 790; cf. L. Fuchs, *op. cit.*, p. 59.

[27] L. Mitteis und U. Wilcken, *Grundzüge und Chrestomathie der Papyruskunde* I, 2, 1912, p. 57.

[28] Bludau, *op. cit.*, pp. 29, 45; cf. Stähelin, *op. cit.*, p. 36; Fischer-Kittel, *op. cit.*, p. 59.

[29] *CPJ* I, p. 249.

that the practices of the Jews in certain professions were a contributing factor to anti-Semitism in the ancient world.

This being so, there is good reason to review the unequivocal information available in the sources pertaining to the economic and social position of the Jews and any influence the latter might have had on the opinion of non-Jews about them. In the first place it is an established fact that there were many wealthy and eminent Jews in the ancient world. The literary and archeological data testify to this. Several of them are mentioned by name, especially by Josephus, who says they often played a very important role under the Ptolemies. One of them was Joseph, son of Tobiah. He had acquired the right to gather taxes.[30] Once he had it, he did not hesitate to collect the taxes by force if necessary, as for example in Ascalon and Scythopolis, where he had the reluctant notables put to death and their property confiscated. Having thus collected great sums of money and made great profits from farming the taxes, he used his wealth to make permanent the power which he now had.[31]

This Joseph had a steward (οἰκονόμος), Arion, who managed all the wealth which he had in Alexandria, amounting to not less than three thousand talents.[32] Earlier Josephus mentions that he was prepared to pay double the amount previously offered by another for the lease of the taxes, not 8000, but 16000 talents.[33] Arion was to negotiate in Alexandria with Joseph's son Hyrcanus, who appears to have needed a considerable amount of money in his youth. Arion hopes to put him off with 10 talents, or a little more, but the young libertine requests 1000. At first Arion refuses, but in the jail awaiting him he changes his mind, especially when he sees that Hyrcanus has the favour of the court.[34] It is not surprising that Joseph encountered quite a lot of problems in his family and had to resort to all sorts of methods to maintain his position. In recording his death, however, Josephus believes he can say of this Jew at the court of the Ptolemies, that he had been an excellent and high-minded man, who had brought the Jewish people from poverty and a state of weakness to more splendid opportunities of life during the twenty-two years he controlled the taxes of Syria, Phoenicia and Samaria.[35]

---

[30] *A*. XII. 169ff.

[31] *A*. XII. 184, 185.

[32] *A*. XII. 200.

[33] *A*. XII. 175f.

[34] *A*. XII. 203, 208.

[35] *A*. XII. 224.

These are a few fragments of Josephus' detailed story about a
very wealthy, powerful Jew. Is he to be believed? The accuracy
of diverse details in such stories is doubted by many. Regarding
the description of the activity of this Joseph, son of Tobiah, it is
frequently pointed out that the statements of Josephus give no
clear and definite information about the monarchs under whom
Joseph held his high position. One suggestion is that this story,
too, was drawn from various sources, whose historical authenticity
greatly differs. The concensus of opinion is that Josephus is inclined
to exaggerate when giving numbers, and certainly in this story.[36] The
laudatory words used by Josephus in recording the death of Joseph
reveal his desire to make the role of this tax-collector of the court
of the Ptolemies appear as prominent as possible. Naturally it is
extremely difficult to tell exactly where exaggeration and deviation
from the historical truth commence. At times Josephus appears to
record relationships very accurately, as can be verified when compara-
tive sources are available. For example, when Josephus says in this
story that all the chief men and magistrates of the cities of Syria
and Phoenicia were coming to Alexandria to bid for the tax-farming
rights, which the king was to sell every year to the wealthy men
in each city,[37] the Zenon papyri confirm that the tax-collectors
of each city were local notables, but that the taxes as a whole were
offered for sale in Alexandria, not in the separate cities.[38] In any
case it may be concluded from the statements of Josephus that certain
Jews filled very important functions under the Ptolemies. Not all
are mentioned by name, of course, but that there were more than
those mentioned personally can be deduced from a parenthetical
remark made by Josephus in the course of his story to the effect
that a brother of Joseph had a marriageable daughter whom he
brought to Alexandria in order that he might marry her to one of
the Jews of high rank ($\tau\iota\nu\grave{\iota}$ $\tau\tilde{\omega}\nu$ $\grave{\epsilon}\pi'\grave{\alpha}\xi\iota\acute{\omega}\mu\alpha\tau\sigma\varsigma$ $\textquoteright Iov\delta\alpha\acute{\iota}\omega\nu$).[39]

Under the Ptolemies the Jews also held important military posts.
Josephus says that Ptolemy Philometor and his consort Cleopatra
entrusted the whole of their realm to the Jews and placed their

---

[36] Cf. R. Marcus, Loeb-ed. VII, p. 103b.

[37] A. XII. 169.

[38] Cf. especially Zenon Papyri (Musée de Caire) 59037; cf. CPJ I, pp. 115ff., Tcherikover, op. cit., pp. 60-73; literature on these papyri : CPJ I, pp. 115, 118ff.; Tcherikover,
op. cit., p. 427.

[39] A. XII. 187.

entire army under the command of Jewish generals, Onias and Dositheus.[40] Though Schürer characterises this statement as an "über-
treibende Schilderung des Josephus", he does take to be an established
fact the one immediately following about a decisive party choice
of the Jews under the command of these two generals in a family
quarrel between the Ptolemies.[41] Another Cleopatra appointed as her
generals Chelkias and Ananias, sons of the Onias who had built the
temple in the nome of Heliopolis, "which was similar to the one
at Jerusalem".[42] This Cleopatra III (116-101), widow of Ptolemy
Euergetes, had to fight a war against her son Ptolemy Lathyrus.
Having entrusted her army to these two commanders, she did nothing
without their approval. According to Strabo, whom Josephus quotes,
the majority of her army deserted to her son. Only the Jews of the
district named for Onias remained faithful to her, because their
fellow-citizens Chelkias and Ananias were held in special favour
by the queen.[43] When her son's power increased, and he ravaged
Judaea and subjected Gazah, Cleopatra decided not to be idle while
he, having grown greater, was at her gates and coveted the throne
of Egypt; and so she at once set out against him with a sea and land
force, appointing as leaders of her entire army the Jews Chelkias
and Ananias. The former was killed while pursuing the enemy.[44]
The statement that Cleopatra gave the two Jews the command over
her entire army could be considered an exaggeration,[45] but there
is no need to doubt that Jewish units and their Jewish commanders
sometimes played a decisive role in the multifarious skirmishes within
the Ptolemy family. Confirmation of the high military office of
Chelkias is perhaps supplied indirectly by an inscription. It contains
a number of lacunae, hence it is not certain whether the Chelkias
mentioned in it was himself strategos or his son. Even if it were the
latter, this honorary inscription, in any case, mentions a Jew as
having been crowned with a golden wreath.[46]

In 3 *Maccabees* a brief comment is made about another important
Jewish personage from the age of the Ptolemies. The author relates

---

[40] *Ap.* ii. 49.

[41] *Ap.* ii. 50; Schürer, *op. cit.* III. p. 131.

[42] *A.* XIII. 285.

[43] *A.* XIII. 286f.

[44] *A.* XIII. 348, 349, 351.

[45] *CPJ* I, p. 24.

[46] Schürer, *op. cit.*, p. 132; *CPJ* I, p. 17[45].

how, on the eve of the battle of Raphia, the life of King Ptolemy IV
Philopator was saved by a renegade Jew Dositheus, son of Drimylus.
He had stationed a lowly man in the king's tent, and he became the
victim of the attack aimed at the king.[47] For a long time doubts
were entertained about the historical value of this statement. Many
have begun to think otherwise, however, now that certain papyri
have been discovered which mention a Dositheus, son of Drimylus.
It is not expressly stated that he was a Jew, but there are diverse
factors which make this highly probable, and so justify his identification with the Jewish renegade mentioned in *3 Macc.* If this is so,
then it can be demonstrated from these papyri that he held very
high office as one of the two heads of the royal secretariat (ὑπομνηματο-
γράφος) and as the eponymous priest of Alexander and the
deified Ptolemies, the highest priesthood in Hellenistic Egypt. One
of the papyri plainly hints that he sometimes accompanied the king
on his travels,[48] and thus it lends credence to the assumption that
this was also the case at the battle of Raphia in 217 B.C.

Sometimes the arguments for identifying an important person
known from the literary sources with a person mentioned in the
papyri are too weak to warrant any far-reaching conclusions. This
is the case with one Onias, evidently addressed as a very important
person in a papyrus and, therefore, assumed by some to be the same
Onias who is known to have built the Jewish temple in Leontopolis.[49]
But the name is not known for sure, and, even if this were established,
it would only provide vague and indirect grounds for identification
with the Onias of Leontopolis. Whatever the truth of this may be,
the statements about persons mentioned by name reveal manifestly
that there were rich and influential Jews in the Egypt of the Ptolemies.

The same holds good for Egypt in the Roman period. Josephus
gives us information on this period, too, although he is no longer
our only source in this respect. In the first place mention must be
made of certain relatives of Philo. It can be deduced from certain
passages in Philo's work that he was not wealthy himself, though
it is quite evident that he was one of the leaders of the Jewish group
in Alexandria, considering he was a member of the embassy sent
to Caligula. In one passage he says that among those who held high

---

[47] *3 Macc.* 1. 3.
[48] *CPJ* I, pp. 230-236.
[49] *CPJ* I, pp. 17, 244ff.

offices of authority there are not a few who, possessing accumulated
goods in vast numbers and abundant resources ..., still sometimes
betake themselves to the use of such things as we poor people use
(ἐφ'ἃ καὶ οἱ πένητες ἡμεῖς).[50] The description of the simple way of
life which Philo then proceeds to give is frequently repeated in his
writings and could be an example of the Stoical-cynical glorification
of such a life which Philo may have personally emulated, but then
like those persons who held high offices of authority (ἐν ταῖς μεγάλαις
ἡγεμονίαις), whose aversion to all forms of extravagance naturally
did not necessarily prevent them from having great power and
influence in their high offices.[51]

Josephus repeatedly mentions a brother of Philo as being a very
wealthy and powerful person. He calls this man Alexander the alabarch,
and so gives him a title that links him with another prominent Jew,
Demetrius.[52] What Tcherikover said of the term alabarch still applies :
"As yet no satisfactory explanation of the enigmatic term 'alabarch'
has been found".[53] Since both Alexander and Demetrius were prominent men, they have been held by some to have been leaders of the
Jewish group in Alexandria and identical with the Jewish ethnarchs.
Nowadays ἀλαβάρχης is usually identified with ἀραβάρχης especially
on the grounds of Schürer's research, which means that he was a
high authority concerned with tax-collecting or the supervision of
it in the region on the Arabian, or eastern, bank of the Nile. Most
likely these were not taxes paid by Jews in particular but taxes in
general.[54] Some believe that for a long time, at least in the first
century A.D., this post was occupied exclusively by Jews.[55] There
is, however, no definite proof of this, though it is remarkable enough
in itself that two Jews held the high post of inspector-general of taxes.

Alexander the alabarch was a very wealthy man, and for this
reason Bludau has called him the Alexandrian Rothschild.[56] He
placed enormous sums of money on loan, for example to the Jewish

---

[50] *Spec. Leg.* ii. 20.

[51] Cf. *So.* ii. 48ff.

[52] Alexander : *A.* XVIII. 159, 259, XIX. 276, XX. 100; Demetrius : *A.* XX.147.

[53] *CPJ* I, p. 49[4].

[54] Cf. Schürer, *op. cit.*, pp. 132f.; Juster, *op. cit.* II, pp. 256f., 311; *CPJ* I, pp. 48f.;
Goodenough, *op. cit.*, pp. 64f.; L.H. Feldman, Loeb-ed. IX, pp. 103ff.

[55] Juster, *op. cit.*, p. 311; cf. *CPJ* I, p. 49[4] : ...in the early Roman period such an
office was sometimes bestowed on wealthy Alexandrian Jews

[56] Bludau, *op. cit.*, p. 68.

king Agrippa when the latter was in dire financial straits. Part of
the sum was paid to him in Alexandria, for fear of the king's tendency
to prodigality. The remainder was to be paid when Agrippa arrived
in Puteoli. Hence Alexander evidently had banking facilities in
Italy as well.[57] This same Alexander had the nine portals of the
temple mounted in gold and silver, a gesture testifying not only
to his great affection for the sanctuary in Jerusalem, but also to
his vast riches.[58] Josephus repeatedly refers to him when emphasising
the importance of the Jewish group in Alexandria. When he says
of Philo that he was a man held in the highest honour, he reinforces
that praise by going on to say that he was a brother of Alexander
the alabarch, even before adding that he was no novice in philosophy.[59] With obvious pride he says that Claudius considered Alexander
his old friend.[60] And when he again mentions Alexander as father
of Tiberius Alexander, he says that he surpassed all his fellow citizens
both in ancestry and in wealth.[61] The other alabarch mentioned by
him, Demetrius, is characterised in much the same way as he who
stood among the first in birth and wealth ($\pi\rho\omega\tau\epsilon\acute{\upsilon}\omega\nu$ $\gamma\acute{\epsilon}\nu\epsilon\iota$ $\tau\epsilon$ $\kappa\alpha\grave{\iota}$
$\pi\lambda o\acute{\upsilon}\tau\omega$).[62]

Mention has already been made above (pp. 20f.) of Tiberius Alexander
as the prefect of Egypt who won Josephus' sympathy because of the
role he played during the period of great turbulence among the
Alexandrian Jews. This Tiberius Alexander is known from other
sources as well as Josephus' works, sources of a literary and archeological nature. In them he also emerges as a very important personage.
In his *Annals* Tacitus says that Tiberius Alexander, a Roman knight
of the first rank (*illustris eques romanus*), together with Corbulo's
son-in-law once entered the camps of Tiridates, partly out of compli-
ment to him, but also, by such a pledge, to remove all fear of trea-
chery.[63] In his *Histories* Tacitus mentions the administration of Egypt
by Tiberius Alexander, "himself an Egyptian".[64] As governor of
that province, he supported Vespasian in the struggle for power

---

[57] *A*. XVIII. 159, 160.
[58] *B*. V. 205.
[59] *A*. XVIII. 259.
[60] *A*. XIX. 276.
[61] *A*. XX. 100.
[62] *A*. XX. 147.
[63] *Ann*. XV. 28.
[64] *Hist*. i. 11.

and administered to his troops the oath of allegiance on the first
of July.[65] According to Suetonius he was the first to compel his legions
to take the oath for Vespasian on the calends of July.[66]

The papyri also contain information about him and, in certain
respects, paint a new picture of this man. On a papyrus the first
40 lines have been recovered of a decree that has also been preserved
intact in a stone inscription. From that inscription it could be inferred
that he was a governor who was prepared to deal severely with all
sorts of malpractices. Another papyrus describes the festivities held
in Alexandria in honour of Vespasian, and the impression received
is that the governor personally welcomed the new emperor and led
the festivities. Another remarkable thing is that Tiberius Alexander
is entitled ἔπαρχος πραιτωρίου in a papyrus, which is the official
Greek term for *praefectus praetorio*. Possibly he was appointed to
this office in order to command the Roman army in the Jewish war
under Titus. Alternatively, he could have been appointed after the
Jewish war and exercised his function in Rome.[67] In any case, the
main details of what Josephus relates about Tiberius Alexander are
confirmed absolutely by data drawn from other literary and archeological sources. It is also quite possible that his father Alexander the
alabarch is called a rich landowner in two papyri,[68] and that on
five ostraca reference is made to his brother Marcus Julius Alexander,
who is also mentioned parenthetically by Josephus.[69]

In his autobiography Josephus mentions one Aliturus, a Jew by
origin and an actor who was highly favoured by Nero. Josephus
struck up a friendship with him and took advantage of it to be
introduced to Poppaea. He assured himself of the assistance of this
Jewish lady, who was very influential at court, in order to attain
his goal, the liberation of a number of priests. After receiving impressive
gifts from Poppaea, he returned to his country.[70]

So the literary and archeological sources have made us acquainted
with several Jews who, by virtue of their power and wealth, were
persons of significance, and it does not appear that, as Jews, they

[65] *Hist.* ii. 74, 79.

[66] *Vespas.* VI. 3.

[67] Cf. *CPJ* II, pp. 188-197.

[68] *CPJ* II, pp. 200ff.

[69] *CPJ* II, pp. 197ff.; *A.* XIX. 276f.; cf. V. Burr, *Tiberius Iulius Alexander*, 1955;
Grant, *op. cit.*, pp. 144f., 199f.

[70] *V.* 16; cf. B. Lifshitz, Du nouveau sur les "sympathisants", *Journal for the Study
of Judaism* 1 (1970), pp. 79, 81; Grant, *op. cit.*, p. 176.

found it particularly difficult to attain their high positions. This also indicates that, in the ancient world, racial theories were not a factor of consideration in this respect. On the other hand it was easier for those about them to accept these Jews as a matter of course in their high position in society when they stopped living according to their laws. Some are said specifically to have done this, others may be assumed to have done so. It is said of the Jew who saved the life of Ptolemy IV Philopator on the eve of the battle of Raphia : a Jew by birth who had subsequently changed his religion and become estranged from his ancestral laws. And if he did, indeed, hold the highest priestly office in Hellenistic Egypt, there can be no doubts about the veracity of this comment.[71] Josephus says of Tiberius Alexander : he did not stand by the practices of his people (τοῖς πατρίοις οὐκ ἐνέμεινεν οὗτος ἔθεσιν).[72] It is a moot point whether these words mean that this Jew, who had such a brilliant career behind him, at a given moment stopped living according to the Jewish precepts. It is also possible that Josephus wishes to show that such a man could not possibly remain faithful to the laws. Moreover, his conduct towards his fellow-Jews was in no way different from that of a Roman commander.[73] The Romans had no grounds for complaint against this renegade, who had adapted himself so admirably to their way of life and methods of war. Some renegades went extremely far in choosing sides against their own people and for the enemy.[74]

Attempts to assimilate with the society about them will certainly have been made repeatedly by the Palestine Jews, and even more so by the Jews in the Diaspora. Inscriptions testify to this. There is extant a list from Jasos, a place on the coast of Asia Minor between Miletus and Halicarnassus, which enumerates those who contributed money to the festivities in honour of Dionysus. One such was Nicetas of Jerusalem, son of Jason. There is no absolute certainty that the person mentioned in this inscription, dating from the middle of the second century B.C., was a Jew. A non-Jew could equally be a man from Jerusalem, but probably this was not what was meant.[75] In

---

[71] *3 Macc.* 1. 3; cf. M. Hengel, *Judentum und Hellenismus*, 1969, p. 60, note 216, see above pp. 68f.

[72] *A.* XX. 100.

[73] *B.* ii. 494-498; *A.* XX. 102.

[74] Cf. e.g. *B.* VII. 46-53.

[75] J.B. Frey, *CIJ* II, 1952, nr. 749; cf. Schürer, *op. cit.* III, pp. 16, 135; J. Klausner. *Von Jesus zu Paulus*, 1950, p. 42; Tcherikover, *op. cit.*, p. 352.

another inscription, a Jew thanks "the God", and a second Jew also gives the reason why he thanks God. He was saved from peril at sea. This inscription was built into a wall of the temple of the god Pan. That in itself is remarkable enough. It would be even more strikingly illustrative of the assimilation process if the two Jews had addressed their thanks to this god, and in my view this is quite possible, considering the situation. Or did they deliberately remain vague about the deity, so that inwardly they could address their thanks to Jahve and still not offend their pagan fellow-citizens?[76] In any case there are as many indications that Jews participated in one way or another in pagan forms of worship. For those who did not wish to become isolated in a pagan society this is understandable. Not eschewing pagan practices easily became part of a way of life aimed at making themselves somewhat acceptable to those pagans. The motivation could have been any of several: a Jew could be partner in a "mixed" marriage; he could desire a Greek education for his children or full citizenship of a town for himself; he could aspire to certain offices; he might even desire to participate in the Greek festivals and games. Any or all of these could be reasons for making adaptations in the language, in the names of his children, in literature and philosophy to the Hellenistic culture, in which he could then participate on equal terms with his fellow-citizens.

Needless to say such aspirations evoked violent reactions in those who wished to live in obedience to the Jewish laws. The author of *3 Macc.*, for instance, speaks bitterly of renegades, betrayors of their people, and is glad when these people come to a bad end after the persecution of Ptolemy Philopator, when the Jews who had remained faithful were finally able to take their revenge.[77] And Philo can scarcely find words enough to express his furious indignation with those who have strayed from the path of the laws of Moses. Ever and again he explains the laws allegorically, but he has only contempt for those who conclude from this method of explanation that the commandments of the laws no longer need to be obeyed literally.[78] Evidently he despises those who participate in the special cult of the Day of Atonement, but who never act religiously in the rest

---

[76] *CIJ* II, nrs. 1537 and 1538; cf. Schürer, *op. cit.* III, p. 50, who suggests an alternative possibility: Ob er Pan oder Jahve heiszt, scheint ihnen nicht von groszem Gewicht gewesen zu sein; Hengel, *op. cit.*, p. 481; Tcherikover, *op. cit.*, p. 352.

[77] Cf. e.g. *3 Macc.* 7. 10ff.

[78] *Migr. Abr.* 89ff.

of their life.[79] He is particularly vexed by those persons who, having become wealthy, forget that nothing is more transitory than good fortune, who look down on their relations and friends and set at nought the laws under which they were born and bred, and subvert the ancestral customs to which no blame can justly attach by adapting different modes of life, and, in their contentment with the present, lose all memory of the past.[80] When recording these words, Philo probably had in mind the lives of many Jews about him and undoubtedly was thinking of the son of his brother, Tiberius Alexander.[81] Atrocious vices are associated with the life of the rebels from the holy laws.[82]

In various respects it is thus evident that the Jews often believed they had better reason to despise their fellow-Jews of high status than the non-Jews who were well aware that it was specifically those aspirations to wealth and power that inevitably must induce the Jews to relinquish their ancestral faith, and to adapt themselves to their surroundings. Since racial distinctions were not deemed significant, in the assimilation of the Jews one of the most important reasons for the pagans to hate and despise the Jews was invalidated.

Naturally that applied not only to the few mentioned in the sources, but also to those rich and prominent Jews who are often referred to only incidentally and not by name. From the passage in Philo about the disastrous economic consequences of the progroms in Alexandria in 38 A.D., it appears that many a Jew in that city had risen to the socially important position of tradesman, $\pi o \rho \iota \sigma \tau \acute{\eta} s$, a man who had stocks and investments to lose, or of shipman, $\nu a \upsilon \kappa \lambda \acute{\eta} \rho o s$, ship-owner, or of merchant, $\dot{\epsilon} \mu \pi \acute{o} \rho o s$, a wholesale dealer who travelled widely and imported his own goods. This passage in Philo therefore confirms that many of the Jews in Alexandria belonged to the well-to-do section of the population by virtue of their businesses and occupations.[83]

The writings of Josephus testify that rich and prominent Jews lived not only in Alexandria, but in many other regions of the Roman

---

[79] *Spec. Leg.* i. 186.

[80] *Mos.* i. 31.

[81] *A.* XX. 100; cf. L. Cohn, *Die Werke Philos von Alexandria in deutscher Übersetzung* I, 1909, p. 229[2]; I. Heinemann, *Philons griechische und jüdische Bildung*, 1932, p. 456.

[82] *Virt.* 181f.

[83] *Flacc.* 57; cf. Safrai-Stern, *op. cit.*, p. 451.

empire as well. This can be inferred, for example, from his statement that his second wife, a woman of Jewish extraction who had settled in Crete, came of very distinguished parents, indeed the most notable people of that country.[84] When terrible massacres broke out in Syria, many were instigated by avarice to murder their adversaries (the Jews); they plundered the property of their victims and transferred it to their own homes.[85] If it is said of a pseudo-Alexander that, on his arrival in Crete, in Melos, in Italy and in Puteoli, that he was loaded with presents by the Jewish colony, then this presumes considerable wealth among the Jews in those places.[86] And when in Cyrene the Roman soldiers receive their commander's permission to plunder all the houses in their greed for loot, this is evidence that many well-to-do Jews lived there, some of whom were even of equestrian rank. Nonetheless the Roman commander had them scourged and nailed to the cross.[87]

These data from literary sources concerning rich and distinghuished Jews are confirmed in part by those from the papyri, though not for each period and each place about which the former provide information. The archeological sources, for example, provide us with no knowledge about Jewish merchants and bankers in Egypt in the period of the Ptolemies, If they did exist, they will have carried on their business operations mainly in Alexandria, and there are no archeological data concerning that city in the Hellenistic period. Moreover the establishment of private enterprises was not promoted by the polity of the realm of the Ptolemies. There must have been a few rich merchants at that time. One of them was Arion, agent of Joseph the son of Tobiah.[88] But for this period and this city the papyri add nothing to our knowledge. For that matter, most of the data available indicate that the rich and prominent Jews were not to be found mainly among the merchants. Philo's list in *In Flaccum* 57 forms an exception to this, but then it applies to the Roman period. To this might be added a passage in *3Maccabees* about the acting in partnership of Greek businessmen with Jews.[89] Not much weight

---

[84] *V*. 427.

[85] *B*. ii. 464.

[86] *B*. ii. 103, 104.

[87] *B*. ii. 305-308; cf. Safrai-Stern, *op. cit.*, pp. 338f.

[88] See above p. 66.

[89] *3 Macc.* 3. 10; cf. *CPJ* I, p. 49: "...a valuable evidence of a vigorous business life triumphing even over fierce national hatred".

can be attached to what is said in a letter ascribed to Hadrian, hence
of a much later date, about money being the only god of the Jews,
for Christians and all other peoples are mentioned in the same breath.
This is more of a general statement than a charge directed specially
against the Jews.[90] Regarding Palestine, Josephus denies explicitly
that the Jews there were a seafaring people. On the contrary, "neither
commerce nor the intercourse which it promotes with the outside
world has any attraction for us".[91] On the other hand he says a
travelling Jewish merchant called Ananias played an important part
in the conversion of Izates and Helena to Judaism.[92]

So the data about Jewish merchants are really scarce, certainly
in the papyri. They do contain certain indications that the Jews
attained high offices in other fields. There were Jews who, as financiers,
put money out on loan. As appeared above (pp. 33ff)., the papyrus from
41 A.D. reveals that certain Jews were known as such in their neighbourhood. The papyri have now disclosed specific instances as well.
In the second half of the third century B.C., a contract concluded
between two Jews stipulated that the one lent the other 108 drachmas
at the customary rate of 2% per month.[93] Another papyrus relates
that a Jew lent out a large sum of money to one of his own people
on mortgage, with the latter's house as security.[94] In a papyrus
dated 174 B.C., a loan contract between two Jews is renewed. The
witnesses to the renewal of this contract were also Jews.[95] Suchlike
contracts prove that there were wealthy Jews. Moreover such documents manifestly disclose how thoroughly and sometimes in all
respects the Jews had adapted themselves to their surroundings.
Not only are there contracts of exactly the same form as those between
non-Jews and the customary rate of 24% per year is stipulated,
but the one Jew accepts, as a matter of course, interest from one
of his own people, though this is explicitly forbidden by their laws :
You may charge interest on a loan to a foreigner but not on a loan
to a fellow-country-man.[96] Apparently assimilation had spread apace
in the Diaspora. Consequently the business relations of the Jews

[90] Reinach, *op. cit.*, p. 327 : *Hist. Aug., Saturn.* VIII. 7.
[91] *Ap.* i. 60.
[92] *A.* XX. 34, cf. L.H. Feldman, Loeb-ed. IX. pp. 406f.
[93] *CPJ* I, pp. 156f.
[94] *CPJ* I, pp. 162ff.
[95] *CPJ* I, pp. 164ff.
[96] *Deut.* 23.20, cf. *Ex.* 22. 25.

were no different than those of the people around them, and so there
was no reason whatsoever for them to avoid such transactions.

It is possible, that a Jew was a high official of the Egyptian police,
chief of police (ἐπιστάτης τῶν φυλακιτῶν).[97] The two ἀρχίατροι mentioned in inscriptions in Ephesus and Venosa were certainly Jewish.
These "chief physicians", appointed by the city were important
men who enjoyed exemption from taxes.[98]

Outside the cities there were also influential persons among the
Jews. Perhaps this is what Philo is alluding to in his description
of the persecution of the Jews in Alexandria, when he relates how
the Alexandrians blockaded the harbours along the river in order
to capture the Jews who anchored there and to seize the wares they
transported for trading purposes. These victims of the pogroms
could have been Alexandrian merchants returning home, but it is
more likely that they were Jewish country land-owners who were
taking a cargo of corn to sell in the city.[99] The contents of certain
papyri have now definitely established that there were wealthy
Jewish landowners in rural Egypt. Two were Alexander and Theodoros,
brothers who owned land in the *chora* of Alexandria.[100] Another
Jew, Chelkias, possessed two lots of land in the Bousirite district.[101]
These landowners are mentioned in papyri from 14 and 13 A.D.,
and ostraca dating from the second half of the first century A.D.
and found in Apollinopolis magna (Edfu) reveal that certain Jews
were probably well-to-do farmers.[102] From another of these ostraca
it appears that a Jew was concerned in the shipment of diverse
merchandise along the Nile. He owned a few ships which must have
been rather large, judging from the number of *amphorae* on board.[103]
From reports on the confiscation of Jewish property following on
the revolt of the Jews in Egypt under Trajan, it appears that in
that period, too, there were well-to-do Jews in Egypt, scattered
throughout various regions.[104]

---

[97] Schürer, *op. cit.* III, p. 132; *CPJ* I, p. 17.
[98] Schürer, *op. cit.* III, pp. 15f., 134; Juster, *op. cit.* II, p. 254.
[99] *Leg.* 129.
[100] *CPJ* II, pp. 5ff.
[101] *CPJ* II, pp. 12ff.
[102] *CPJ* II, p. 138, no. 241, p. 151, no. 294.
[103] *CPJ* II, p. 176, no. 404.
[104] *CPJ* II, pp. 251f., no. 445, pp. 255ff., no. 448.

As seen above (p. 70), two alabarchs held very high offices as tax-farmers. The papyri also mention several Jews concerned with the collection of taxes. They were probably not as rich as Joseph, son of Tobiah, who had the farming of taxes in vast areas, but they must have had money. These τελῶναι were not the people who collected the taxes, but they were much concerned with the timely receipt of them, for in the age of the Ptolemies they were bound by contract to hand over a given amount of money to the king. If there was a deficit, they were obliged to make this good together with their partners (μέτοχοι) and their guarantors. Needless to say the tax-farmers had to be men of considerable wealth themselves and must have had acceptable partners and guarantors among their wealthy friends. In the papyri it is not always stated clearly whether certain Jews were tax-farmers or tax-collectors. The former were the more important, of course. The use of certain terms ἐξειληφώς, ἔχω παρά σου, μέτοχοι, often clearly indicates that they were also farmers, though at times the impression is that the Jews were both collectors and farmers of taxes.[105] According to a receipt of 153 B.C., Simon, son of Jazaros, delivered 90 artabai of wheat to the granary and in that same document is said to be a tax-farmer, so he, in any case, was a wealthy enough landowner to have an income high enough to qualify him as a financially perfectly safe tax-farmer in the eyes of the government. Another Jew called Simon, son of Horaios, delivered the same amount of wheat and probably was likewise a well-to-do farmer.[106]

All these instances suffice to demonstrate that in the Jewish population groups of the ancient world there were certainly eminent personages. The question, however, is what percentage they formed of the Jewish people as a whole, whether this percentage was remarkably high compared with the percentage of wealthy people among the Gentiles. Various scholars have emphasised that the number of wealthy Jews was slight and that they constituted a small minority. Juster, who studied the data available in his time in order to ascertain the social status of the Jews, says: "tous ces riches ne formaient qu'une minorité", and further on he calls the Jews 'un pauvre petit monde' ".[107] Bell says of the Jews of Alexandria: "Mehrere Alexandrinische

---

[105] *CPJ* I, p. 18.
[106] *CPJ* I, pp. 198, 217, nrs. 90 and 91.
[107] Juster, *op. cit.* II, pp. 318, 319.

Juden waren bekanntlich im Besitze gewaltigen Reichtums; aber im Ganzen waren die Juden wohl keine reiche Gemeinde. Im Gegenteil zeigt manches von erheblicher Armut unter ihnen".[108] Tcherikover's opinion of this people under the rule of the Ptolemies is that "the majority of the Jewish people of Egypt was not rich", and of the Jews in Egypt under the Romans he says "the poor ones constituted the majority of the Jewish population".[109] In another work he says: "Wealth was gathered in the hands of exceptional individuals who had been successful in their commercial dealings or in tax-collecting, and the vast majority lived humbly by the sweat of their brows".[110]

There are exceptions to such descriptions of the economic situation of the Jews in ancient times. Of the Jewish community in Alexandria, for example, Lazare says "armateurs, commerçants, agriculteurs, la majorité était riches; la somptuosité de leurs monuments et de leur synagogue en témoignait", and those in Rome he calls "une colonie puissante et riche", though he does not fail to add that many Jews lived in the poorer quarters of Rome on the other side of the Tiber.[111] The residential areas of the Jews in Rome are not the only proofs at hand to demonstrate their poverty. But the information about the poverty of the great majority of the Jews is much more incidental, indirect, than that about the wealth of a few of them. This is quite understandable. Powerful, influential and wealthy people were inte-resting subjects for the ancient historiographers—in the "pauvre petit monde" not much happened that was worth mentioning. Apart from anything else, it is logical that the number of paupers in the ancient world was much higher than stated in so many words by contemporary historiographers. All the more reason, then, to pay scrupulous attention to the information imparted indirectly.

Philo enumerates the privileges granted by Augustus to the Jews, and one was that when the monthly dispensation of money and food in Rome fell on a Sabbath, the dispensers were instructed to reserve the allotment to the Jews till the following day.[112] From this can be deduced that these Jews must have been in possession of full Roman citizenship and also that very many of them belonged to

---

[108] Bell, *J.u.G.*, p. 14.
[109] *CPJ* I, pp. 11, 50.
[110] Tcherikover, *op. cit.*, p. 343; see above p. 59.
[111] Lazare, *op. cit.*, pp. 26f., 31f.
[112] *Leg.* 158; cf. Jos. *A.* XII. 120.

the urban proletariat which had to depend on the monthly distribution of grain for the barest subsistence.

The inscriptions in the Jewish catacombs of Rome provide more indirect than direct confirmation of the above. The profession of the deceased is given only a few times, a painter (ζωγράφος), a teacher (διδάσκαλος), a Torah scholar (νομομαθής), a father of synagogues (πατὴρ συαγωγίωνν), a student of the sages (μαθητὴς σοφῶν). A Latin inscription mentions a butcher from the market (bubularus de macello) who is praised as a good soul, the friend of everyone (anima bona omniorum amicus). The Latin here is faulty, but even more so is that of the conclusion—this kindly man will sleep among the righteous (dormitio tua inter dicaeis)—which, with its mixture of Latin and Greek intended to reproduce the Greek formula μετὰ τῶν δικαίων, does not give a very favourable impression of the linguistic ability of those who commissioned the composition of this inscription. There is no doubt that, on the grounds of this paucity of information about professions, the comment must be : Manifestly, no conclusions are justified on the basis of these scanty data.[113] Consequently the indications contained in the linguistic mistakes and confirmed by the physical appearance of the inscriptions are all the more significant. Some of the inscriptions clearly testify to the prosperity of those who commissioned them. They are enscribed on marble, evidently by able craftsmen, and placed in private and beautifully painted tombs containing priceless sarcophagi. But by far the greatest number are scratched roughly in the wall or on loose, formless pieces of marble and in such clumsily executed letters that they are sometimes difficult to decipher. The difference in language usually accords with that in appearance; the former often contain no errors in spelling or grammar, the latter abound with them. All this proves that there were, indeed, well-to-do persons in the Jewish community of Rome, but that the great majority were simple, unlettered people.

The literary sources strengthen this impression. One might go so far as to say that, if the Roman authors were our only source of information, we would be inclined to assume that the Jews in Rome were nothing more than a group of miserable paupers. They could deliberately be giving a one-sided, satirical description, a possibility suggested above (p. 61), but it is significant that they never found matter for their satires in the wealth of the Jews. Persius

---

[113] H.J. Leon, *The Jews of Ancient Rome*, 1960, p. 234.

describes the sad sobriety of the celebration of the Sabbath, when
the lamps wreathed with violets and ranged round the greasy window-
sills have spat forth their thick clouds of smoke, when the floppy
tunnies' tails are curled round the dishes of red ware, and the white
jars are swollen out with wine, you silently twitch your lips, turning
pale at the Sabbath of the circumcised.[114] Martial mentions among
all the noise that contaminates Rome that of a Jew who learned
begging from his mother.[115] According to Cleomedes, Epicurus learned
his particular way of putting things in the synagogue, or among
the individuals who begged in its vicinity : "a Jewish jargon of poor
quality, lower than all that creeps on the ground".[116] And Juvenal
bitterly depicts the degradation of a once holy place, now the camp
of all sorts of poor Jews who possess a basket and a truss of hay
for all their furnishings. According to him the synagogues are also
places where diverse disreputable characters congregate. And in the
passage in his biting satire about the Roman women describing
how ladies have their fortunes told by various persons, he also mentions
a Jewish woman, a trusty go-between of highest heaven, who will
tell you dreams of any kind you please for the minutest of coins.[117]
All these writers agree as to their allusions to the miserable poverty
of the Jews. This they must have seen about them, not merely
imagined.[118]

Both in the period of the Ptolemies and of the Romans in Egypt,
there were various rich and distinguished Jews. The literary sources
especially, and archeological sources in part, have made this manifest.
But the latter reveal even more clearly that the majority of the Jews
were definitely neither rich nor distinguished. It has already been
noted that Philo and Josephus inadvertently, sometimes quite deliberately, extolled the social status of the Jews in Egypt. Still, their
writings sometimes obliquely reveal that all was not wealth and
luxury among the Jews and that writers who were not favourably
disposed to the Jews commented on this. In Josephus' enumeration
of the serious and repugnant accusations made by Apion against

---

[114] Reinach, *op. cit.*, pp. 264f. : Persius, *Sat.* V. 176ff.

[115] Reinach, *op. cit.*, p. 289 : Martial, *Epigr.* XII. 57. 13f.

[116] Reinach, *op. cit.*, pp. 212f.

[117] Reinach, *op. cit.*, pp. 290-292 : *Sat.* iii. 10ff., VI. 542ff.; cf. G. Highet, *Juvenal the Satirist*, 1954, p. 253.

[118] Cf. Baron, *op. cit.*, I, ⁴1962, p. 194 : Jewish poverty rather than wealth attracted the attention of most satirists of stage and literature.

the Jews of Alexandria, he begins with his insinuation that the Jews
came from Syria and settled by a sea without a harbour, close beside
the spot where the waves break on the beach. What Apion probably
wished to insinuate is that it was a place where all sorts of rubbish
thrown overboard washed up on the beach. In any case Josephus
feels obliged to answer Apion's accusation by remarking that the
Jews of Alexandria lived in the finest residential quarter.[119] When
Philo proclaims to his readers that people owe their lack of earthly
possessions to their own injustice and impiety, to their lack of respect
for the laws and ancestral customs, and that they therefore fall into
the hands of money-lenders and usurers who charge high rates of
interest, then he is clearly thinking of his own people, admitting
explicitly that many of them were in a very difficult position socially.[120]
The papyri testify abundantly to this. Certain papyri were referred
to above (pp. 62ff.) which, in their description of the daily life of ancient
times, mention Jews who were anything but rich : the man who
stole a lady's cloak, the Jew concerned in the delivery of a horse,
the group of Jews who stole grapes from a vineyard. Many more
such examples could be cited. The dowry of Apollonia, daughter
of Sambathion, amounted to the rather meagre sum of 60 drachmas.[121]
The three Jews who together borrowed 140 drachmas and promised
to repay it in 14 monthly instalments must have been paupers in
bitter financial straits.[122] The Jewish woman who acted as a wet
nurse for a foundling slave for a pre-arranged period in return for
8 drachmas and an amount of olive oil per month cannot be said
to have done this out of luxury.[123] Her friend called Martha and
therefore Jewish, was evidently terribly disappointed when she failed
to obtain such a contract as wet nurse, ar appears from the stipulations
of the new agreement, in which a promise is extracted that neither
Martha, nor anyone acting for her, shall refer back to this matter
or demand any financial compensation.[124] And the terms of a contract,
set forth in another papyrus, concerning a loan made by a Jew and
his two sons could be a practical example of what Philo relates about
members of his own people who fall prey to usurers. Superficially the

---

[119] *Ap.* ii. 33f.
[120] *Praem.* 105ff.
[121] *CPJ* II, pp. 10ff.
[122] *CPJ* II, pp. 22ff.
[123] *CPJ* II, pp. 15ff.
[124] *CPJ* II, pp. 19ff.

said Jews would seem to have made a good bargain : a Roman
cavalry man lends a sum of money, 600 drachmas, without interest
(ἀτόκους). But the loan is made in the form of a deposit (παραθήκη).
That was anything but easy for the borrowers to repay, being lent
on a very short term, two months only, and involving serious financial
consequences in the form of extra charges for failure to pay on time.
The papyrus is quite clear on this point.[125]

In his description of the extent to which the economic life of
Alexandria was disrupted by the pogroms that paralysed the activities
of the Jewish citizens, Philo does not mention just the notable Jews.
As appeared above (p. 75), Philo first mentions the groups who manage
economically important business concerns, but in the same context
he also mentions simple workmen τεχνῖται, artisans, and γεωργοί,
farmers.[126] The latter could, of course, have included well-to-do
landowners. The papyri reveal that there were some, as shown above,
but the majority must have been hard-working, common people.
Sometimes there were Jewish soldiers who, like all foreign soldiers
under the Ptolemies, were allotted a piece of land. Officially such
land remained the property of the king and could at any time be
taken from the owner, but in practice the land was passed down
from one generation to the other. Moreover it may be assumed that
there were also Jewish landowners who lived on the yields of their
land, but had it worked by native farmers. Two such owners were
Jews mentioned by name in a papyrus, of the first hipparchy, dating
from 174 B.C., and both were 80-arourai holders.[127] Statements about
the business transactions of Jewish military colonists also reveal
that some of them were well-to-do.[128] But other Jews were of quite
a different class of landworkers. In a papyrus from 240 B.C. a whole
list of Jewish hired land-workers is given (γεωργοὶ μισθῷ).[129] Once
mention is made of Jewish wine-growers who hired a 60-arourai
vineyard from Zeno.[130] Jewish shepherds frequently are named in
the papyri. Some of them were both sheep-owners and wool-dealers,
but definitely not always wealthy. Testimony of the questionable
business practices of such a Jewish shepherd is to be found in a few

---

[125] *CPJ* II, pp. 186ff.; cf. *CPJ* I, p. 36.

[126] *Flacc.* 57.

[127] *CPJ* I, p. 165, lines 26f.; cf. Jos., *A.* XII. 151.

[128] *CPJ* I, pp. 147-178.

[129] *CPJ* I, p. 182.

[130] *CPJ* I, p. 141ff., 143ff.

papyri.[131] Sometimes the tax returns tell us something about a profession. In the ostraca from Apollinopolis Magna (Edfu), for example, it is said that a Jew paid all the usual taxes of a peasant, the taxes on wheat, cattle, wine and an ass.[132] Sometimes, too, the Jews appear to have operated as tax-collectors. Josepos was a government official who was employed in a barn where chaff was stored, a ἀχυροθήκη. Another papyrus mentions a number of Jewish σιτόλογοι, who were concerned with the gathering of corn in the royal barns.[133] Although these Jews may have been important locally, they must not be qualified eminent and wealthy personages. Similarly the Ἰουδαῖος φυλακίτης, who is expressly called a Jew at the end of a loan contract in a papyrus from 173 B.C. was probably just an ordinary policeman.[134] And though for many who came into contact with Onias the secretary, γραμματεύς, he may have been envelopped in the nimbus of a man who could write, in reality he was just a person of little significance, attached as clerk to a higher government official.[135] Whereas the arabarchs were very eminent and wealthy Jews, this certainly did not always apply to the lower revenue officials, such as the numerous Jews mentioned in the papyri in connection with the charge of the river (ποταμοφυλακία). It was already known from the writings of Josephus that many Jews were concerned with this *fluminis custodia*, an example given by the author as proof of the great faith placed in the Jews formerly by the kings and later by the emperors.[136] Nowadays it is generally assumed that this surveillance of the river had to do with the collection of the duties that were levied on river navigation. If it is true that, for some time, the Jews were involved in this revenue control, it means they must have been hated by the indigenous population, Revenue officials are not usually classified among the most popular groups of society. But there is nothing in the papyri to suggest hostility towards this group of officials, and certainly nothing of any transference of such a feeling to Jews in general.

---

[131] *CPJ* I, pp. 185f., pap. No. 38; Jewish shepherds are also mentioned in the papyri nrs. 9, 39, 412.

[132] *CPJ* II, p. 110.

[133] *CPJ* I, p. 220; *CPJ* II, pp. 215f.; cf. Tcherikover, *op. cit.*, p. 341.

[134] *CPJ* I, pp. 167f.

[135] *CPJ* I, pp. 251f.

[136] *Ap.* ii. 64; cf. Juster, *op. cit.* II, p. 257; Schürer, *op. cit.* III, pp. 133f.; Bludau, *op. cit.*, p. 31; *CPJ* I, p. 53[14].

Among the Jews whose work was brought to a standstill by the pogroms in Alexandria, Philo also mentions the artisans, τεχνῖται. As one of the many striking peculiarities of the Jewish people which non-Jews try to emulate, Josephus mentions "our devoted labour in the crafts" (τὸ φιλεργὸν ἐν ταῖς τέχναις).[137] The inference is that many Jews must have been highly skilled in diverse crafts. Unfortunately few traces of the existence of such Jewish craftsmen are to be found in the papyri. One papyrus containing an agreement about the joint use of a pottery in a Syrian village in the Fayûm mentions Jewish potters belonging to a family in which this trade evidently was passed down from father to son.[138] Another one from Upper Egypt mentions a Jewish weaver.[139] The fact that once there existed a Jacoubis, son of Jacoubis, a flute player (αὐλητὴς), was by chance preserved for us, because this flute-player's name occurs in a list of owners of sheep and goats from Samareia in the Fayûm, dating from 155 or 144 B.C.[140] Since in this case his profession is mentioned expressly, he must have been a professional musician who could easily find employment in the military colony of Samareia. Considering that this is all the papyri have to say about Jewish artisans, the yield can only be called very meagre indeed. Moreover, these few data were definitely not given in order to draw attention to these few representatives of certain professions, but, because they played some role in the compilation of an agreement, they briefly and vaguely appear before the footlights before disappearing forever into obscurity. Understandably enough, the lower their position in society, the briefer and vaguer their appearance. After all, these few people were involved, in some way or another, in special circumstances, and so they momentarily become visible to us. But how numerous must be all those who were employed in all sorts of "humble" professions, who, because of this "humbleness", never appeared above the horizon of history. Obviously we cannot expect to hear anything of that great majority of poor and insignificant people, proletarians of the urban and the rural areas. Their existence must be assumed, if an accurate picture of the social status of the Jews in the ancient world is to be formed. The data at our disposal prove, in any case, that

---

[137] *A*. ii. 283.
[138] *CPJ* I, pp. 190ff.
[139] *CPJ* I, pp. 218f., no. 95.
[140] *CPJ* I, pp. 171f.

the Jewish groups in the urban and rural societies were not of a homogeneous, but of a heterogeneous social composition. Rightly, therefore, scholars have long insisted that the Jews must be assumed to have been engaged, on the average, in about the same professions as other population groups in ancient times. Tcherikover, for instance, writes : Generals, soldiers, policemen, officials, tax-farmers, estate-owners, agricultural labourers, slaves, craftsmen, merchants, money-lenders, and doubtless also members of the free professions such as physicians, scribes and the like—all these types of people were to be found in the Diaspora, and if we had numerous sources at our disposal we should certainly discover a still greater variety.[141] I should like to emphasise the last comment and add that the variety would probably then be expanded mainly in the lower social levels.

Naturally the economic situation of the Jews in the ancient world could not have been the same at all times and in all places. There are, for example, indications that the position of the Jews in Egypt slowly and gradually deteriorated under the rule of the Romans, as compared with that of the Ptolemies. The causes can be sought in the peculiar form of government of the Romans, in the general economic deterioration of their position because of exploitation by the Roman administration, and probably also in the increasing ani-mosity of large groups of Jews against Rome.[142] It is also probable that the professions of the Jews in the various countries were not everywhere equally divided between "high" and "low" ones. Klausner, for example, criticises Tcherikover on this point for postulating that the social strata and classes were equally distributed in Palestine and in the Diaspora. Klausner is of the opinion that the same social strata occurred in both areas, but that proportionately they were not equally distributed. In the Diaspora there were Jews who were agricultural labourers, in Palestine there were Jews who were mer-chants, but in Palestine the number of agricultural labourers was very large whilst the merchants formed the minority. The ratio was the other way round in the Diaspora.[143] In my opinion, the

---

[141] Tcherikover, *op. cit.*, p. 343; cf. Juster, *op. cit.* II, pp. 292ff., 310; L. Fuchs, *op. cit.*, pp. 50-68; M. Rostovtzeff, *The Social and Economic History of the Roman Empire*, [2]1957, pp. 270. 663f.; J. Jeremias, *Jerusalem zur Zeit Jesu*, [3]1962, pp. 1-33, 101-135; Simon, *op. cit.*, pp. 241f.; M. Avi-Yonah, *Geschichte der Juden im Zeitalter des Talmud*, 1962, pp. 20-25; J. Neusner, *op. cit.*, pp. 88-93; Safrai-Stern, *op. cit.*, pp. 482f.

[142] Cf. *CPJ* I, pp. 54f.

[143] Klausner, *op. cit.*, pp. 39f.

data are too scarce and too undiversified to make such a postulation, especially with respect to the number of agricultural labourers in relationship to that of the entire Jewish population group. That data on the farm workers among the Jews of Egypt are scarce is only to be expected. But this in no way implies of necessity that there were, indeed, but a few.

The information available clearly demonstrates, in any case, that the economic status of the Jews was very diversified and that there was no special reason for hating them for their wealth, or their economic power. Obviously the rich Jews known to us from literary and archeological sources must sometimes have aroused hatred, but the same applies to wealthy non-Jews, and certainly no proof can be drawn from the data that the Jews in particular met with hostility for this reason. Perhaps an allusion to the envy of the non-Jewish Alexandrians for the Jews can be discerned in a letter from Emperor Claudius to the Alexandrians, urging the Jews quietly to enjoy what they already possess, an abundance of all good things in a city which is not their own. Bell thinks that here he hears "an echo of the envy felt by the Greeks for their wealthy enemies".[144] The context in which these words are placed, however, makes it more likely that the reference is to the political privileges enjoyed by the Jews of Alexandria, rather than to their wealth. This political situation is discussed in greater detail below.

Now it happened more than once that the social status of the Jews was very diversified and that their enemies, nonetheless, very one-sidedly emphasised the wealth and the power of a few of them, and on these grounds fulminated against the Jews. Here, again, we see how significant it is that a biological theory of race was not applied to the Jews in the ancient world. When that does finally happen, all the wealth and power of individual Jews is used as an excuse for opposition to them, even though it is realised prefectly well that, in this way, a very biased picture is given of the social relationships. Thus the lack of an economic situation as root of anti-Semitism is related to the lack of racial discrimination. The most fundamental cause of anti-Semitism in the ancient world must be sought for elsewhere.

---

[144] Bell, *J. and C.*, p. 11³; *CPJ* II, pp. 41, 43.

CHAPTER THREE

STRANGENESS

On closer consideration, the most fundamental reason for pagan anti-Semitism almost always proves to lie in the strangeness of the Jews midst ancient society. They were strange in the sense that in practically all the countries of the ancient world they were immigrants. This was a strangeness they had in common with various other peoples, but the strangeness that astonished and very soon offended the people in whose midst they lived lay in their way of life and their customs, which always forced a certain degree of segregation upon them. The Jews were never quite like the others; they were always inclined to isolate themselves; they had no part in the morals and customs of the people about them, nor in that syncretism that was meant to be so tolerant. There was always something exceptional about the religion of the Jews, and this made them difficult in social intercourse, ill-adapted to the pattern of ancient society. Pagan anti-Semitism in the ancient world is fundamentally of a religious character, even though its attacks were usually directed against the day-to-day way in which Jews lived, dictated as it was by the prescripts of their religion. The Jews always entertain those bothersome scruples about participating in the rites and customs of a country's cult, and often, because of such ridiculous idiosyncrasies, they shun all those festivities in which all the others join in so joyously.

Sharp criticism of the Jews because of their $,\dot{a}\mu\iota\xi\iota a,$ non-mingling with the Gentiles, which was also well-known to Jewish writers (cf. 2 *Macc.* 14:38), resounds in a whole scale of tones in the literature of ancient writers. It is even present in writers who may certainly not be accounted violent anti-Semites and who, in many respects, comment favourably on Judaism. Hecataeus of Abdera, for example, obviously sympathises with the Jews on different points. What he finds attractive about their religion is that it gives no anthropomorphical description of their god. Many Jewish laws appeal to him, because they accord with those of the Egyptians, whom he particularly admires. He knows very well that their marriage and funeral rites are quite

different from those of their neighbours, but the establishment of
this fact elicits no sharp criticism from him. Even Hecataeus' story
about the departure of the Jews from Egypt which, in the description
of Exodus, was felt to be insulting to the Egyptians and therefore
often reproduced in a greatly divergent version by ancient writers,
is scarcely insulting to the Jews.[1] But he does not ignore their exceptional way of life and clearly condemns it : Moses introduced an
unsocial and intolerant mode of life (ἀπάνθρωπόν τινα καὶ μισόξενον
βίον). However, he is prepared to explain this away as the result
of their own expulsion from Egypt.[2]

This reproach aimed at the Jews by Hecataeus, probably before
the end of the fourth century B.C., recurs frequently in the course
of many succeeding centuries. Manetho states that the Jews in
Egypt swore to obey all the commands of Osarsiph, one of the priests
of Heliopolis, whom they had chosen for their leader. By his first
law he ordained that they should not worship the gods, nor abstain
from the flesh of any of the animals held in special reverence in Egypt,
but should kill and consume them all and that they should have
no connexion with any save members of their own confederacy.[3]

According to Diodorus, Posidonius said that the majority of the
friends of Antiochus Sidetes advised the king to take the city by
storm and to wipe out completely the race of Jews, since they alone
of all nations avoided dealings with any other people and looked
upon all men as their enemies. They pointed out, too, that the ancestors
of the Jews had been driven out of all Egypt as men who were impious
and detested by the gods. The refugees had occupied the territory
about Jerusalem and having organised the nation of the Jews had
made their hatred of mankind (τὸ μῖσος τὸ πρὸς τοὺς ἀνθρώπους) into

---

[1] Reinach, op. cit., pp. 14-20 : Diod. Sic. XL. 3. 4.

[2] Reinach, op. cit., p. 17 : Diod. Sic. XL. 3. 5. The translations of ἀπάνθρωπόν τινα καὶ
μισόξενον βίον differ considerably. Reinach's version is : "un genre de vie contraire à
l'humanité et à l'hospitalité"; Tcherikover translates the words as follows : "a form
of life encouraging seclusion from humankind and hatred of aliens", op. cit., p. 361;
Radin's version is : "an inhospitable and strange form of living", and writes then :
"The two words μισόξενον and ἀπάνθρωπον form a doublette or rhetorical doubling of
a single idea. That idea is 'inhospitality', lack of the feeling of common humanity,
a term which for Greeks and Romans embodied a number of conceptions not suggested
by the word to modern ears", op. cit., pp. 182f. This description fails to express the
touch of hatred which is definitely implied in the very first word and which emerges
more manifestly in the statements of other ancient writers.

[3] Jos., Ap. i. 238, 239; According to Ap. i. 250, Osarsiph is a reference to Moses.

a tradition and on this account had introduced utterly outlandish laws : not to break bread with any other race nor to show them any goodwill at all. His friends reminded Antiochus also of the enmity that in times past his ancestors had felt for this people. Antiochus called Epiphanes, on defeating the Jews had entered the innermost sanctuary of the god's temple...Finding there a marble statue of a heavily bearded man seated on an ass, with a book in his hands, he supposed it to be an image of Moses... who had ordained for the Jews their misanthropic and lawless customs (τὰ μισάνθρωπα καὶ παράνομα ἔθη). And since Epiphanes was shocked by such hatred directed against all mankind (τὴν μισανθρωπίαν πάντων ἔθνων) he had set himself to break down their traditional practices... Rehearsing all these events, his friends strongly urged Antiochus to make an end of the race completely, or, failing that, to abolish their laws and force them to change their ways.[4]

According to Josephus, Apollonius Molon also called the Jews atheists (ἄθεοι) and misanthropes (μισάνθρωποι) and condemns them for refusing admission to persons with other preconceived ideas about God and for declining to associate with those who have chosen to adopt a different mode of life.[5] Elsewhere Josephus says that, according to Lysimachus, Moses instructed the Jews when they reached inhabited country to show goodwill to no man (μήτε ἀνθρώπ-ων τινὶ εὐνοεῖν), to offer not the best but the worst advice.[6] Similar to this imputation made by Lysimachus is the statement by Juvenal in one of his satires, charging the Jews with being forbidden by law to point out the way to any not worshipping the same rites, and conducting none but the circumcised to the desired fountain.[7] This accusation of showing no goodwill to a single alien, above all to Greeks, also occurs in Apion.[8]

According to Pompeius Trogus, the Jews anxiously avoided all contact with aliens. The original reason for this was fortuitous, but Moses made of it a fixed rule and a religious prescript.[9] Sharp criticism of the Jews because of their separateness (ἀμιξία) continued far

---

[4] Reinach, *op. cit.*, pp. 56-59 : Diod. Sic. XXXIV, fragments 1-4 (Vol. XII, pp. 52ff.); cf. Jos. *A.* xiii. 245ff. and ed. Loeb on the spot VII, pp. 350f.; see also p. 139.

[5] Jos. *Ap.* ii. 148, 258.

[6] Jos., *Ap.* i. 309.

[7] Reinach, *op. cit.*, p. 292 : *Sat.* XIV. 102ff.

[8] Jos., *Ap.* ii. 121; Like Lysimachus Apion also uses the word εὐνοεῖν.

[9] Reinach, *op. cit.*, p. 255 : M. Junianus Justinus XXXVI. 2.

into the centuries after Christ. At the beginning of the third century
A.D., Philostratus wrote : "The Jews have long been in revolt not
only against the Romans, but against humanity; and a race that
has made its own a life apart (βίον ἄμικτον) and irreconcilable,
that cannot share with the rest of mankind in the pleasures of the
table nor join in their libations or prayers or sacrifices, are separated
from ourselves by a greater gulf than divides us from Susa or Bactra
in the most distant Indies".[10] And in a travel journal from the beginning
of the fifth century A.D. Rutilius Namatianus grumbles that his
rapture about an idyllic landscape was thoroughly spoiled by the
presence of an inn-keeper who owned this rural manor, a quarrelsome
Jew, *humanis animal dissociale cibis,* an unsociable fellow to whom
human fare is loathsome.[11] Namatianus "requires twelve verses to
give vent to his feelings about the Jews and to ridicule their customs
and religious practices". Sizoo is probably right in his opinion that
Namatianus' rage was incited by a bill for damages presented to
him. But the expression *animal dissociale* for a Jew evidently sprang
to his mind exceptionally quickly.[12]

Roman writers, and not only they, frequently draw attention
to the fact that the Jews, who seclude themselves so completely
from others, do not intermingle with the outside world and behave
unsociably towards non-Jews, form among themselves a serried and
cohesive group. Tacitus' well-known charge against the Jews that
towards every other people they feel only hate and enmity (*adversus
omnes alios hostile odium*) is preceded by the statement that they
are extremely loyal toward one another and always ready to show
compassion (*apud ipsos fides obstinata, misericordia in promptu*).[13] In
his defence of Flaccus, Cicero suggested that the Jews in Rome always
display a special concord and can therefore often operate as a pressure
group.[14]

Josephus thinks it very strange that Apion should bring charges

---

[10] Reinach, *op. cit.,* p. 176 : Philostratus, *Vit. Apoll.* V. 33.

[11] Reinach, *op. cit.,* p. 358 : *De reditu suo* i. 377ff.

[12] A. Sizoo, *Reizen en trekken in de oudheid,* 1962, p. 117.

[13] Tac., *Hist.* V. 5. 2; cf. R. Syme, *Tacitus,* Vol. II, 1958, p. 530 : "His anger bears
most heavily upon the Greeks and the Jews... The Jews asserted another kind of
superiority and held aloof from the comity of nations, deaf to persuasion and recalcitrant
even against compulsion. Their 'odium humani generis' put them beyond the pale".

[14] Reinach, *op. cit.,* pp. 237f. : *Pro Flacco* XXVIII. 66 : "*illa turba...scis quanta
sit manus, quanta concordia, quantum valeat in concionibus*"; see above p. 50.

against the Jews specifically because of their notorious concord.[15]
Elsewhere he comments that of all the aspects in which the non-Jews
endeavour to emulate the Jews, their unanimity is one of the most
important (τὴν πρὸς ἀλλήλους ἡμῶν ὁμόνοιαν).[16] But he emphatically
refutes the contention that this mutual solidarity is supposed to
result in an unfriendly attitude towards others. He refers to diverse
humane actions prescribed by the Jewish law, such as sharing with
others, furnishing fire, water, food to all who ask for them, pointing
out the road, not leaving a corpse unburied, showing consideration
even to declared enemies.[17] The fact that Josephus mentions the
prescript about pointing out the road to non-Jews could indicate
that he was familiar with such charges against the Jews as that of
Juvenal, *non monstrare vias*, mentioned above. In that case it is not
by chance that he generalises a commandment laid down in Deut. 27:18
concerning the blind and makes of it a prescript to point out the road
to those who are ignorant of it.[18] By the same token it is definitely
a matter of polemics that, in his praises of the Jewish laws, he includes
the one inviting men not to hate their fellows, but to share their
possessions.[19] And when, in this same context, he attests that the
laws teach not impiety, but the most genuine piety, he must have
had in mind the repeated charges of ἀσέβεια made against the Jews.

In a like manner, Philo indignantly refutes all sorts of imputations
against the Jews. He, too, says the accusation of misanthropy
(μισανθρωπία) is defamatory. Although those clever libellers accuse
the Jewish nation of misanthropy and charge the laws with enjoining
unsociable and unfriendly practices (ἄμικτα καὶ ἀκοινώνητα), these
laws so clearly extend their compassion to flocks and herds, and
our people through the instructions of the law learn from their earliest
years to correct any wilfulness of souls to gentle behaviour.[20] The
pagans would do better to look to their own behaviour. For example,
does not the exposure of infants, forbidden by the Jews but a frequent
practice among numerous peoples, testify to an ingrained inhumanity
(φυσικὴ ἀπανθρωπία)? Who more deserves to be called men-haters
(μισάνθρωποι) than these enemies, these merciless foes of their off-

---

[15] *Ap.* ii. 68.
[16] *Ap.* ii. 283; cf. Lazare, *op. cit.*, pp. 19f.
[17] *Ap.* ii. 211.
[18] *A.* IV. 276.
[19] *Ap.* ii. 291.
[20] *Virt.* 141.

spring?[21] It astonishes Philo to see that some people venture to accuse of inhumanity the nation which has shown so profound a sense of fellowship and goodwill to all men everywhere, by using the prayers and festivals and first fruit offerings as a means of supplication for the human race in general and of making its homage to the truly existent God, in the name of those who have evaded the service which it was their duty to give, as well as of itself.[22]

Heinemann believes that Philo "den Vorwurf der Menschenfeindschaft geschickt zu parieren weiss" and speaks of "dem sehr geschickten Angriff auf 'die Unmenschlichkeit' derer, die den Juden $\dot{\alpha}\pi\alpha\nu\theta\rho\omega\pi\dot{\iota}\alpha$ (inhumanity) vorwerfen".[23] True, Josephus and Philo frequently reiterate the argument that, if the eyes of the pagans were open to the facts, they would discover that what they charge the Jews with occurs to a worse degree among themselves. This may be considered a correct apology and a clever argument, but it is questionable whether it was very efficacious. In any case, it appears from numerous testimonies of pagan writers that the charge of separateness was made throughout many centuries against the Jews and that for a long time the strangeness of the Jews in the midst of other peoples developed "zum ununterbrochenen Stein des Anstosses".[24] And in my opinion we may be sure that the annoyance engendered by this separateness of the Jews, which is manifest in many literary testimonies, was also a reflection of an "animosité des masses contre ceux qui ne vivent pas comme tout le monde".[25] Those masses undoubtedly were terribly annoyed by "the exceptional gestures of this never-assimilated little people".[26]

The pagans who were averse to all those peculiarities of the Jews must at times have felt, more or less consciously, that this separateness was engendered by living in obedience to the god of the Jews. They realised that in this obedience lay the root of what to them was contempt for other gods. In the midst of his various interesting, neutral comments on the topography, flora and fauna of Palestine, Pliny the Elder suddenly inveighs bitterly against the Jews: we give, he says, a certain sort of dates as an offer to the honour of the gods,

---

[21] *Spec. leg.* iii. 110, 113, 36; cf. iii. 119.

[22] *Spec. leg.* ii. 167.

[23] I. Heinemann, *Philons griechische und jüdische Bildung*, 1932, pp. 453, 522.

[24] Hengel, *op. cit.*, pp. 473f.

[25] Simon, *op. cit.*, p. 244.

[26] Bolkestein, *op. cit.*, p. 166.

but not the Jews, a race remarkable for their contempt for the divine powers (*gens contumelia numinum insignis*).[27] In Claudius' edict, cited by Josephus, the emperor discloses his wish to continue the policy of Augustus and to maintain the privileges of the Jews. Throughout the whole world the Jews should observe the customs of their fathers without let or hindrance. But Claudius felt it necessary to enjoin upon the Jews to avail themselves of this kindness in a more reasonable spirit and not to set at nought the beliefs about the gods held by other peoples, but to keep their own laws.[28]

Similarly in his edict to the Alexandrians, which has been preserved in a papyrus, the Jews are warned not to aim at more than they have previously had, probably a reference to the acquisition of more political privileges. Claudius evidently felt that any presumptuousness, also among the Jews, was pernicious, and so he exhorted the Alexandrians and the Jews to give up their present ways and to live in gentleness and kindness with one another ($\mu\epsilon\tau\grave{\alpha}$ $\pi\rho\alpha\acute{o}\tau\eta\tau\sigma\varsigma$ $\kappa\alpha\grave{\iota}$ $\phi\iota\lambda\alpha\nu\theta\rho\omega\pi\epsilon\acute{\iota}\alpha\varsigma$). For him that must also have implied that the Alexandrians had to respect the customs observed in the worship of the god of the Jews, and equally that the Jews were not to show disrespect to the religious customs of the Alexandrians.[29] That was not easy for the Jews. When Apion irritatedly asks why the Jews, if they are citizens, do not worship the same gods as the Alexandrians, Josephus answers with the counter-question why the Alexandrians, though Egyptians, wage with one another bitter and implacable war on the subject of religion. They should realise that the Jews have difficulty in calling them all Egyptians, or even collectively men, because they worship and breed with so much care animals that are hostile to humanity.[30]

Lysimachus believed that Moses instructed his people to overthrow any temples and altars of the gods which they found. According to him he was therefore not surprised they called their capital Hierosyla ($`I\epsilon\rho\acute{o}\sigma\upsilon\lambda\alpha$), because of their sacriligious propensities.[31] Dio Cassius says of the Jews that they are distinguished from the rest of mankind in practically every detail of life, and especially by the fact that they do not honour any of the usual gods, but show extreme reverence

---

[27] Reinach, *op. cit.*, p. 281 : *Hist. Nat.* XIII. 4. 46.

[28] *A.* XIX. 289. 290.

[29] *CPJ* II, p. 41, ll. 82ff.; cf. above p. 88.

[30] *Ap.* ii. 65.

[31] *Ap.* i. 309, 311.

for one particular divinity.[32] And Tacitus knows that, unlike the
Egyptians who worship many animals and monstrous images, the
Jews conceive of one god only, and that with the mind alone, and that
they regard as impious those who make from perishable materials
representations of gods in man's image.[33]

In various ways, therefore, it emerges that the people of the ancient
world had some idea of what was behind the ἀμιξία, separateness,
of the Jews. The exclusive worship of the God of Israel and obedience
to this one god led to their strange way of life and to their violent
resistance to the worship of other gods, to their refusal to participate
in the cult of those gods. As a result the Jews were the targets of
all sorts of imputations which implied an indictment of their manner
of belief. The pagans saw nothing but *superstitio* in this belief. It
was pointed out above (pp. 55f.) that, on several occasions, Tacitus
speaks of the superstition of the Jews, although, like Suetonius,
he did not confine his use of this term to the Jewish religion.[34] Such
charges against this people who are particularly "addicted to superstition",[35] are to be found in several writers. Cicero believes it praiseworthy of Flaccus that he resisted this *barbara superstitio*.[36] Augustinus
says of Seneca that with other superstitions of the civil theology,
he also mentions the sacred institutions of the Jews, especially the
Sabbath.[37] Quintilianus speaks of the *perniciosa ceteris gens*, who
embrace the *Judaica superstitio*.[38] And even in the second century
A.D., Apuleius mentions the *Judaei superstitiosi*.[39]

Their rejection of the cult prevailing in the polis or country left
the Jews open to the charge of atheism. If this rejection manifested
itself in demonstrable, visible behaviour, the charge could be made
against them formally and legally. That did not always mean a
charge of denying the existence of a deity. It did not often happen
that atheism was professed in the sense of a philosophical doctrine.
Among those who incurred difficulties with the authorities of Athens,
Josephus mentions Diagoras of Melos, who was reported to have

---

[32] Reinach, *op. cit.*, p. 182 : *Hist. Rom.* XXXVII. 17.

[33] *Hist.* V. 5.

[34] *Hist.* V. 8, 13; *Ann.* ii. 85; Sueton., *Tib.* XXXVI. 1.

[35] *Gens superstitioni obnoxia, Hist.* V. 13.

[36] Reinach, *op. cit.*, p. 238 : *Pro Flacco* XXVIII. 67.

[37] Reinach, *op. cit.*, p. 262 : Augustinus, *De civ. Dei* VI. 40.

[38] Reinach, *op. cit.*, pp. 284f. : *Institutio oratoria* iii. 7. 21.

[39] Reinach, *op. cit.*, p. 336 : *Florida* i. 6.

jeered at the mysteries of the Athenians.[40] It is possible that this contemporary of Anaxagoras, who in ancient days was called "the atheist", ridiculed belief in gods in general, but in practice he would seem to have directed his ridicule against the gods of the polis. Usually a charge of atheism referred to non-participation in the prevailing cult, to deviating from the religious ceremonies of the polis, to not believing in the gods the state believed in, as in the charge against Socrates.[41] Sometimes the word ἄθεος acquires a much broader significance, approximating the sense of 'evil' or 'bad'. The use of the superlative is remarkable, as for example when Xenophon calls Tissaphernes ἀθεότατος καὶ πανουργότατος.[42]

The pagans were certainly not the only ones to accuse the Jews of atheism. This accusation was also sometimes reversed, for Philo repeatedly expresses his contempt for Egyptian atheism.[43] Often his remarks on the ἀθεότης of the Egyptians were undoubtedly aimed at the worship of animals, which evoked his outbursts of profound scorn.[44] Consequently the Jews were sometimes reproached with lack of respect for the gods because of what, for them, was precisely the reason for the godlessness of the pagans. Manetho states that Moses ordained that his followers should not worship the gods, meaning the repudiation of the animal cult by the Jews.[45]

Apollonius Molon was the first to use the term ἄθεοι in reference to the Jews.[46] Much later Dio Cassius stated that Flavius Clemens and his wife Flavia Domitilla were accused of ἀθεότης.[47] This passage

---

[40] *Ap.* ii. 266.

[41] *Apology* 26B, cf. 24B.

[42] *Anab.* ii. 5. 39; cf. D.R.A. Hare, *The Theme of Jewish Persecution of Christians in the Gospel according to St Matthew*, 1967, p. 172; sometimes the superlatives her; are not translated, e.g. Paul Masqueray, *Xenophon, Anabase*, Tome I, 1952, p. 117: cet impie, ce scélérat...

[43] *Leg.* 163; *Mos.* ii. 196. Philo speaks of a τῆς Αἰγυπτιακῆς ἀθεότητος ζηλωτὴς ; cf. ii. 193, *Post. Cai.* 2 : the ἀθεότης of the Egyptians; *Leg. All.* iii. 112 : ὁ ἄθεος καὶ φιλήδονος τρόπος; *Heres* 203; *Fug. et inv.* 114, 180.

[44] *Vita cont.* 8, 9.

[45] *Ap.* i. 238, 239; cf. above p. 90; for the charges of atheism see : A. Harnack, *Der Vorwurf des Atheismus in den drei ersten Jahrhunderten, Texte und Untersuchungen*, Bd. 28, 1905; A.B. Drachmann, *Atheism in Pagan Antiquity*, 1922, for the atheism of the Jews see especially pp. 9f., 126ff.; Böhl, *op. cit.*, pp. 480f.; E. Stauffer, Art. θεός *Th.W.N.T.*, iii, pp. 120-122.

[46] *Ap.* ii. 148.

[47] Reinach, *op. cit.*, pp. 195f. : Xiphil., *Epitome* LXVII. 14.

has only been preserved in a summary of Dio Cassius' book that was made by an eleventh century monk, Xiphilinus. Consequently it is not absolutely certain whether he cites Cassius literally here, or uses that word to give his own personal impression of what he had read of this ancient writer in terms familiar to him from his own day, or dictated by his personal judgment of the situation. Moreover some have held Clemens and Domitilla to have been Christians. It is practically certain, however, that they were proselytes, judging from the very clear indicatives in the context. According to Xiphilinus, Dio Cassius said they were both accused of ἀθεότης, the reason for the condemnation of many others who had strayed towards Jewish customs. If there had been any question of conversion to Christanity, Xiphilinus would not have failed to make this clear[48] and to comment on the expression τὰ τῶν Ἰουδαίων ἔθη read in Dio Cassius.[49]

Although the term atheism does not often occur in the accusations made by the ancient writers against the Jews, that reproach is unmistakably implied in the word ἀσέβεια. It is remarkable, for instance, that shortly after the citation of the aforesaid passage in Dio Cassius concerning the action of Domitianus against ἀθεότης, Xiphilinus says that, according to this ancient writer, Nerva radically altered this policy. He had those accused of ἀσέβεια brought back from exile, and he forbade accusations being made on the grounds of ἀθεότης or of the Jewish way of life. The obvious assumption is that here the Jewish way of life was referred to as an example of godlessness. It is also highly probable that an allusion is made here to an injunction of Nerva, expressed in the legend on coins as *Fisci Judaici calumnia sublata*. Nerva put an end to libellous accusations made against all sorts of people for the sake of the reward paid to the informers.[50] In any case it is evident that the ἀσέβεια mentioned here means approximately the same as the aforesaid ἀθεότης [51] Above (pp. 90f.) Posidonius is mentioned as having spoken

---

[48] Today the general assumption is that the reference is to proselytes; cf. Juster, *op. cit.*, I, p. 257[1]; Schürer, *op. cit.*, III, pp. 117f.; Radin, *op. cit.*, pp. 334ff.; Guterman, *op. cit.*, p. 106, 124[14].

[49] Hengel, *op. cit.*, p. 486[60] believes that precisely because of this expression no decision should be made as to whether it was a question of conversion to Judaism or to Christianity.

[50] Schürer, *op. cit.*, III, p. 118; Radin, *op. cit.*, pp. 332-337.

[51] Cf. Philo, *Mos.* ii. 193, 196; *Leg.* 163, where ἀσέβεια and ἀθεότης are mentioned together; for the charge of ἀσέβεια in the ancient world see also Drachmann, *op. cit.*,

of the Jews as impious and detested by the gods since time immemorial and of Antiochus Epiphanes as one of those who detested
the nation of the Jews. Similarly Apion,[52] Tacitus,[53] and Porphyry[54]
in the third century A.D. mention this king as a shining example of
vigorous action against that people. The man who practised the
worst godlessness in the eyes of the Jews is sometimes represented
by the opposing party as a powerful personage who made short work
of the customs and morals of that nation of godless, "this basest
of peoples", characterised by Tacitus as follows: the Jews regard
as profane all what we hold sacred; on the other hand, they permit
all what we abhor.[55]

Another term used to express the godlessness of the Jews is ἀνόσιοι
Ἰουδαῖοι. This expression is used especially in papyri concerning
the revolt of the Jews under Trajan. It is understandable that it
occurs in the collection known as the *Acts of the Alexandrian Martyrs*,
in which the leaders of the Alexandrians are depicted as intrepid
martyrs who defended proudly their city and their ideals, and therefore
did not hesitate mercilessly to tell the truth straight to the emperor's
face. Hermaiskos openly reproaches Trajan that his Council is filled with
impious Jews. And when the emperor says that this is a shameless,
insolent remark, Hermaiskos angrily replies that, if this word is
apparently such an offensive name to the emperor, he ought to help
his own people and not play the advocate for the impious Jews.[56]
The *Acts of the Alexandrian Martyrs* is not the only source in which
this term occurs, for it suddenly appears in two other papyri written
in the thick of the fight against the rebel Jews. In the first one it
is frankly admitted that the Jews were winning in an alarming fashion
and that all resistance offered had failed. The only hope and expectation
left was a push of the massed villagers from the district against the
impious Jews, but the opposite had happened. One ray of hope was

---

pp. 6-8, 25, 27, 39, 64f., 74; G. Delling, *Studien zum Neuen Testament und zum hellenistischen Judentum*, 1970, p. 47; N.J. McEleney, Conversion, Circumcision and the Law,
NTS, April 1974, pp. 324, 326.

[52] *Ap.* ii. 79ff.; Reinach, *op. cit.*, pp. 56, 57: Diod. Sic. XXXIV, fragments 1ff.;
cf. above pp. 90f.

[53] *Hist.* V. 8.

[54] Reinach, *op. cit.*, p. 204: Περὶ ἀποχῆς ἐμψύχων i. 14.

[55] *Hist.* V. 8, 4.

[56] *CPJ* II, pap. 157, Col. III, ll. 41ff., 47ff., cf. pap. 158, Col. VI, ll. 11ff.; cf. L. Fuchs,
Die Juden Aegyptens in ptolemäischer und römischer Zeit, 1924, pp. 25f.; Musurillo,
op. cit., pp. 168-172; cf. above p. 33.

the reported approach of Roman legions.[57] The second papyrus in which the ἀνόσιοι Ἰουδαῖοι are mentioned contains a letter from a strategos to the prefect of Egypt, in which he speaks of the attack of the 'impious Jews'.[58] Now Fuks has deduced from this last-mentioned papyrus that the expression towards the end of the revolt was "an official designation".[59] Heinemann's opinion is that ἀνόσιος has lost its religious significance in many respects, and, like *impius*, applies to every criminal.[60] To support this view, Fuks argues that an official would not air his personal hatred of the Jews to the prefect of Egypt. A perusal of the rest of this missive, however, reveals that this communication between the one authority and the other is of a very personal nature and concerns the private affairs of the strategos : he reports to the prefect that, owing to his long period of absence, his private affairs have been completely neglected. Now, because of the attack of the impious Jews, practically all he possesses in the villages of the Hermoupolis district and in the metropolis urgently requires his attention. He therefore would like to have 60 days leave to regulate his affairs. He respectfully submits this request to his superior. Such being the contents, this communication between two officials may reasonably be termed a private letter, in which case it does not prove that ἀνόσιοι Ἰουδαῖοι had become "an official designation". Like the first papyrus, this second one shows that especially during this revolt with its atrocious cruelty the bitter feelings against the Jews were also expressed in these words. Now more strongly than ever they naturally lay on the tongues of the pagans, for the Jews had totally ravaged various sanctuaries of pagan gods.[61] For this reason, I believe there is more truth in Wilcken's comment than Fuks thinks : "In jener Prägung des ἀνόσιοι Ἰουδαῖοι sehe ich einen Beweis dafür, wie tief der religiöse Gegensatz empfunden wurde".[62] And it is also very doubtful whether that expression belongs

---

[57] *CPJ* II, pap. 438, ll. 1ff.

[58] *CPJ* II, pap. 443, Col. II, ll. 4f.

[59] A. Fuks, *CPJ* II, p. 249; cf. V.A. Tcherikover, The Decline of the Jewish Diaspora in Egypt in the Roman Period, *The Journal of Jewish Studies* 14 (1963), p. 30; Hopfner, *op. cit.*, p. 51; L. Fuchs also thinks it strange that this term here "in einem amtlichen Schriftstücke sich findet", *op. cit.*, p. 30.

[60] Heinemann, *op. cit.*, p. 20.

[61] Cf. *CPJ* I, pp. 89f., 96, II, p. 249. I consider it very dubious whether the term also contains an allusion to the Messianic character of the revolt, *CPJ* I, pp. 89f.

[62] U. Wilcken, *op. cit.*, p. 786.

exclusively to a certain period and a certain region. Perhaps, more than we can demonstrate directly on the grounds of the sources, it belongs to that whole complex of charges of superstitio, atheism, impiety. Perhaps it is not a mere coincidence that, in the same passage in which Manetho uses the word ἀνοσίως (sacrilegious) for the behaviour of the Jews, the word ἀσεβήματα (impieties) also occurs.[63] Possibly, too, Philo is parrying a reproach made by the opposition when he calls God the avenger of unholy (ἀνοσίων) men and deeds.[64] As for ἀσέβεια, he employs those polemics openly, and not merely tacitly: "If someone bring against you an indictment for impiety (ἀσέβεια) ..." And regarding this matter he confesses that, in his judgment and in that of his friends, preferable to life with impious men (-τῆς μετὰ ἀσεβῶν ζωῆς-) would be death with pious men (μετὰ εὐσεβῶν).[65] Josephus likewise feels obliged to state emphatically that the Jewish laws teach not impiety, but the most genuine piety.[66] Evidently, then, these Jewish writers were extremely sensitive about the charges of atheism and impiety. Josephus thinks it grossly unfair that the Jews are accused of not worshipping the same gods as other people,[67] and that Apollonius condemned the Jews for refusing admission to persons with other preconceived ideas about God.[68] Apparently on this point there was continually being waged an open or latent fight, in which the charges of both sides were often very similar. At times the Jews accepted, with a certain degree of pride, a charge made by the pagans. Josephus relates that Antiochus Sidetes lay down certain conditions for the surrender of the besieged Jews, one of which was that they should admit a garrison in their towns. But this was a condition the Jews refused to accept, since they did not come into contact with other people, because of their separateness (διὰ τὴν ἀμιξίαν οὐκ ἐφικνούμενοι πρὸς ἄλλους).[69] Here, then, was voiced a charge of separateness against the Jews, but clearly Josephus records this word with a certain degree of pride and unmistakably admits there was some truth in the pagans' indictment. The Jews had every reason to pride themselves on the fact that they were not

---

[63] *Ap.* i. 248.
[64] *Flacc.* 104.
[65] *Post. Cai.* 38f.
[66] *Ap.* ii. 291.
[67] *Ap.* ii. 79.
[68] *Ap.* ii. 258; cf. above p. 91.
[69] *A.* XIII. 245-247; cf. above pp. 90f.

permitted to mingle with other peoples. They were aware of their strangeness and went out of their way to accentuate it, sometimes even fanatically demanding it of fellow Jews who threatened to forget their fidelity to the laws.

There were occasions when the separateness of the Jews proceeded more from a self-chosen isolation than from special measures taken by their pagan opponents. There was no question of a ghetto, for example, in the later sense of that word. Various authors do use this word for quarters in certain cities where Jews lived. Reinach says of Persius' description of the life of the Jews in Rome on the Sabbath : "C'est un croquis un peu superficiel, mais vivant et pittoresque, du ghetto de Rome un soir de sabbat".[70] Lazare briefly sketches the life of the Jews in the squalid quarters of Rome on the other bank of the Tiber, where they carry on their miserable little trades, and goes on to say : "Le juif du ghetto est déjà là".[71] The quarters where the Jews lived in Alexandria are sometimes called a ghetto.[72] The existence of a ghetto in Alexandria has even been used as an argument to support the postulation that the Jews of that city really did not possess civil rights.[73] A ghetto in Edfu is also assumed on the grounds of papyrus findings.[74]

Nonetheless it would be incorrect to use this word to indicate the manner of Jewish society in certain urban areas in ancient days. The term 'ghetto' would only be properly applicable if the Jews were allotted these urban sectors as compulsory residential areas, outside of which they were not allowed to live. Neither the literary nor the archeological sources provide any such proof. True, the Jews often lived in certain sectors of the cities, as is evidenced by many indications. In his description of his voyage to Rome, Philo says that a large district of Rome beyond the river Tiber was owned and

---

[70] Reinach, op. cit., p. 265, note 3.

[71] Lazare, op. cit., p. 32.

[72] U. Wilcken, op. cit., p. 788; B. Brüne, Flavius Josephus und seine Schriftten in ihrem Verhältnis zum Judentume, zur griechisch-römischen Welt und zum Christentume, 1969, p. 77; Hopfner, op. cit., p. 8 speaks of a "ghettoartige Absonderung der Juden"; Baron, op. cit., I, p. 188 : a sort of ghetto; see, on the other hand, L. Fuchs, op. cit., pp. 104f.

[73] H. Willrich, Art. on Caligula in Klio III (1903), p. 406.

[74] C. Wessely, Das Ghetto von Apollinopolis Magna, Studien zur Paläographie und Papyruskunde, XIII (1913), pp. 8ff.; Wilcken, op. cit., p. 788.

inhabited by the Jews.[75] Philo therefore states expressly that the Jews of Rome had their own district. They were not compelled to live there, however, but enjoyed the privilege of living together wholly in accordance with their customs. One gets the impression that this living together was entirely the choice of the Jews and not in any way compulsory. Research carried out in the catacombs where the Jews of Rome were buried confirms this impression. The earliest settlement of Jews was, indeed, very probably located on the other bank of the Tiber, i.e. on the right bank in the bend of the river. In those days that was on the outskirts of the city, which lay almost entirely along the left bank. In later times the Jews continued to reside together in separate quarters, so that they might live in complete obedience to the prescripts of their laws and avoid contact with non-Jews, who often made it extremely difficult for them to fulfil their rules conscientiously. Frey ascribes the concentration of Jews in certain parts of Rome to their own choice : "- les Juifs ont toujours eu la tendance de se séparer des autres races et de rester groupés entre eux. Dans l'ancienne Rome où toutes les institutions et les habitudes sociales étaient pénétrées de pratiques polythéistes, les raisons qui les poussaient à se réunir dans les quartiers distincts étaient particulièrement pressantes".[76]

Other cities also had quarters inhabited permanently by Jews. Josephus possibly alludes to the existence of such districts in Sardes and Antioch in Syria,[77] and presumably they were to be found elsewhere, too.[78] More is known about the special Jewish quarter of Alexandria, but there is not a single statement about it which warrants the opinion that it was a ghetto in the more modern sense of the word, with the exception of one single comment on a temporary measure taken by the prefect Flaccus. Philo says that the city had five quarters named after the first letters of the alphabet; "two of these were called Jewish, because most of the Jews inhabited them (or because most of the inhabitants were Jews)". But he proceeds at once to add that in the rest, also, there were not a few Jews scattered about.[79] When describing the attacks on the Jews by the

---

[75] *Leg.* 155, 156; In Martial and Juvenal are also indications that in Rome the Jews lived in certain rather poor quarters; cf. Juster, *op. cit.*, II, p. 177, note 3.

[76] *CIJ* I, p. LVI.

[77] *A.* XIV. 235; *B.* VII. 43ff.

[78] Cf. Juster, *op. cit.* II, p. 177, note 3.

[79] *Flacc.* 55.

rabble of Alexandria, he mentions the destruction by the angry masses of their synagogues, "of which there are many in each section of the city".[80] Here, again, Philo naturally assumes there were synagogues in all five sections of the city and that, normally in his age, there was no question of the Jews being confined to two separate districts.

Josephus likewise mentions that the Jews lived in certain districts of Alexandria, but he always represents this as a privilege said to have been granted them by Alexander or, according to another statement, by his successor.[81] As we saw above (p. 83), he considered this Jewish residential area to be one of the most beautifully situated of the whole city.[82] In this regard, Josephus also mentions the division of the city into districts, named after the first letters of the alphabet.[83] According to him, Strabo said that, in Egypt, territory had been set apart for a Jewish settlement, and in Alexandria a great part of the city had been allocated to this nation. The reason for this was that the Jews could then better observe the national laws.[84] Josephus himself mentions a similar reason: "in order that, through mixing less with aliens, they might be free to observe their rules more strictly".[85] How little this had to do with any compulsory isolation in a ghetto, even according to the opponents of the Jews, is demonstrated by a comment of Apion, cited by Josephus, to the effect that the Jews owed their occupation and subsequent undisturbed tenure of their quarter in Alexandria to force of arms.[86]

Only once is there any question of a forceful herding of Jews in a very small part of Alexandria. According to Philo, that took place under Caligula. During the severe persecutions under this emperor, the Alexandrians drove many thousands of men, women and children out of the whole city into a very small part of it ($\epsilon i s\ \mu o \hat{\imath} \rho a \nu\ \dot{\epsilon} \lambda a \chi \dot{\imath} \sigma \tau \eta \nu$), like sheep or cattle into a pen. They supposed that within a few days the Jews would die either of starvation or of overcrowding and suffocation.[87] Here Philo attributes this herding together of

---

[80] *Leg.* 132.

[81] *Ap.* ii. 35; *B.* ii. 488.

[82] *Ap.* ii. 33, 34; cf. J.N. Sevenster, *Do you know Greek*, 1968, p. 92.

[83] *B.* ii. 495.

[84] *A.* XIV. 116, 117.

[85] *B.* ii. 488.

[86] *Ap.* ii. 35.

[87] *Leg.* 124.

the Jews to the unbridled rage of the Alexandrian rabble, but elsewhere he suggests that Flaccus first gave this measure a certain
legal basis by issuing a proclamation in which he denounced the
Jews as foreigners and aliens, which meant they had no right to live
in Alexandria, apart from the district originally allocated to them.[88]
This may, indeed, be termed a violent and compulsory isolation
of the Jews in a given part of the city which they were not permitted
to leave, "a compulsory ghetto, the first known to us in the Roman
world".[89] But this action was part of a wild outburst of hatred against
the Jews, and Caligula's successor Claudius immediately put an end
to it. Only of this short period in Alexandria can it be said : "Hier
treffen wir zum ersten Mal den Gedanken des Ghetto,[90] or : "with
unremitting severity the Jews were driven out of the Greek city
and shut away in a ghetto".[91]

The evidence of the papyri accords with the literary data. Here
and there the papyri clearly reveal that the Jews often lived together
in certain quarters, though here, too, there is no indication that
they were forced to do so by the authorities. It was stated above (p. 102)
that some believe there was a ghetto in Edfu (Apollinopolis Magna).
Apparently this city was divided into several quarters ($\check{\alpha}\mu\phi o\delta a$), the
fourth of which was the Jewish quarter. Numerous ostraca found
there contain mention of Jews, and always from that district (δ
$\dot{\alpha}\mu\phi\acute{o}\delta o\upsilon$). Practically all of them date from the period 70-116 A.D.,
but that in no way proves there was a ghetto in Edfu at that time.[92]
There appears to have been such a $\check{\alpha}\mu\phi o\delta o\nu$ of the Jews in Oxyrhynchus
as well, as is manifested by the registration of the sale of a sixth
part of a house in the Jewish quarter ($\dot{\epsilon}\pi$'$\dot{\alpha}\mu\phi\acute{o}\delta o\upsilon$ '$Io\upsilon\delta a\ddot{\iota}\kappa o\hat{\upsilon}$) in
85 A.D.[93] Plots of land in a Jewish street of that same city were
sold in 133 A.D. The term '$Io\upsilon\delta a\iota\kappa\grave{\eta}$ $\lambda a\acute{\upsilon}\rho a$ was probably used in
that papyrus. Since ,however, the expression "in the Cretan quarter"
($\dot{\epsilon}\pi$'$\dot{\alpha}\mu\phi\acute{o}\delta o\upsilon$ $K\rho\eta\tau\iota\kappa o\hat{\upsilon}$) is used in practically the same breath, it
can hardly be said to indicate a ghetto. Other ethnic groups as well

---

[88] *Flacc.* 54; cf. H. Box, *Philonis Alexandrini In Flaccum*, 1939, pp. xxi f.; Smallwood, *op. cit.*, pp. 215f.

[89] Smallwood, *op. cit.*, p. 216, cf. p. 21; Grant, *op. cit.*, p. 123.

[90] Bell, *J.u.G.*, p. 19.

[91] *CPJ* I, p. 66.

[92] *CPJ* II, pp. 108f.; cf. Safrai-Stern, *op. cit.*, pp. 18, 123, 466, 477, 478f., 484.

[93] *CPJ* II, p. 210; Wilcken, *op. cit.*, p. 788 concludes from this that there once
was a ghetto in Oxyrhynchus.

as the Jews apparently had their own urban district.[94] The term "Jewish street" (᾽Ιουδαϊκὴ λαύρα) is manifestly used for a Jewish street in Hermoupolis.[95] The exact difference between "ἄμφοδον" and "λαύρα" is not quite clear. Often it is assumed to be the distinction between "street" and "quarter", but just how these two meanings must be allocated to the two Greek words is not certain.[96] In any case what is apparent is that the Jews lived in separate quarters or streets, but that this applied to other ethnic groups as well.

There is one passage in the *Acts of the Alexandrian Martyrs* which has led various scholars to assume that there is, nevertheless, some reference to a ghetto in the papyri; though usually these are the same scholars who believe they have discovered traces of the existence of a ghetto in the literary sources. The precise significance of the words in question is, however, absolutely uncertain, and consequently very divergent interpretations have been given. Antonius, one of the Alexandrians, says to emperor Hadrian that already the Alexandrians have written him many letters, in which they state : "διέταξ'ἀνοσίους ᾽Ιουδαίους προσκατοικεῖν οὗ οὐ παραβόλως ἔσχον ἀναπίπτειν καὶ πολεμεῖν τὴν εὐπροσώνυμον ἡμῶν πόλιν..."[97] The different translations of these words reveal the different interpretations placed on them. Reinach's translation is, for example : "On avait ordonné aux Juifs impies d'aller s'établir dans un endroit d'où ils ne pourraient plus, à l'improviste, tomber sur notre très renommée cité et la combattre..."[98] Tcherikover's translation is : "(the prefect) had ordered the impious Jews to transfer their residence to a place from which they could not easily attack and ravage our well-named city..."[99] What exactly is meant by these words ? The answer to this question depends largely on the interpretation of the προσκατοικεῖν. Does this mean that the prefect wanted to round up the Jews once more in a ghetto, in order to prevent them from suddenly attacking the city (Reinach, Juster) ? Or must we add ἡμεῖν, so that the prefect, on the contrary, wanted to abolish the ghetto and have the Jews live among the Alexandrians, so that they could not again attack the city in compact groups (Wilcken) ? Or is reference made to an entirely

---

[94] *CPJ* III, pp. 10ff.; cf. *CPJ* I, p. 5, note 14.

[95] *CPJ* III, pp. 29f.

[96] *CPJ* III, p. 12.

[97] *CPJ* II, p. 93, ll. 13-18.

[98] Reinach, *op. cit.*, p. 226; see also Juster, *op. cit.* II, p. 178.

[99] *CPJ* II, p. 95.

new settlement of the Jews, who had fled their homes during the
revolt under Trajan and had sought asylum in Alexandria, but who
had no right to live there and consequently had to be assembled
somewhere outside the city (Tcherikover)? To a certain extent what
Tcherikover says of his solution applies to them all : of course, this
is a mere suggestion, that cannot be proved. Whatever the case
may be, it seems highly improbable that there is here any question
of a ghetto. If two scholars, both of whom assume there were ghettos
in the ancient world, draw such diametrically opposite conclusions
from these words as Reinach and Wilcken, it is clear that this passage
contains no proof positive of a ghetto in or outside Alexandria.[100]

In periods of violent clashes, the Jews will have been forced into
a situation closely resembling a ghetto, but if so, it was of a very
temporary nature. Neither the literary nor the archeological sources
contain anything to indicate that Jews were forced to live together
for a longer period in an isolated area. No doubt they longed for
a city quarter or street where they could feel at home, where undisturbed they could live communally according to their laws, where they
could practice their trades in peace, where they also sometimes
could seek protection in a world often hostile to them. Consequently
they felt it a privilege, right from very early times, to be allocated
certain streets and quarters : "C'était un privilège qu'on leur accordait
et non une dechéance dont on les frappait".[101]

The separateness of the Jews, therefore, often resulted from their
own choice and originated in their obedience to the laws. That deliberate self-isolation is classically formulated in the words which the
author of the book *Esther* places in Haman's mouth : "there is a
certain people, dispersed among the many peoples in all the provinces
of your kingdom, who keep themselves apart. Their laws are different
from those of every other people; they do not keep your majesty's

---

[100] Reinach, *op. cit.*, p. 226, note 1; Juster, *op. cit.* I, p. 127; Wilcken, *op. cit.*,
pp. 819f.; *CPJ* II, p. 98; cf. Bell, *J.u.G.*, pp. 42f.

[101] Juster, *op. cit.* II, p. 178; In 1 Kings 20 : 34 there is already some question of
חֻצּוֹת, which were allotted them in Damascus. The reference here is to a quarter where
the Jews could live together. "Handelswijk" (= Trading quarter), Transl. N.B.G.,
suggests too strongly that there was a specific reason for designating such a quarter.
Brongers is also of the opinion that reference is made here to trading facilities, trading
concessions, H.A. Brongers, *1 Koningen*, 1967, p. 209. But that is not clear from the
text and the context. In my opinion this would restrict the purpose of such a privilege
too much.

laws. It does not befit your majesty to tolerate them" (*Esth.* 3:8).
Josephus quotes these words of Haman, but not literally. He has
Haman speak of a nation which was unfriendly and unsocial and
neither had the same religion, nor practised the same laws as others,
of a nation that, both by its customs and practices, is the enemy
of your people and of all mankind.[102] Josephus adapts the terminology
even more closely to the pagan accusations of separateness ($\dot{\alpha}\mu\iota\xi\acute{\iota}\alpha$)
and of hostility to the human race as revealed in the peculiar customs
and practices of that people. But he agrees entirely with the text
of *Esther* when he says that the reason for the isolation of the Jews
was their living according to their laws. The Jewish writers did not
have to let only the enemies of their nation say that herein lay the
foremost reason for their strangeness in the ancient world. Only
too well did they know that this was true, and they repeatedly and
clearly said so, and so with pride.

Essentially the conflict with the ancient world was always centred
on the law. In using this word, one must always bear in mind that
it does not completely and adequately reflect the meaning of the
Hebrew Torah. It was very soon realised that there really is no word
which reproduces its full significance, and so the Hebrew word is
left untranslated.[103] The use of the Greek νόμος could easily lead
to an incorrect limitation of the meaning of the Torah, even for the
ancient Jew. But when both Jewish and pagan writers speak of νόμος,
that can hardly be translated as anything other than "law". Consequently what is meant at times is a whole complex of legal rules
which must be obeyed in practice, though often it is wise to remember
that in νόμος there echo subtle tones of the Hebrew Torah.
The struggle about the position of Jewry was often a struggle
about the law, often even within Jewry itself, as is clearly enough

---

[102] *A.* XI. 212.

[103] See, for example R. Travers Herford, *Das Pharisäische Judentum*, 1913, pp. 48ff.
In the original English edition T.H. says that no English word can reproduce the full
meaning of Tora, and in a note Perles says the same holds good for German, p. 49.
J. Parkes, *The Conflict of the Church and the Synagogue*, 1934, p. 35, also notes that
tora is only partially expressed by "law". He quotes the statement made by Travers
Herford : "It is near the truth to say that what Christ is to the Christian, Torah is
to the Jew", and further on he also says : "The written Law was the basis of Torah,
but Torah itself was the complete revelation of the life of the holy community or nation
through which the individual in every act could fulfil the purpose of God in His creation",
p. 36; cf. Bergmann, *op. cit.*, pp. 94-119; K. Schubert, Das Selbstverständnis des
Judentums in der rabbinischen Theologie, *Judaica* 12 (1956), pp. 220ff.

evidenced by all sorts of Jewish writings. A few examples follow. In the time of the Maccabees the supporters and opponents of the law were sharply divided. The latter were the lawless men (ἄνδρες παράνομοι), the Jews who wanted to assimilate as far as possible with their Hellenistic environment, who believed all the misery of the Jews was due precisely to their isolation. These criminal folk from Israel, as they are called in *1 Macc.*, who hated their nation, said : "Let us go and make a covenant with the Gentiles round about us, for since we separated from them many evils have come upon us".[104] Their aim was that the Jews should forget the law and change all the ordinances.[105] The books of the law which they found they tore to pieces and burned with fire. If the book of the covenant were found in possession of anyone, or if anyone adhered to the law, the decree of the king condemned him to death.[106] With regret and indignation, the author records that many of the people, every one who forsook the law, joined them.[107] The Greek customs (τὰ Ἑλληνικά) were extremely attractive to many Jews.[108] They were prepared to go at any length, even to denying the law, in order to participate in the society about them, in the Hellenistic culture, in the education of the gymnasium. It is difficult to determine the actual number of these renegades in the age of the Maccabees. The obvious assumption is that they were most numerous in the upper social circles. It goes almost without saying that such a wave of assimilation with the pagan surroundings evoked a strong counter-stream of strict adherence to the law and a consequent sharp isolation from the pagan environment.

Great emphasis is placed on the separation of Jews and pagans by the book *Jubilees*. Israel alone is the chosen people of God. There are many nations and many peoples, and all are His, and over all has He placed spirits in authority to lead them astray from Him. But over Israel He did not appoint any angel or spirit, for He alone is their ruler.[109] The dying Abraham gives his last warning to Jacob : "Do thou, my son Jacob, remember my words, and observe the commandments of Abraham thy father : separate thyself from the

---

104 *1 Macc.* 1. 11; ἄνδρες παράνομοι; *1 Macc.* 10. 61; 11. 21.
105 *1 Macc.* 1. 49.
106 *1 Macc.* 1. 56f.
107 *1 Macc.* 1. 52.
108 *2 Macc.* 6. 9; 11. 24.
109 *Jub.* 15. 31f.

nations, and eat not with them : and do not according to their works
and become not their associate; for their works are unclean and all
their ways are a pollution and an abomination and uncleanness".[110]
Marriage with a pagan is a scandalous matter. Failure to circumcise
children, or an attempt to undo circumcision, is a horrible thing.
The Sabbath must be strictly observed. The readers are continuously
told that the law has not become obsolete, that nothing in it may
be 'modernised' and brought up to date. Against all forms of Hellenising
moderation or abolition of the law it is repeatedly postulated that
the law is of divine origin and worthy of absolute authority both
now and in the future. All falling away from the law resulting from
assimilation with pagan customs, regardless of degree, inevitably
calls down the wrath of God.[111] Placed in the second half of the second
century B.C., this book shows how fiercely certain circles of that
time condemned any form of intermingling or assimilation and insisted
on the strict observance of the law in all degrees. That meant they
formed a strong impulse towards strict isolation from their pagan
environments, and in practice this must have been very obvious
to the non-Jews.

The Mishnah contains repeated evidence of just how serious was
the Jewish vigilance against any contamination by pagan worship
and pagan vices. Particularly in the tract *Avoda zarah* are the lines
of distinction sharply drawn, evidently with an eye to very concrete
instances in daily life. All actions which could be seen as anything
approaching participation in pagan sins, or even as offering an opportunity for such, must be avoided. All deeds and actions which in no
way engender any risks of that nature are proclaimed permissible.
A scrupulous investigation is made into possible sources of contamination by pagan idolatry in the contacts with the pagans in the neighbourhood. For example there are places and moments in which the Jews
must strictly avoid contact via all sorts of relationships with their
pagan surroundings. For three days before the festivals of the Gentiles,
specified by name, it is forbidden to have business with them—to
lend to them or to borrow from them, to lend them money or to
borrow money from them, to repay them or to be repaid by them.
Rabbi Ishmael even says that this rule also applies to the three days

---

[110] *Jub.* 22. 16.

[111] Warning against the "mixed marriage" *Jub.* 30. 7-17; on circumcision *Jub.*
15. 11-24; on the Sabbath *Jub.* 50. 6-13; cf. *Letter of Aristeas* 130, 139-142.

following those festivals.[112] A precise list is given of what may not be sold to pagans. In it attention is paid to a possible participation, indirectly, in the pagan cult, for the list includes a white cock. But Rabbi Judah says: "one may sell a Gentile a white cock among other cocks, or, if it is by itself, cut off its spur and sell it to him, because they do not sacrifice to an idol what is defective.[113] Where the custom is to sell small cattle to Gentiles, they may sell them; where the custom is not to sell them, they may not sell them. Nowhere may they sell them large cattle.[114] Assistance may not be given to build certain buildings, though for others it may, as for example public baths; yet when they have reached the vaulting where they set up the idol, it is forbidden to help them to build".[115] The list gives a long series of such injunctions, and especially interdictions. They refer to leaving cattle behind in the inns of the Gentiles, assistance given by a Jewish woman at the birth of a pagan child, which is forbidden, since she would be assisting to bring to birth a child for idolatry,[116] the foodstuffs permitted and forbidden,[117] the images of idols,[118] the libation-wine.[119] This last subject, in particular, is discussed in the minute detail appropriate to subtle casuistry. It is said, for instance, that one may buy the contents of a trodden winepress from a Gentile, even though the Gentile took the grapes in his hand and put them on the heap, for the wine cannot become libation-wine until it flows down into the vat. If some had flown down into the vat, what is in the vat is forbidden, but the rest is permitted.[120] If a Gentile hired an ass of an Israelite to bring thereon libation-wine, its hire is forbidden, but if he had hired it to ride upon, even if the Gentile rested his flagon of libation-wine upon it, the hire is permitted. [121]

---

[112] *Avoda Zarah* 1. 1-3.

[113] *Av. Zar.* 1. 5.

[114] *Av. Zar.* 1. 6, cf. *Pesaḥim* 4. 3; in *The Damascus Document* the sale of clean beasts or fowl to the pagans was forbidden, lest they use them for sacrifices; similarly, under no circumstance whatsoever was it permitted to sell anything from the threshing-floor or the winepress to the pagans, *CD* XII. 8-10.

[115] 1. 7.

[116] 2. 1.

[117] 2. 5ff.

[118] 3. 1ff.

[119] 4. 8ff.

[120] 4. 8.

[121] 5. 1.

Obviously, the criterion employed in enumerating such injunctions and interdictions is the degree of contact with the pagan cult. Such rules, when observed obediently and strictly, deeply affected the day-to-day coexistence of the Jews and the pagans about them and inevitably contributed to the isolation of the Jewish groups. In many ways they could not but suffer practical disadvantages as a result— in trade and commerce, for example.[122] Not all Jews were prepared to bear the detrimental effects of living according to the laws. Some certainly did not hesitate to participate fully in the social and cultural life of their neighbourhood, to give their children a Hellenistic education, to eat at one table with pagans, to enter a "mixed" marriage. The Jews were prevented by law from having intercourse with a foreign woman,[123] from building up a good career, from participating in festivities and amusements which inevitably were correlated with a certain cult. There must always have been those of whom it could be said οἱ ποτὲ Ἰουδαῖοι, as can be read in an inscription on a marble tablet found in Smyrna. They are named in a list of citizens who had donated gifts to the city. These Jews, who had forsworn their faith and received citizenship, had contributed 10,000 drachmas.[124] It is known from another inscription deriving from Miletus that Jews had their own reserved places in the theatres, which were clearly indicated : "τόπος <Ε>ιουδ(αί)ων τῶν καὶ θεοσεβ(ῶν)". Frey's translation of these words runs : "Place des Juifs qui s'appellent aussi craignant Dieu".[125] But this text is sometimes read and interpreted differently :"τοπός τῶν Εἰουδαίων φιλοσεβάστων", the finest translation of which is the English "Reserved for His Imperial Majesty's most loyal Jews", especially when it is added that reference is made here to "some extremely desirable seats in the very front rows".[126] In any case these culture- or pleasure-loving Jews did not hesitate to reserve permanent seats in a theatre where the performances were not independent of a pagan religious setting. We have seen above (pp. 72ff.) that it was very tempting for eminent Jews to renounce their ancestral religion for the sake of a successful or pleasant life in a pagan community. The same sort of temptation

---

[122] Cf. Hengel, *op. cit.*, p. 101; Bergmann, *op. cit.*, pp. 10-24.

[123] Jos., *A.* XII. 187.

[124] *CIJ* II, nr. 742.

[125] *CIJ* II, nr. 748.

[126] Radin, *op. cit.*, p. 331; cf. A. Deissmann, *Licht vom Osten*, ⁴1923, pp. 391f.; Lifshitz, *op. cit.*, pp. 81f.; McEleney, *op. cit.*, pp. 326f.

must have been felt in less exalted circles as well. In a list of night guards occurs the name of Jacob, son of Achilleus and a Jew. He apparently was not disturbed by the fact that his profession involved the responsibility for guarding a temple of Serapis; earning a little extra was more important.[127]

The examples of apostasy given here and on pp. 72ff. concern different times and places and mainly certain circles of Jewry. This is, of course, no proof that there were numerous renegades and assimilators, even though *1 Macc.* does suggest this for a certain period. With regard to this question, it must again be borne in mind that the data collected derive from widely divergent places and periods of time. Naturally one could argue that the material available is very incomplete and that there must have been many more apostate Jews than we know of. An inscription from Hypaepa, to the south of Sardes, bears the words Ἰουδαίων νεωτέρων,, which probably signify that these Jews belonged to the group of juniors, according to the ephebes system of athletes.[128] How large was that group of Jews? How many Jews voluntarily participated in the Greek system of the *paideia*? Did that occur in many cities and in many different periods? The material available seems to support Tcherikover's statement, made with reference to certain archeological data about the assimilation of the Jews: "Such cases are, of course, very rare, and far-reaching conclusions should not be drawn from them... the overwhelming majority of them (the Diaspora Jews) did not incline to assimilation".[129] Only the words "of course" might possibly be queried. The data are too scarce to admit of such positiveness. The impression that the number of anti-law advocates was large and that for a time they were influential is given not only by the books of *Maccabees*, but also by Philo, whose indignation at the violation of the prescripts of the law is so great that one must perforce conclude that he must have encountered quite a number of such apostates.[130] After quoting Gen. 11. 1-9 he vents his vexation with his fellow Jews in Alexandria, who cherish a dislike of the institutions of the fathers and make it their constant study to denounce and decry the laws and who find in these and similar passages openings, as it were, for their godlessness (ἀθεότης). "Can you still", say these

---

[127] *CPJ* III. nr. 475.

[128] *CIJ* II, nr. 755.

[129] Tcherikover, *op. cit.*, pp. 352, 354; cf. Safrai-Stern, *op. cit.*, pp. 185, 451.

[130] *Mos.* i. 31; cf. above pp. 74f.

impious scoffers, "speak gravely of the ordinances, as containing
the canons of absolute truth? For see your so-called holy books
contain also myths, which you regularly deride when you hear them
related by others". Numerous examples of such can, if necessary,
be found scattered about the Law-book.[131] The Jews in question
here probably no longer took the laws too seriously and consequently
violated them with a clear conscience in order to make it easier for
themselves to live, work and succeed in the pagan world about them.
Perhaps, too, something of the religious apathy of that world infected
Jewry. On this point Heinemann says: "die Stimmung sehr weiter
griechischer und römischer Kreise, zumal der Gebildeten, die mit
einem Augurenlächeln über den Kult sprachen und ihm, auch wenn
sie ihn äusserlich mitmachten keine religiöse Bedeutung zumassen,
mag auch auf gebildete jüdische Kreise von Einfluss gewesen sein".[132]
In that case, what he says just before this passage could be true:
"Natürlich mussten auch religiöse Lauheit und Gleichgültigkeit, wie
wir sie für gebildete Kreise der hellenistischen Zeit durchaus voraus-
zusetzen haben, jüdischer Gesetzestreue gefährlich werden".[133]

In any case, it was Philo's belief that the Jew's way of thought
and life had to be determined by obedience to the prescripts of the
laws and that such an attitude irrevocably made the position of the
Jew in ancient society difficult in many respects and one he was
not permitted to evade by assimilation. He realises that this inevitably
involved a degree of loneliness and strangeness. Josephus also was
aware of this and was convinced that the life of the Jews, both
individually and as a nation, was centred on obedience to the prescripts
of the laws. David may be termed an example in this respect. Despite
the sin he committed with Bathseba, he was a righteous and god-
fearing man, who strictly observed the laws of his fathers.[134] This
φυλάσσειν τοὺς πατρίους νόμους is what Josephus also means when
he speaks of the τηρεῖν or φυλάσσειν of the πάτρια ἔθη.. These expressions are sometimes interchanged in use.[135] Love of the laws of the

---

[131] *Conf. ling.* 2f.; cf. A.D. Nock, *Essays on Religion and the Ancient World*, I, 1972,
p. 446: Philo knew and disapproved of contemporary liberals who, feeling, as he did,
that they knew the inner meaning of the Law, concluded, as he did not, that they
were emancipated from the obligation of observing the letter. See also II, 1972, pp. 574,
945f.

[132] I. Heinemann, *Philons griechische und jüdische Bildung*, 1932, p. 455.

[133] *Ib.*, p. 454.

[134] *A.* VII. 130.

[135] *A.* XIX. 290; cf. *A.* XIV. 223.

fathers surpasses all else. If necessary the Jews are prepared to risk their lives for them.[136]

Throughout our history, Josephus says, we have kept the same laws, to which we are eternally faithful.[137] The fairest defence we can offer in reply to the numerous false accusations which are brought against us is to be found in the laws which govern our daily life.[138] Moses the legislator proved himself the people's best guide and counsellor; and after framing a code to embrace the whole conduct of their life, induced them to accept it and to observe it for all time.[139] Josephus is convinced that, to those who observe the laws and, if they must needs die for them, willingly meet death, God has granted a renewed existence and, in the revolution of the ages, the gift of a better life.[140] Consequently the only evil which can befall them is to be compelled to do any act or utter any word contrary to their laws.[141] Robbed though they be of wealth, of cities, of all good things, their Law at least remains immortal; and there is not a Jew so distant from his country, so much in awe of a cruel despot but he has more fear of the Law than of him. [142]

Is it so strange, then, that the Jews refused to mingle with those who chose a different sort of life ? When Apollonius Molon reproached them for this, he should have read Plato carefully. He would have read that he, too, took precautions to prevent foreigners from mixing with fellow-citizens at random.[143] Undeniably there were Jews who did not shun such intercourse. But they were people who renounced the laws of their fathers and the God to whom they owe them,[144] who abandoned the observance of their fathers' customs.[145] On the other hand, the Jews who do not abandon their faith hearken to and observe the laws.[146]

Josephus, therefore, testifies again and again that the entire life and society of the Jews are centred on the maintenance of the prescripts

---

[136] *A.* XVIII. 84, 263; see above pp. 25f.; cf. *A.* XVIII. 55, 59; *Ap.* i. 212.

[137] *Ap.* ii. 82.

[138] *Ap.* ii. 147.

[139] *Ap.* ii. 156.

[140] *Ap.* ii. 218.

[141] *Ap.* ii. 233.

[142] *Ap.* ii. 277; cf. *B.* iii. 356, VII. 343; *A.* iii. 317.

[143] *Ap.* ii. 258.

[144] *A.* IV. 130.

[145] *A.* VIII. 190; cf. *A.* VIII. 192, 229f., XIII. 121; here the word ἀσεβής is used.

[146] *A.* IV. 183, 306, 309.

of the law. He is acutely aware of the fact that this determines their
place in ancient society and that it irrevocably involves conflict
with those about them, with all the resultant dangers. But only
renegades would attempt to evade such conflicts. He believes, however,
that the hatred for the Jews is founded on misunderstandings. When
enumerating the many decrees that testify to the tolerance of the
Roman authorities for the Jewish customs, he says he cites these
decrees so often, because "it is to reconcile the other nations to us
and to remove the causes for hatred which have taken root in thought-
less persons among us as well as among them. For there is no nation
which always follows the same customs, and it also happens that
there are great differences among cities. And it is most profitable
for all men, Greeks and barbarians alike, to practise justice, about
which our laws are most concerned, and, if we sincerely abide by
them, they make us well disposed and friendly to all men. We therefore
have a right to expect this same attitude from them, for one should
not consider foreignness (τὸ ἀλλότριον) a matter of indifference in
practice, but of whether there is a proper attitude to goodness. For
this is common to all men and alone enables society to endure".[147]
Josephus must have known he was painting here a much too optimistic
picture of the state of affairs.[148] What he says elsewhere about living
in accordance with the Jewish law proves that he realised that the
fidelity of the Jews to their laws could not but arouse the hostility
and hatred of the non-Jews and would always be an impediment
in the way of reconciliation between his people and the other nations.
As long as the observance of the laws led to such a strange attitude
among the Jews, to such separateness and segregation, the pagans
certainly did not think it justified to expect them to feel goodwill
towards the Jews. The ideas about the attitude to goodness (καλο-
καγαθία), which Josephus sees as a possible means of binding all
nations together,[149] differed so radically that the Jews could not
but remain a strange element in ancient society.

As last example of the central position occupied by the law in the
Jewish way of life, might be mentioned the inscriptions in the Jewish
catacombs. It is remarkable enough in itself that the Jews were buried

---

[147] A. XVI. 174-178; cf. R. Laqueur, *Der jüdische Historiker Flavius Josephus*,
1920, pp. 221-223; Brüne, *op. cit.*, pp. 215ff.

[148] Two passages from the writings of Polybius could possibly have had something
to do with this digression, cf. Brüne, *op. cit.*, p. 216

[149] A. XVI. 178.

together in a separate place. "Le séparatisme confessionel", says Frey, "des cadavres est absolu : les Juifs de Rome, comme d'ailleurs les Chrétiens, n'admettent aucune promiscuité avec ceux qui n'appartiennent pas à la même foi : la communauté reste unie dans la mort comme dans la vie".[150] The determining factor was, indeed, the faith. Those who were not Jewish by birth, but who had been converted to the Jewish religion, could be buried alongside of those who were full-Jews by parentage. This is once more a testimonial of the fact that membership of a certain race was not a factor of consideration. In the Jewish catacombs of Rome, seven inscriptions were found which definitely refer to a proselyte. But evidently only those proselytes were buried in a Jewish burial place. Nothing has been found to indicate that God-fearers, $\phi o\beta o\acute{u}\mu\epsilon\nu o\iota$ $\tau\grave{o}\nu$ $\theta\epsilon\acute{o}\nu$ ($\sigma\epsilon\beta\acute{o}\mu\epsilon\nu o\iota$ $\tau\grave{o}\nu$ $\theta\epsilon\acute{o}\nu$, *metuentes*), were ever admitted.[151] According to the statements of certain pagan authors, it was common knowledge in the ancient world that the Jews observed special customs in burying their dead. Hecataeus of Abdera says that the laws of the Jews concerning marriage and burial were quite different from those of other people.[152] According to Tacitus the Jews bury the body rather than burn it, thus following the Egyptians' custom; they likewise bestow the same care on the dead, and hold the same belief about the world below; but their ideas of heavenly things are quite the opposite.[153]

A closer study of the contents of the inscriptions reveals the remarkable frequency with which the law and the deceased's fidelity to the law are mentioned. Frey rightly points out that in the more than 500 Jewish inscriptions of Rome which he collected, God is only mentioned once as $\delta\epsilon\sigma\pi\acute{o}\tau\eta\varsigma$, but that the law "se retrouve partout". These mortuary inscriptions provide further evidence that the law was the rule of the religious, social and political life of Jewry. The law was also "le premier objet de son culte et de sa piété".[154] All sorts of laudatory adjectives describe primarily the observance of the law, which is evidently the highest honour accorded the deceased : $\phi\iota\lambda\acute{o}\nu o\mu o\varsigma$, $\phi\iota\lambda\acute{\epsilon}\nu\tau o\lambda o\varsigma$.. In Latin inscriptions the deceased is called *juste legem colens* or is praised for his *observantia legis*. It can also

---

[150] *CIJ* I, p. cxxx.

[151] Cf. Juster, *op. cit.*, I, pp. 480f.; *CIJ* II, p. xiii, cxxx; H.J. Leon, *The Jews of Ancient Rome*, 1960, pp. 253ff.

[152] Reinach, *op. cit.*, p. 19 : Diod. Sic. XL. 3.

[153] *Hist.* V. 5.

[154] *CIJ* II, p. cxlii.

be inferred from the inscriptions that the teaching and the study
of the law were highly honoured in the Roman community of the
Jews. And that, too, is mentioned in praise of some of the deceased :
νομοδιδάσκαλος, νομομαθεῖς, διδάσκαλος νομομαθὴς, μαθητὴς σοφῶν".[155]

Needless to say, the close ties between the deceased and the synagogue are often noted, as for example in the following legend : "Here
lies Pancharius, Father of the synagogue of Elaea, aged 110 years,
lover of his people, lover of the Commandments. He lived a good
life. In peace his sleep".[156] The synagogue was the place where Moses
was read every Sabbath (*Act.* 15.21), as is written in the famous
Theodotus inscription from a synagogue in Jerusalem. Theodotus
built this synagogue for the teaching of the law and the instruction of
the commandments (εἰς ἀναγνωσίν νόμου καὶ εἰς διδαχὴν ἐντολῶν).[157]
Since the law constituted the very nucleus of Jewish life and the
meetings in the synagogue, it is not surprising that often a scroll
of the law is reproduced at the entrance to a tomb or on the marble
of the epitaphs. The direct association with the synagogue appears
from representations of the holy ark and the synagogue rolls.

Diverse sources, both literary and archeological, thus demonstrate
how the law dominated the life and community of the Jews and
hence their position in society. There can be little doubt that the reason
for their strangeness in the ancient world lay in their obedience to
the commandments of the law. Some non-Jewish authors probably
understood something of this, as for example Hecataeus of Abdera,
who is reported by Josephus as having said : "neither the slander
of their neighbours and of foreign visitors, to which as a nation they
are exposed, nor the frequent outrages of Persian kings and satraps
can shake their determination; for these laws, naked and defenceless,
they face tortures and death in its most terrible form, rather than
repudiate the faith of their forefathers". Josephus repeats a few
examples given by Hecataeus of their obstinacy in defending their
laws.[158] Dio Cassius speaks of those who, although of alien race
(ἀλλοεθνεῖς), affect the customs (τὰ νόμιμα) of the Jews.[159] In general,
however, the pagan writers did not probe the innermost motifs of
the Jewish way of life and thought, and certainly not when their

---

[155] *CIJ* II, p. cxlii.
[156] *CIJ* I, p. 372; Leon, *op. cit.*, p. 340.
[157] *CIJ* II, p. 333; J.N. Sevenster, *op. cit.*, p. 131.
[158] *Ap.* i. 191f.
[159] Reinach, *op. cit.*, p. 182 : *Hist. Rom.* XXXVII. 17.

attitude was hostile. Even when they accuse the Jews of superstition, they do not begin a discussion about fundamentals, but immediately start discussing very concrete points. When Seneca deals with the superstition of the civil theology (*civilis theologiae superstitiones*), he at once cites as example the religious ceremonies of the Jews, particularly the Sabbath.[160] When Dio Cassius states that Flavius Clemens and his wife Flavia Domitilla were accused of atheism, he classifies them with the numerous others who were proved to have allowed themselves to be converted to the customs of the Jews (ἐς τὰ τῶν Ἰουδαίων ἔθη).[161] In a way it is not surprising that the pagan writers immediately pick on the morals and customs of the Jews whenever they describe their life and society. These were the aspects which made them stand out, in practice, in ancient society, which first made non-Jews notice that there was something special, something strange about this nation which distinguished, and hence often segregated them from all others. The result, however, is that they aimed their criticism and ridicule, often hatred as well, against what they saw as strangely divergent customs without enquiring into a possible deeper connection. Consequently the entire scale of polemics between Jews and non-Jews usually disintegrates into separate, concrete points, and the manner in which the controversy is waged warrants the comment of Tcherikover : It is sufficiently clear from anti-Semitic literature that Jewish religious customs—circumcision, the Sabbath, the festivals and the dietary laws—were the first things to attract the attention of the Gentiles, serving as signs which made the Jew immediately recognizable.[162] This is why the anti-Semitic controversy in the ancient world almost always resembled a spiteful scuffle about separate, concrete points.

One of the points repeatedly brought up by pagan writers is the Jewish repudiation of any form of image-worship. This, in addition to abstention in eating the meat of swine and the rigorous observance of the Sabbath, are accounted by Schürer to be the three things which particularly formed the target of the ridicule of the civilised world of that day.[163] In my opinion it is doubtful whether these three things can be considered on a par. I believe that the absence

---

[160] Reinach, *op. cit.*, p. 262 : August., *De civ. Dei* VI. 11; cf. above p. 96.

[161] Reinach, *op. cit.*, pp. 195f. : Xiphilinus, *Epitome* LXVII. 14; cf. above pp. 97f.

[162] Tcherikover, *op. cit.*, p. 354.

[163] Schürer, *op. cit.* III, p. 153.

of images in Jewish worship evoked less virulent ridicule than the other two points. Opinion is divided as to whether certain statements about this matter are intended to be favourable or not. Attention was drawn above (pp. 10f.) to the remarkable contradiction between Tacitus' comments on this subject: on the one hand he states that the Jews worshipped the image of an ass, and on the other he says the Jews worshipped no images whatsoever.[164] One of these statements about the absence of images is interpreted in divergent ways, viz. *Hist.* V. 5.8, 9, the passage quoted on p. 10. Moreover, on p. 11 it was said that, according to Isaac, this Tacitus is the one "pour qui les Juifs ne sont pas idolâtres" in contra-distinction to the Tacitus "qui les veut idolâtres de l'âne". Here Isaac apparently reasons that the first Tacitus took a favourable view of the non-participation of the Jews in image-worship. Heinemann would seem to hold the same opinion, for it is precisely this text which he cites as proof that in Tacitus, who, for the rest, merely serves up "eine Sammlung wirrer Märchen", can be heard "der leise Nachklang griechisch-wissenschaftlicher Wertungen".[165] Hospers-Jansen likewise discerns appreciation, not adverse criticism in this passage.[166] Heinisch, on the contrary, discerns an undertone of criticism in Tacitus' pronouncements on the lack of image-worship, for he writes "Tacitus konnte nicht begreifen, warum die Juden in ihrem Tempel keine Götterbilder aufstellten",[167] Schürer believes that here he expresses himself "auffallend kühl, ja, nicht ohne Beimischung von Tadel".[168]

My opinion is that the first group of critics are right in this instance. Indeed, the friendly, understanding, to say the least of it neutrally recording way in which Tacitus comments on the repudiation of image-worship by the Jews might be termed striking, and all the more so when account is taken of the fact that he, personally, could not possibly have agreed with this repudiation. As a Roman with an important administrative career behind him, he could hardly have approved of what he says of the Jews never having honoured kings and emperors with statues. His comparison between the Jewish and

---

[164] *Hist.* V. 3, 4, 5, 9.

[165] Heinemann, *op. cit.*, p. 36.

[166] Hospers-Jansen, *op. cit.*, p. 133; cf. Bergmann, *op. cit.*, p. 72: "Wenn Tacitus von der Verehrung des einzigen, höchsten und ewigen Gottes bei den Juden spricht, dann schweigt sein Hass gegen sie".

[167] P. Heinisch, *Griechentum und Judentum*, 1908, p. 36.

[168] Schürer, *op. cit.*, III, p. 153.

the Egyptian manner of worship gives the impression that he preferred
the former. It would even seem that Tacitus understands the reasons
why the Jews refuse to admit divine images in their temples. There
is certainly no question here of any remarkable coolness mixed with
criticism. That is why this particular statement stands out among all
his other ones and makes it very probable that, in this instance,
Tacitus concurs with a source he consulted. In any case, there are
several writers whose judgment of the Jewish repudiation of images
is not unfavourable. Hecataeus says of Moses : He made no manner
of image of gods, for he did not believe that God is in human form
(διὰ τὸ μὴ νομίζειν ἀνθρωπόμορφον εἶναι τὸν θεόν,), but that "the
heaven that surrounds the earth is alone divine and rules the universe".[169] It is obvious in the latter part of this pronouncement
that Hecataeus gives a completely false representation of what,
according to the Torah, Moses taught. His attribution to Moses of
this pantheism could have been intended as praise rather than censure,
for then the Jews were not so far removed from certain Greek concepts.
Consequently the repudiation of an image cult is placed in a favourable
light, certainly the underlying motif for it which is sought by Hecataeus
in Moses. Not thinking of God in anthropomorphic terms presumes
considering Him too exalted to be portrayed.

A similar judgment of the repudiation of image-worship is to be
found in Strabo : Moses said and taught that the Egyptians were
mistaken in representing the Divine Being by images of beasts and
cattle, as were also the Libyans; and that the Greeks were also wrong
in modelling gods in human form (ἀνθρωπομόρφους τυποῦντες); for
according to him, God is this one thing alone that encompasses us
all and encompasses land and sea, the thing which we call heaven
or universe or the nature of all that exists. What man then, if he
has any sense, could be bold enough to fabricate an image of God
resembling any creature amongst us ? Nay, people should leave off
all image-carving, and, setting apart a sacred precinct and a worthy
sanctuary, should worship God without an image.[170]

Here we find the same misconceptions as in Hecataeus, but also,
essentially, the same judgment about image worship. An unequivocally
favourable statement about the representation of this worship by

---

[169] Reinach, *op. cit.*, p. 16 : Diod. Sic. XL. 3. 4.

[170] Reinach, *op. cit.*, p. 99 : *Geogr.* XVI. 2. 35; Jos. *Ap.* i. 199; "Srabo had a positive
attitude towards the Jews", M. Stern, *Immanuel*, Summer 1972, p. 43.

the Jews is given by Varro and has come down to us via Augustine. Varro said that "the ancient Romans for more than one hundred and seventy years worshipped the gods without an image. If this usage had continued to our own day", he says, "our worship of the gods would be more devout". And in support of his opinion Varro adduces, among other things, the testimony of the Jewish race. According to Augustine he concludes this passage by saying that those who first set up images of the gods for the people diminished reverence (*metus*) as they added error (*error*).[171] It would be difficult to determine in how far Augustine's citation of Varro is affected by the special purposes to which he bent it, but it may be taken for granted that Varro was very critical of image-worship and therefore set the Jews up as example for their repudiation of it.

When viewed in the light of the monotheism of the Jewish religion, the pagan opinion about the repudiation of images will be less favourable. In that monotheism, that "not worshipping the same gods as other people",[172] they almost always discerned an intolerable self-conceit and obstinacy on the part of the Jews. That Jewish nation was the only one to recognise but one god and to consider him the only true god : Dio Cassius says that the Jews are distinguished from the rest of mankind especially by the fact that they do not honour any of the usual gods, but show extreme reverence for one particular divinity. Then he goes on to say at once : "They never had any statue of him even in Jerusalem itself, but believing him to be unnamable and invisible, they worship him in the most extravagant fashion on earth".[173] Not fabricating images is here associated with the unnamableness and invisibility of god and godhead. The Jews are not commended for such a faith. On the contrary, the relationship with the one god, of whom no image may be made, nor of any other god, is in the eyes of Dio Cassius an outward token of a vexatious intolerance that compels the Jews to isolate themselves from all other nations and peoples.

"Besides", the pagans queried, "does this repudiation of images not mean the loss of a bit of concrete, lively and colourful religiousness ? Does it not make the worship of God more unreal, dull and gloomy" ? Juvenal believes that, already in the first stage, the drift towards Judaism is characterised by the tendency to worship nothing but

---

[171] Reinach, *op. cit.*, p. 242 : August., *De civ. Dei* IV. 31.

[172] Apollonius Molon according to Jos., *Ap.* II. 79.

[173] Reinach, *op. cit.*, p. 182 : *Hist. Rom.* XXXVII. 17.

the clouds and the divinity of the heavens.[174] Here again the counter-
claim could be a lack of true insight into Judaism on the part of
the writer. He makes no mention of the attitude of the Jews to
images in this context. He could, however, have had this in mind
when he said it was incomprehensible and vexatious that the path
of proselytes begins already with that vague adoration of clouds
and heaven. Perhaps the same thought was entertained by Petronius
when he unmistakably jested about the clamour in the ears of high
heaven caused by a Jew, who also worships his pig-god.[175]

In practice the repudiation of images was a matter of bitter gravity
in the ancient society, where the worship of images was taken for
granted and often even emphatically demanded. In the first case
the social position of the Jews in the community was rendered extremely difficult and they suffered great damage; in the second they
were placed in a position of great danger, sometimes even of life.
Little wonder that the tract *Avoda Zarah* endeavours to delineate
as precisely as possible what was permitted to a Jew and what was
not in this field,[176] and that, throughout the centuries, all discussions
on the explanation of the prescripts of the law have dealt with these
problems at length. Philo and Josephus discuss the erection of statues,
not because of any theoretical interest, but because of the bitter
necessity of ruthless practice. Josephus reacts to a charge of Apion
that the Jews do not erect statues of the emperors. Among other
things, he says that the legislator of the Jews forbade the making
of images, alike of any living creature and much more of God, who
is not a creature, not in order to put, as it were, a prophetic veto
on honours paid to the Roman authority, but out of contempt for
a practice profitable to neither God nor man. The complete absence
of the first motive is manifested by the many tokens of homage paid
by the Jews to the emperors and the people of Rome.[177] One of the
things Philo aims at demonstrating is that Augustus was never elated
or made vain by extravagant honours and to prove this cites his
refusal even to be addressed as a god, his annoyance if anyone so
addressed him, his approval of the Jews who, as he knew very well,
eschewed all such language on religious grounds.[178] Suetonius con-

---

[174] Reinach, *op. cit.*, p. 292 : *Sat.* XIV. 97.

[175] Reinach, *op. cit.*, p. 266 : Fragment 37.

[176] *Avoda Zarah* 3. 1-10.

[177] *Ap.* ii. 73, 75-78; cf. Philo, *Leg.* 157; Delling, *op. cit.*, pp. 47f.

[178] *Leg.* 154.

firms Philo's contention in his own way when he says of Augustus
that he would not accept a temple even in a province save jointly
in his own name and that of Rome. In the city itself he refused this
honour most emphatically, even melting down the silver statues
which had been set up in his honour in former times.[179] But in Philo
this remark is placed in the context of a life and death struggle for
the Jews. He wrote at a time when Caligula had decided to have
a statue of himself erected in the temple in Jerusalem, when the
rabble in Alexandria razed many synagogues, in others, which they
had to leave standing, placed portraits of the emperor and in the
largest and most famous a bronze statue. When the Jews violently
resisted, Flaccus ordered their extermination without mercy. In this
period of unbearable anxiety, violent disturbances and cruel massacre
in Alexandria, the Jews had to prove in word and deed the worth
of their repudiation of any form of image-worship, which made them
so annoyingly strange in the ancient world. An end was put to this
desparate period for the Jews by the violent death of Caligula. Le
bras de Chéréas fut providentiel pour les Juifs, says Juster.[180] Understandably the Jews repeatedly referred to the privileges granted
them by several emperors with regard to the form of homages to
the emperor permitted them and emphatically urged the maintenance
of those privileges.[181] But for the pagans, these privileges were the
sign of the separateness of the Jews in society. As we shall see below,
they were often terribly vexed about these. Precisely the attitude
of the Jews in practice, one that could not escape the notice, aggravated
the aversion to this race remarkable for their contempt for the divine
powers (*gens contumelia numinum insignis*), to the nation which even
Claudius felt he had to admonish not to set at nought the beliefs
about the gods held by other peoples.[182]

The celebration of the Sabbath occupied a central position in
Judaism. The attention devoted to it in Jewish writings from the

---

[179] Sueton., *Aug.* LII : "*-nisi communi suo Romaeque nomine*"; cf. The Letter of
Claudius to the Alexandrians, ll. 48-51 and 28, 29, *CPJ* II, pp. 39, 40, 42.

[180] Juster, *op. cit.* I, p. 352; these dramatic events are described in detail by Philo
and Josephus : *Leg.* 132ff., 184-348, 353-357, 366, 367; *Flacc.* 41ff.; *A.* XVIII. 216-310;
B. ii. 184-203; cf. Tacitus, *Hist.* V. 9; a good summary of what happened is given by
Smallwood, *op. cit.*, pp. 19ff., 31ff.

[181] Cf. Juster, *op. cit.* I, pp. 348-354.

[182] Pliny the Elder, Reinach, *op. cit.*, p. 281 : *Nat. hist.* XIII. 4.46, see above pp.
38, 94f.; Claudius, Jos. *A.* XIX. 290.

Torah on is proportionately large. Two tracts of the Mishnah, *Shabbat* and *Eruvin* for example, are devoted entirely to it and another, *Bezah*, for the greater part. From what Jewish writers say about the Sabbath, it appears that the degree of strictness[183] of the precept about rest on that day varied according to times and groups, but the rest occasioned by abstention from work on the Sabbath was, in any case, one of the characteristic features of Jewish life and society which first struck outsiders. Certain consequences of the prescripts about the Sabbath must have affected them deeply in practice, as for example the attitude of the Jews on the Sabbath during wartime. This often formed a problem for the Jews. At the beginning of the revolt of the Maccabees a group of Jews offered no resistance when attacked by the enemy on the Sabbath. On that day thousands of men, women, children and cattle died.[184] But Mattathias and his friends quickly realised that the Jews would soon be wiped out if they continued to refuse to fight on the Sabbath. He therefore resolved on that day : "Let us fight against every man who comes to attack us on the Sabbath day; let us not all die as our brethren died in their hiding places".[185] Josephus also mentions this event, and according to him Mattathias says, inter alia, that, if the Jews offer no resistance on the Sabbath, they would be their own enemies, for then they would all inevitably die. He goes on to say that Mattathias persuaded his followers, and that to this day the Jews continue the practice of fighting even on the Sabbath whenever it becomes necessary.[186] Sometimes the enemies of the Jews are therefore disappointed in their expectation that the Jews will not fight on the Sabbath. They learn by bitter experience that they have miscalculated, and they meet heavy opposition.[187] The specification "whenever it becomes necessary" ($\epsilon\ddot{\iota}$ $\pi o\tau\epsilon$ $\delta\epsilon\acute{\eta}\sigma\epsilon\iota\epsilon$) could be interpreted in different ways. One is that only defence when attacked, and not attack itself is permissible on the Sabbath. But the enemy could take advantage of this application of the rule to improve his military position. When

---

[183] Cf. E. Lohse, Art. σάββατον, *Th.W.N.T.* VII, pp. 8ff.

[184] *1 Macc.* 2. 34-38.

[185] *1 Macc.* 2. 39-41.

[186] *A.* XII. 274-277; this problem is also considered in various places in the Talmud; cf. M. Wolff, Het oordeel der Helleensch-Romeinsche schrijvers over oorsprong, naam en viering van den sabbath (The Opinion of the Hellenic-Roman Writers about the Origin, Name and Celebration of the Sabbath), *Theologisch Tijdschrift* 44 (1910), p. 169.

[187] *A.* XVIII. 319, 354; XIII. 12f.

Pompey besieged Jerusalem, the Jews could have prevented the construction of all sorts of defence-works, which went on under their very eyes, if they had not idly stood by on the Sabbath. The Romans were well aware of this : they did not shoot at the Jews or meet them in hand to hand combat, but instead they raised earth-works and towers and brought up their siege-engines in order that these might be put to work the following day.[188] Little wonder that during the revolt the Romans were massacred even on the Sabbath, though Josephus thinks it necessary to add that this took place on the Sabbath, a day on which from religious scruples (διὰ τὴν θρησκείαν) the Jews abstain even from the most innocent acts.[189] He says the Jews were completely ruled by their passion in battle when launching a heavy attack near Jerusalem, though he must admit that the same passion which shook them out of their piety, brought them victory in the battle.[190]

It frequently happened that the Jews were at a disadvantage and even had to sacrifice their lives when surprised and overwhelmed by an enemy attack on the Sabbath,[191] as when the rabble of Caesarea massacred them on that day.[192] During the siege of Jerusalem, the labours of the Romans would have been endless, had not Pompey taken advantage of the seventh day of the week.[193] Several pagan writers therefore cite the disaster which the Jews bring upon themselves by not fighting on the Sabbath as the best illustration of the folly of the Jewish Sabbath. Josephus says that Ptolemy Soter entered Jerusalem on the Sabbath as if to sacrifice. The Jews did not oppose him, for they did not suspect any hostile act and because of this lack of suspicion and the nature of the day were enjoying idleness and ease. Ptolemy became master of the city without difficulty and ruled it harshly. Josephus adds that Agatharchides of Cnidus speaks scornfully of the pious scrupulousness of the Jews, on account of which they lost their liberty. He quotes him thus : there is a nation called Jews, who have a strong and great city called Jerusalem, which they allowed to fall into the hands of Ptolemy by refusing to take up arms and instead through their untimely superstition

---

[188] *A.* XIV. 63f.
[189] *B.* ii. 456.
[190] *B.* ii. 517f.
[191] *A.* XIII. 337.
[192] *B.* VIII. 362ff.
[193] *B.* i. 146.

submitted to having a hard master.[194] In another passage he quotes
Agatharchides at greater length, and there it appears that, because
of this disaster, the writer taxes the Jews for their adherence to
their insane practices. The absurdity of their law had now become
manifest. That experience has taught the whole world, except that
nation, the lesson not to resort to dreams and traditional fancies about
the law, until its difficulties are such as to baffle human reason.[195] This
oldest known attack on the practice of the Sabbath recurs in other
forms in several writers. Plutarch relates that when the Jews were
attacked on the Sabbath during a siege, they sat in their places
immovable while the enemy were planting ladders against the walls
and capturing the defences, and they did not get up, but remained
there fast bound in the toils of superstition as in one great net.[196]
According to Dio Cassius, the Romans profited from this Jewish
custom of not doing any sort of work on the day of Saturn to batter
down the wall. He, too, is convinced that if the Jews had defended
the city every day with equal strength Pompey could never have
gained command of it. During the battle against Titus, Jerusalem
was lost in the same way on the day of Saturn, which Jews honour
most of all.[197]

Hence we see that the non-Jewish writers had not the least respect
for this attitude of the Jews in wartime, of which Josephus says
in his autobiography that the laws of the Jews forbid the carrying
of arms on that day, however urgent the apparent necessity may
be.[198] Whatever Josephus may mean by 'being forbidden by our
laws' (κωλυόντων ἡμᾶς τῶν νόμων), the Torah or the law of oral
tradition, the pagans understood nothing of the holy constraint
behind the attitude of the Jews, and thought it foolish, ridiculous,
completely irrational. They considered the whole Sabbath a ludicrous
affair. Apion gives a remarkable explanation of the word 'Sabbath':
after a six days' march the Jews developed tumours in the groin,
and that is why, after safely reaching the country now called Judaea,
they rested on the seventh day and called that day *sabbaton*, pre-

---

[194] *A.* XII. 4-6.

[195] *Ap.* i. 209-211.

[196] Reinach, *op. cit.*, p. 136 : *De superstitione* 8; here Plutarch uses the same word
as Agatharcides : δεισιδαιμονία.

[197] Reinach : *op. cit.*, pp. 180f., 194f. : *Hist. Rom.* XXXVII. 16; cf. p. 186 and Nic.
of Damascus, p. 81.

[198] *V.* 161.

serving the Egyptian terminology; for disease of the groin in Egypt is called *sabbo*. Josephus even takes the trouble to demonstrate that such a derivation of the word betrays either gross impudence or shocking ignorance.[199] Perhaps Lohse is right in saying of Apion's etymology : "Apion hat offensichtlich einen schnodderigen Ausdruck aus den Gassen Alexandrias aufgenommen, mit dem man den jüdischen Sabbat lächerlich machen wollte".[200] Similarly Pompeius Trogus and Tacitus connect the origin of the Sabbath with the exodus, though not on the grounds of linguistics. The former relates how Moses and his people marched through the deserts of Arabia for seven days filled with fatigue and fasting and dedicated the seventh day, called the Sabbath by this people, to fasting, for this day marked the end of their hunger and wandering.[201] And Tacitus notes that the Jews first chose to rest on the seventh day, because that day ended their evils.[202] Some found the Jewish customs on the Sabbath so foolish that they endeavoured to induce the Jews to cease such silly habits. Philo speaks of one of the ruling class who, when he had Egypt in his charge and under his authority, proposed to disturb the ancestral customs of the Jews and especially to do away with the law of the seventh day. In veiled threats this high official said : "An end must now be put to that foolish superstition of which the keeping of the Sabbath is a manifest sign".[203]

In one of his satires Juvenal refers to the fornication committed by the barbarian Agrippa with his sister, for which he gave her a diamond ring. But then that happened in that country where kings celebrate festal sabbaths with bare feet.[204] This pure figment of the imagination, *mero pede*, is probably intended to make the Sabbath seem even more ridiculous. How is it possible, Juvenal asks in amazement, that there are Romans who are in sympathy with these sabbatical customs. The keeping of this day is often the first step along the

[199] *Ap.* ii. 20, 21, 26, 27.

[200] Art. σάββατον, *Th.W.N.T.*, VII, p. 18. note 138.

[201] Reinach, *op. cit.*, p. 254 : M. Junianus Justinus XXXVI. 2.

[202] *Hist.* V. 4.

[203] *So.* ii. 123-129. It is not quite clear who the ruler is who is introduced here as speaker, Flaccus or another prefect; cf. Loeb-ed. Philo, Vol. V. p. 609.

[204] Reinach, *op. cit.*, p. 291 : *Sat.* VI. 156ff.; cf. L. Friedlaender, *D. Junii Juvenalis Saturarum Libri V*, 1895, pp. 301f.; on the relationship between Agrippa and Berenice Jos., *A.* XX. 145 and the commentary on this passage by Feldman, Loeb-ed. Vol. IX, p. 467.

path from bad to worse and, ultimately, complete surrender to Judaism.[205] Ovid's remarks on the religious ceremonies of the Syrian Jew are scornful. The Sabbath is one of the days which are not bad for beginning an amorous affair.[206] When Horace is desirous of getting rid of the company of a man whom he does not like, he is fortunate in that his friend Fuscus Aristius happens to pass by. He calls to him : "Surely you said there was something you wanted to tell me in private". "I mind it well", Fuscus says, "but I'll tell you at a better time. Today is the thirtieth sabbath. Would you affront the circumcised Jews" ? Horace replies that he has no scruples whatsoever on this point. Fuscus answers : "But I have. I'm a somewhat weaker brother, one of the many. You will pardon me; I'll talk another day".[207] It is not quite clear what the significance was of the thirtieth Sabbath, and it will never be.[208] In any case Fuscus was one of those Romans called 'sabbatisants' by Reinach, and who are also mentioned by Tibullus and Juvenal.[209] Obviously Horace is jestingly giving vent in this satire to his annoyance with a friend who is taking part in all those Jewish goings-on.

In Juvenal's opinion the rest of the Sabbath was nothing but the indulgence of a natural human laziness. Such a "sabbatisant" gives every seventh day to idleness, keeping it apart from all the concerns of life.[210] He had a predecessor of the same opinion in Seneca, who, according to Augustine, along with other superstitions of the civil theology, censured the sacred institutions of the Jews, especially

---

[205] Reinach, op. cit., p. 292 : Sat. XIV. 96ff.; cf. above pp. 122 f.

[206] Reinach, op. cit., p. 248, nrs. 134a, 134b : Ars amatoria I. 75, 415; see above p. 52.

[207] Reinach, op. cit., p. 246 : Sat. 1. 9. 60ff.; Radin, op. cit., p. 246.

[208] Radin, op. cit., p. 247 : The "thirtieth Sabbath" will probably remain an unsolved riddle. He associates the expression with the Day of Atonement, pp. 399ff. Lohse prefers to separate the words as follows : hodie tricesima, sabbata and to translate them as : "heute ist Neumond, also Sabbatruhe", op. cit., p. 17, note 136; cf. M. Friedländer, Das Judenthum in der vorchristlichen, griechischen Welt, 1897, p. 45; Fairclough says of this passage in a note : "This is probably pure nonsense, no particular Sabbath being intended. Perhaps, however, the Sabbath fell on the thirtieth of the month, Horace, Satires, Epistles and Ars Poetica with an English Translation by H.R. Fairclough, 1961, p. 111.

[209] Reinach, op. cit., pp. 246f., 292f.; Radin, op. cit., p. 247 speaks of a metuens sabbata.

[210] Sat. XIV. 105f.; P. Green, Juvenal, The Sixteen Satires, Penguin Books, 1967, p. 267 translates the words et partem vitae non attigit ullam as "taboo for all life's business"; R. Humphreis, The Satires of Juvenal, 1958, p. 164 : "setting this day apart from life"; Reinach, op. cit., p. 293 : sans prendre aucune part aux devoirs de la vie.

the Sabbath. Seneca declares that their practice is inexpedient, because by introducing one day of rest in every seven, they lose in idleness almost a seventh of their life, and by failing to act in time of urgency they often suffer loss.[211] Tacitus is the only one who also mentions a sabbatical year, and explains its institution, after deciding to rest on the seventh day, as follows : "after a time they were led by the charms of indolence to give over the seventh year as well to inactivity".[212] Similarly Rutilius Namatianus is of the opinion that a Jew spends the Sabbath in scandalous sleepiness with the weakly picture of his tired god in mind.[213]

Rutilius Namatianus was not the first to describe the Sabbath as a chilly day. The Jew celebrates that cold day with his heart, but his heart is even colder than his religion.[214] Meleager had already said the Sabbath was a cold day, and his use of $\psi\nu\chi\rho\delta s$, "cold", probably also meant "boring". Nevertheless Eros can bring a little warmth, even on such a cold day, if one is seized by a $\sigma\alpha\beta\beta\alpha\tau\iota\kappa\delta s$ $\pi\delta\theta os$, une passion sabbatique (Reinach).[215] Seneca's opinion is : let us forbid lamps to be lighted on the Sabbath, since the gods do not need light, neither do men take pleasure in soot.[216] Persius' comment about smoky Sabbath lamps behind greasy window-sills does not suggest a joyous day.[217]

It is very remarkable that many non-Jewish writers apparently assumed the Sabbath was a day of fasting. One might indeed say there was "une confusion ordinaire" among the writers of the age of Augustus.[218] In his description of the capture of Jerusalem by Pompey, Strabo says that he chose as the day for the attack $\tau\dot{\eta}\nu$ $\tau\hat{\eta}s$ $\nu\eta\sigma\tau\epsilon\iota\alpha s$ $\dot{\eta}\mu\epsilon\rho\alpha\nu$, the day of fasting, no doubt meaning the Sabbath, since he continues : "on which the Jews abstained from all form of work".[219] According to Suetonius, Augustus prided himself

---

[211] Reinach, *op. cit.*, p. 262 : August., *De civ. Dei* VI. 11.

[212] *Hist.* V. 4.

[213] Reinach, *op. cit.*, p. 358 : *De reditu suo* I. 391f.

[214] *Ibid.* I. 389f.

[215] Reinach, *op. cit.*, p. 55 : *Anthol.* V. 160.

[216] *Ep.* XCV. 47.

[217] Reinach, *op. cit.*, 264 : *Sat.* V. 179ff.; according to Guttmann this description of the Sabbath of Persius is reminiscent of the way this day was ridiculed in the plays of the pagan theatres, as mentioned in Jewish sources, M. Guttmann, *Das Judentum und seine Umwelt*, 1927, pp. 92f.; see above pp. 81f.

[218] Reinach, *op. cit.*, p. 244, note 1.

[219] Reinach, *op. cit.*, pp. 103f. : *Geogr.* XVI. 40.

before Tiberius on fasting more strictly on the Sabbath day than any Jew.[220] Pompey Trogus mentions that Moses dedicated for ever the seventh day to fasting.[221] Similarly Petronius, a contemporary of Nero, takes for granted that the Jews had to keep a law which imposed on them fasting on the Sabbath.[222] Martial speaks of *ieiunia sabbatariarum*, of the fasting of the women who keep the Sabbath.[223]

This frequently recurring assumption that the Sabbath is a day of fasting is striking. In the Old Testament and in Jewry it was definitely not so. On the contrary, it is a day of joy, a day when there must be plenty of opportunity for good eating and drinking. There were more meals on that day than others. Judith fasted all the days of her widowhood, except the day before the Sabbath and the Sabbath itself.[224] The author of *Jubilees* lists fasting as one of the many things expressly forbidden on the Sabbath.[225] The rabbinical pronouncements are all of the same trend. They set many rules for fasting on all sorts of occasions, public, general and in personal, private life. The Sabbath, like certain feast days however, is definitely excepted from fasting.[226] Nowadays the consensus of opinion is that the belief held by diverse pagan writers that the Sabbath is a day of fasting is a misconception.[227] The question is how such a misconception, evidently quite common though Plutarch forms an exception,[228] came into being. As explanation, reference is sometimes made to Tacitus' statement that the Jews by frequent fasts even now bear witness to the long hunger with which they were once distressed.

---

[220] Reinach, *op. cit.*, pp. 243f. : *Aug.* LXXVI

[221] Reinach, *op. cit.*, p. 254 : M. Junianus Justinus XXXVI. 2.

[222] Reinach, *op. cit.*, p. 266 : Fragment 37.

[223] Reinach, *op. cit.*, p. 287 : *Epigr.* IV. 7.

[224] *Judith* 8. 6.

[225] *Jub.* 50. 12.

[226] See Str. Bill. I, pp. 611ff.; G.F. Moore, *op. cit.*, II, pp. 37f.; J. Behm, Art. νῆστις *Th.W.N.T.* IV, pp. 928ff.; E. Lohse, Art. σάββατον, *Th.W.N.T.* VII, pp. 15f.; Bergmann, *op. cit.*, pp. 98-102; Böhl, *op. cit.*, pp. 490-494.

[227] Cf. e.g. Reinach, *op. cit.*, p. 104, note 1, 244, note 1, 254, note 3, 266, note 4; Radin, *op. cit.*, p. 399; J.H. Freese, *Suetonius, History of Twelve Caesars*, 1930, Notes and Annotations, p. 38; E. Lohse, *op. cit.*, p. 18.

[228] Reinach, *op. cit.*, pp. 144f. : *Quaest. conv.* IV. 5, 6. According to Plutarch, the celebration of the Sabbath was in some way connected with Bacchus, as appears from the nomenclature of the day. The Jews exhort each other on the Sabbath to drink and to get drunk; Persius' remark about the paleness (*pallere*) on the Sabbath has been interpreted in various ways and hence, too, his description of Jewish meals on that day, Reinach, *op. cit.*, p. 265, note 3; Radin, *op. cit.*, p. 399.

Tacitus immediately goes on to describe the rest of the seventh day, although he does not associate the Sabbath rest with fasting.[229] The argument is therefore that the pagans were so deeply impressed by the amount of fasting of the Jews that they naturally assumed it was also a feature of such an exceptional day as the Sabbath. Besides, there was a continual increase in the number of rules about, and appreciation for fasting, which non-Jews could not help but notice in their intercourse with the Jews. When Behm says: "dahin gehört auch das Nüchternbleiben am Sabbatmorgen" under reference to a remark made by Josephus, he draws, in my opinion, too far-reaching conclusions.[230] In this passage Josephus says it was the custom of the Jews to eat their midday-meal ($\dot{\alpha}\rho\iota\sigma\tau\sigma\pi\sigma\iota\epsilon\hat{\iota}\sigma\theta\alpha\iota$) on the sixth hour on the Sabbath. All he means to say, however, is something about the moment when the most important meal of the Sabbath was eaten, probably after the service on that day. His comment does not imply, however, that the preceding period was one of fasting.[231]

Conceivably the fact that it was forbidden to cook on the Sabbath led to the conclusion about fasting.[232] Of greater significance for the explanation of the misconception, however, is perhaps the identification of the Sabbath with the day of Saturn. This occurs in Dio Cassius, Tibullus and Tacitus.[233] The day of Saturn was held to be a day of misfortune. According to Dio Cassius Jerusalem was repeatedly taken specifically on this day of disaster. Work done on that day, *dies ater* and *nefastus*, could not possibly be beneficial. That day of Kronos was inevitably labelled as gloomy and threatening, surrounded by taboos and hence the day par excellence for fasting.[234] Regardless of how one explains the pagan writers' notion of the Sabbath, it does give the impression that they were often only superficially acquainted with Judaism and took little trouble to fathom it.

Circumcision often formed the butt of the derision of pagan writers. In his description of the separate laws, Philo says he wishes to begin with the one made ridiculous by the great majority, the law concerning

[229] *Hist.* V. 4.

[230] J. Behm, *op. cit*, p. 929; Jos., *V.* 279.

[231] E. Lohse, *op. cit.*, S. 16; Str.-Bill. II, p. 615.

[232] Cf. Heinemann, *op. cit.*, pp. 31ff., Wolff, *op. cit.*, p. 171

[233] Reinach, *op. cit.*, pp. 180f., 186, 194, 247: *Hist. Rom.* XXXVII. 16, XLIX. 22, LXVI. 6; Tib., *Eleg.* I. 3. 17f., Tac., *Hist.* V. 4; cf. Heinemann, *op. cit.*, p. 31.

[234] Cf. E. Lohse, *op. cit.*, pp. 17f.; Reinach, *op. cit.*, pp. 180f., 359, note 3.

circumcision.[235] Josephus mentions that Apion derides the practice of circumcision, and with some degree of satisfaction he describes how Apion met his just deserts for his attack on circumcision, which was particularly foolish since the Egyptians not only practise circumcision, but they have taught others to adopt circumcision, as Herodotus has already said. A fitting punishment had to follow, and it did : an ulcer on his person rendered circumcision essential; the operation brought no relief, gangrene set in and he died in terrible tortures.[236]

This ridicule observed by Philo and Josephus does indeed echo throughout the works of non-Jewish writers. When they speak of the Jews as circumcised, their tone is almost always slightly scornful. When Martial showers down reproaches on a Jewish rival, culminating in the accusation that this Jew, although born in the very midst of Solyma, directed his pederasty in a most annoying way towards his own favourite, he addresses him four times as 'circumcised poet' (*verpus poeta*). When this circumcised poet passionately denies any such relationship as charged by Martial, swearing by the Thunderer's Temple, the latter simply does not believe him.[237] To a mistress called Caelia he furiously protests : You grant your favours to Parthians, you grant them to Germans, you grant them, Caelia, to Dacians, and you do not spurn the coach of Cilicians and Cappadocians nor do you shun the lecheries of circumcised Jews (*recutiti Judaei*).[238] The friend of Horace, who was not at all against Jewish customs, speaks of the *curti Judaei*.[239] In describing the Sabbath, Persius uses the same word as Horace, *recutitus*.[240] Petronius says of a Jew that, unless he cuts back his foreskin with the knife, he shall go forth from the holy city cast forth from the people.[241]

The term circumcised is often interpreted as applying exclusively to Jews. Tacitus remarks that the Jews adopted circumcision to distinguish themselves from other peoples by this difference, *ut diversitate noscantur*.[242] Namatianus believes that circumcision is at the

---

[235] *Spec. leg.* i. 1f.

[236] *Ap.* ii. 137, 142, 143.

[237] Reinach, *op. cit.*, p. 288 : *Epigr.* XI. 94; cf. I. Heinemann, *Philons griechische und jüdische Bildung*, 1932, p. 283; Juster, *op. cit.*, I, p. 263f.

[238] Reinach, *op. cit.*, p. 287 : *Epigr.* VII. 30.

[239] Reinach, *op. cit.*, p. 246 : *Sat.* i. 9. 70.

[240] Reinach, *op. cit.*, p. 264 : *Sat.* V. 184.

[241] Reinach, *op. cit.*, p. 266 : Fragment 37.

[242] *Hist.* V. 5.

root of all the folly of the Jews (*radix stultitiae*).[243] Juvenal thinks
the nadir of a Roman's fall has been reached when, after adopting
diverse other customs of the Jews, he has himself circumcised.[244]
Strabo, already, had looked upon circumcision as one of the fruits
of the superstition into which the Jewish religion had degenerated
when it fell under the influence of superstitious men who were appointed
to the priesthood, and then tyrannical people.[245]

Really it is somewhat strange and perhaps characteristic of latent
anti-Semitism, that this ridicule was aimed specifically at the circumcision of the Jews and not, or hardly, at that of other nations. It
was well enough known that circumcision was not applied exclusively
among the Jews. When Philo states that the circumcision of the
Jews is often ridiculed, he clearly hints at how foolish this really
is by mentioning that circumcision is an institution that is very
zealously observed by many other nations, particularly by the Egyptians. Research carried out on mummies appears to confirm Philo's
remark.[246] As noted above, Josephus pointed this out to Apion.[247]
Elsewhere he quotes the passage in which Herodotus discusses the
origins of circumcision : the Colchians, the Egyptians and the Ethio-
pians are the only nations with whom the practice of circumcision
is primitive. The Phoenicians and the Syrians of Palestine admit
that they learnt it from the Egyptians.[248] Diodorus Siculus says
that the Colchians and the Jews are descended from the Egyptians
and from them learnt circumcision.[249] Celsus likewise states that
circumcision came from the Egyptians. The Jews must not, therefore,
fancy that they are holier than other people, because they are circumcised; for the Egyptians and the Colchians did this before they did.[250]

The general assumption, therefore, was that circumcision derived
from the Egyptians and, in any event, was practised by other nations
as well as the Jews. Nonetheless it was the Jews who, because of it,

---

[243] Reinach, *op. cit.*, p. 358 : *De red. suo* I. 389.

[244] Reinach, *op. cit.*, pp. 292f. : *Sat.* XIV. 99.

[245] Reinach, *op. cit.*, pp. 101f. : *Geogr.* XVI. 2. 37.

[246] *Spec. Leg.* i. 2; cf. note to this text in L. Cohn, *Die Werke Philos von Alexandria*,
II, 1910, p. 13.

[247] *Ap.* ii. 142; see above p. 133.

[248] *Ap.* i. 169; see Loeb-ed., Vol. I, p. 231, note c on the Syrians of Palestine.

[249] Reinach, *op. cit.*, p. 69 : I. 28. 3; 55. 5 cf. A. Burton, *Diodorus Siculus, Book I,
A Commentary*, 1972, p. 121.

[250] Origen, *Contra Celsum*, i. 22, V. 41, cf. note to i. 22 in H. Chadwick, *Origen,
Contra Celsum*, 1953, p. 22.

had to bear ridicule and hostility, sometimes even persecution. Antiochus Epiphanes strictly forbade the Jews to circumcise their sons. Women who had their children circumcised and their families and those who circumcised them were put to death and they hung the infants from their mothers' necks.[251]

Up to the first half of the second century A.D. the Romans took no action against the practice of circumcision. True, Domitian forbade castration, but there are no indications that circumcision was equated with it.[252] Suetonius says of this emperor further on that, if necessary, he had the Jews carefully examined for circumcision. But that was to discover any evasion of the tax, the *fiscus Judaicus*, or didrachma that had to be paid annually for the new Roman cult in Jerusalem after the temple had been destroyed. There were non-Jews who had been circumcised, and there were Jews who tried to conceal their circumcision. Suetonius says, "he recalled being present in his youth when the person of a man ninety years old was examined before the procurator and a very crowded court, to see whether he was circumcised".[253] The purpose of this measure, however, was to ensure that the *fiscus Judaicus* was collected as strictly as possible in order to relieve the financial worries of an emperor who was chronically in need of money, and it was not directed against circumcision in itself. Only under Hadrian did this change. According to the *Historia Augusta*, this emperor forbade the circumcision of the Jews during his journey in Asia, and this prohibition was the cause of the revolt of the Jews under Bar-Cochba.[254] Hadrian's successor, Antoninus Pius, once more permitted the circumcision of Jews by birth, but the interdiction remained valid for non-Jews. When Septimius Severus threatened severe punishment for conversion to Jewry, this certainly implied as well the circumcision practised by non-Jews.[255] And the statement that Alexander Severus *Judaeis privilegia reservavit* may be assumed to include circumcision.[256]

---

[251] *1 Macc.* 1. 48, 60f.; cf. *2 Macc.* 6. 10; Jos., *A.* XII. 254.

[252] Suet., *Domit.* VIII.

[253] Suet., *Domit.* XII; cf. Dio Cass., Reinach, *op. cit.*, pp. 194f. : *Hist. Rom.* LXVI. 7.

[254] Reinach, *op. cit.*, p. 343 : *Hist. Aug.*, Hadrianus XIV; here circumcision is identified with self-mutilation (*mutilare genitalia*). The historical truth of this statement is strongly doubted by Radin, *op. cit.*, pp. 343ff.; cf. Böhl, *op. cit.*, p. 495.

[255] Reinach, *op. cit.*, p. 346 : *Hist. Aug.*, *Sept. Severus* XVII.

[256] Reinach, *op. cit.*, p. 348 : *Hist. Aug.*, *Alex. Severus* XXII; cf. Schürer, *op. cit.*, III, pp. 118f.

This rapidly alternating succession of measures concerning circumcision demonstrates how acutely aware the emperors were of the extreme significance of this rite for Jewry as a whole and of the fact that any attack on it was considered by the Jews as an attack on their nation and their religion. The interdiction of circumcision struck at the core of their faith and rendered impossible the observance of the law. Little wonder, then, that the Jews experienced Hadrian's measure as a provocative challenge and retaliated with revolt. Just as the emperor realised more or less clearly to what degree this "circumcision, sans laquelle il n'y a pas de Juif" was fundamental to the Jews and consequently was "le rite liminaire"[257] for them, so did all those writers who poured forth their scornful ridicule on circumcision know perfectly well that, in doing so, they gravely offended that strange people and struck at the very core of their faith and their way of life.

The majority of the pagans probably thought the Jewish abstention from eating the flesh of swine a great folly. It was a conspicuous custom often witnessed by them. If they made no study of its background, but looked on it as an isolated peculiarity of Jewish life, it is understandable that they frequently ridiculed it. Where did the Jews get the idea that that meat could not be eaten, the meat of an animal that was fitted for the food of man and that nature made the most prolific of all her offspring,[258] that could be deemed the most legitimately destined for consumption?[259] Such an animal could have no other purpose than to serve for food.[260] Little wonder that all sorts of witticisms were circulated about this custom of the Jews. Plutarch relates that several witty sayings of Cicero were told which he passed during the lawsuit against Verres. One was as follows: when a certain Caecilius, who was suspected of Jewish practices, tried to constitute himself the prosecutor of Verres, Cicero said: what has a Jew to do with a Verres? The words used by Plutarch here are in Greek: "Τί 'Ιουδαίῳ πρὸς χοῖρον"; When translated into Latin, the pun assumed by Plutarch here, according to what preceded, is clear: "Quid Judaeo cum verre"? Verres is the Roman word for a castrated porker and was used as invective.[261] These words thus

---

257 Simon, op. cit., p. 127.

258 Cicero, De nat. deorum ii. 160.

259 Reinach, op. cit., p. 138: Plutarch, Quaest. Conv. IV. 5: τὸ δικαίοτατον κρέας.

260 Reinach, op. cit., p. 203: Porphyry, Περὶ ἀποχῆς ἐμψύχων I, 14.

261 Reinach, op. cit., p. 150; Cicero, Verr. i. 121; Plutarch, Cicero VII. 5; cf. Quaest. Conv. IV. 5-6.

contain a venomous anti-Semitic derision of this ἄνθρωπος ἔνοχος τῷ ἰουδαΐζειν.

Macrobius says of Augustus that, when he heard that Herod king of the Jews had ordered boys in Syria under the age of two years to be put to death and that the king's son was among those killed, he said : "I'd rather be Herod's pig than Herod's son".[262]

When Philo and a Jewish delegation went to Rome to champion the cause of the Jews of Alexandria, they spent endless hours following around after emperor Caligula, who took his time about giving instructions about diverse buildings under construction. Suddenly he put to the Jewish company, as Philo says, an important and solemn question. "Why do you not eat pork"? The members of the rival pagan delegation from Alexandria burst into violent peals of laughter, partly because they were really amused and partly because they made it their business as flatterers to let his remark seem witty and entertaining. One of the servants attending Gaius was annoyed at the scant respect being shown to the Emperor, in whose presence it was not safe for people who were not his intimate friends even to smile quietly. Philo, however, took the question seriously and explained that different people have different customs. The Jews are forbidden to use some things, just as their adversaries are forbidden to use others. Someone then said : "For instance many people do not eat lamb, which is a very ordinary kind of food". At that Gaius laughed and said : "Quite right too. It is not nice". It is not surprising that Philo bitterly remarks that he and his companions were thoroughly fed up with such derision and jesting and that they were at their wits' end (ἐν ἀμηχάνοις ἦμεν).[263] What clearly emerges from the description of this scene is that the very mention of this custom of the Jews was enough to arouse the laughter of non-Jews and to make them seem a strange and unusual people in the eyes of the pagans. Juvenal thinks it is one of the critical stages in the decline towards total proselytism when no difference is made between eating swine's flesh and that of a man. He therefore ridicules the land of Agrippa as the land where the long-established clemency suffers pigs to attain old age.[264]

Once more the remarkable thing is that the ridicule was directed especially against the Jews, whereas it is evident from various sources

---

[262] Reinach, op. cit., p. 357 : Macrobius, Saturnalia ii. 4. 11.

[263] Leg. 361-363.

[264] Reinach, op. cit., pp. 292, 291 : Sat. XIV. 98; VI. 160.

that they were not the only people to abstain from eating pork.
When Apion denounces the Jews for not eating pork, Josephus
reminds him that the Egyptian priests also abstain from swine's
flesh and that even among the rest of the Egyptians there is not
a man who sacrifices a pig to the gods.[265] The fact that the Egyptians
ate no pork, except on special occasions, was mentioned already
by Herodotus.[266] Sextus Empiricus says that a Jew or an Egyptian
priest would rather die than eat pork.[267] Celsus follows Herodotus in
stating that the Egyptians abstain from pigs because they loathe them,
in addition abstain also from goats, sheep, oxen and fish.[268] Porphyry
couples the Phoenicians and Jews as people who eat no swine's
flesh.[269] Obviously then in ancient days many knew the Jews were
not the only people to abstain from pork, and yet they formed the
special butt of ridicule. This custom is sometimes associated with
events in Jewish history. Tacitus says the Jews abstain from pork
in recollection of a plague, for the scab to which this animal is subject
once afflicted them.[270] Here Tacitus is probably alluding to the
tradition that the exodus from Egypt was connected with a leprosy
epidemic. Plutarch also refers to something similar in his statement
that the Jews apparently abominate pork, because barbarians especially abhor skin diseases like lepra and white scale and believed
that human beings are ravaged by such maladies through contagion.
Now, every pig is covered at the under side by lepra and scaly erup-
tions.[271] This entire discussion is held by Plutarch on the question
whether the Jews abstain from pork because of reverence or aversion
for the pig. Plutarch describes the dirtiness and unattractiveness of
the pig in too much detail to support the first motive.[272]

---

[265] *Ap.* ii. 137, 141.

[266] *Hist.* ii. 47.

[267] Reinach, *op. cit.*, p. 170 : *Hypotyp.* III. 24. 223.

[268] Origen, *Contra Celsum* V. 34, 41; cf. Plutarch, *Moralia* 353f.; Aelian, *De natura animalium* X. 16; Anaxandrides in Athenaeus, *Deipnosophistai* VII. 300a; Seneca is also acquainted with *alienigena sacra*, who agreed that they were supporters of *quorundam animalium abstinentia*, *Ep.* CVIII. 22

[269] Reinach, *op. cit.*, p. 203 : Περὶ ἀποχῆς ἐμψύχων i. 14.

[270] *Hist.* V. 4.

[271] Reinach, *op. cit.*, p. 140 : *Quaest. conviv.* IV. 5. 3.

[272] Reinach, *op. cit.*, pp. 137f. : *Quaest. conviv.* IV. 5, 6; Petronius speaks of the worship of *porcinum numen* by the Jews, Reinach, *op. cit.*, p. 266 : Fragment 37. Likewise Philo who naturally was acquainted with the commandments of the law on this point (*Lev.* 11. 2-8, *Deut.* 14. 3-8), took into account the reasons for this prohibition.

Abstention from eating pork occasioned a great deal of mockery and worse. The Jews must have been vexed beyond measure when Antiochus Epiphanes built altars in Jerusalem on which swine and other unclean animals were sacrificed. The king wanted to force the Jews to eat unclean meat. But many in Israel stood firm and were resolved in their hearts not to eat unclean food. They chose to die rather than to be defiled by food or to profane the holy covenant; and they did die.[273] The aged and pious Eleasar was being forced to open his mouth to eat swine's flesh. But he, welcoming death with honour rather than life with pollution, spitted out the flesh.[274] Josephus likewise mentions this sacrifice of swine on altars built in Jerusalem.[275] The scandalous maltreatment to which the Jewish women were subjected included, Philo says, the compulsory eating of pork. Some gave way in fear of punishment. But the more resolute were delivered to the tormentors to suffer desperate ill-usage.[276] The Jewish writers were not the only ones who chronicled such persecution of the Jews by the enforced eating of pork. Posidonius says that in Jerusalem Antiochus sacrificed before the image of the founder and the open-air altar of the god a great sow, and poured its blood over them. Thus having prepared the flesh, he ordered that their holy books should be sprinkled with the broth of the meat and that the high priest and the rest of the Jews should be compelled to partake of the meat.[277]

It goes without saying that abstention from eating pork had significant consequences in social contact at meals. A reproach frequently uttered by pagan writers is that Jews refuse to sit at the same table as strangers.[278] They do not mention in this context the reason for refusing to sit at one table, but for the Jews it was the fear of κοινοφαγία, eating unclean food, and this included pork.[279]

When directed against the imageless cult, the Sabbath, the circumcision, the abstention from pork, the ridicule and hatred of the non-Jews did, indeed, have as target existing customs of the Jews.

[273] *1 Macc.* 1. 47, 62ff.

[274] *2 Macc.* 6. 18ff.; cf. Hengel, *op. cit.*, p. 534.

[275] *A.* XII. 253, XIII. 243.

[276] *Flacc.* 96.

[277] Reinach, *op. cit.*, p. 58 : Diod. Sic. XXXIV, Fragments 4; cf. above p. 91.

[278] Posidonius : Diod. Sic. XXXIV, Fragments 1; Apoll. Molon : Jos., *Ap.* ii. 258; Philostr., *Vita Apoll.* V. 33; Pomp. Trogus : M. Junianus Justinus XXXVI. 2, Reinach, *op. cit.*, pp. 57, 64, 176, 255; Tacitus, *Hist.* V. 5 : *separati epulis.*

[279] Jos., *A.* XI. 346; cf. Brüne, *op. cit.*, pp. 77ff.; Böhl, *op. cit.*, pp. 488ff.

Although the pagan writers misunderstood and misrepresented them, they nevertheless attacked in their own way what struck them as unusual in the life and society of the Jews. In addition, however, they often resorted to all manner of foolish and libellous contentions which they imagined themselves or copied from predecessors. These contentions are sometimes encountered in one or two writers, sometimes in so many that one must consequently conclude there must have been an established tradition. The first is the case, for example, with the story of the ritual murder. Apion relates that when Antiochus penetrated the temple he found there a Greek who told him of the horrible things the Jews planned to do with him. He was, while travelling about in the province, kidnapped by men of a foreign race and conveyed to the temple; there he was fattened on feasts of the most lavish description. At first he enjoyed them immensely, but then he heard from the attendants what was going on. Annually at a fixed season the Jews kidnapped a Greek foreigner, fattened him up for a year and then conveyed him to a wood, where they slew him, sacrificed his body with their customary ritual, partook of his flesh, and while immolating the Greek, swore an oath of hostility to the Greeks.[280] Tcherikover says: This is Apion's story. It is of special interest as the first of a long series of tales of this kind, whose tragic role in Jewish history is all too well known.[281] Reinach had already said something similar when quoting this story, though in his time he believed the Middle Ages in particular should be mentioned as example of the horrible use of this legend: "Tel est le premier germe de l'accusation du meurtre rituel, qui a fait couler au Moyen Age tant de sang innocent".[282]

This story cannot be said to have been widespread in the ancient world. The only other source where it is mentioned is Damocritus. Suidas says the latter wrote a book about the Jews in which he relates how, every seven years, they capture a foreigner, take him to the temple, chop his flesh into pieces and offer him.[283] In a few words it is the same story as in Apion, with this difference, that the ritual murder occurred annually in Apion and once in seven years in Damo-

---

[280] *Ap.* ii. 89ff.
[281] Tcherikover, *op. cit.*, p. 366.
[282] Reinach, *op. cit.*, p. xvii; cf. Böhl, *op. cit.*, pp. 479f.
[283] Reinach, *op. cit.*, p. 121 : Suidas s.v. Δαμόκριτος

critus. Opinions vary as to who is the originator of this story, particularly since it is not known when Damocritus lived.[284]

It might be considered significant that this story is not repeated by other anti-Semitic writers, such as Juvenal and Tacitus, especially since these two writers are assumed to have read Apion. Is it not strange that it does not appear in times when mutual hatred was inflamed to extremes, as during the revolts under Trajan and Hadrian? The Roman authors were certainly not hesitant about saying such things concerning people they despised. In his fifteenth satire directed especially against the Egyptians, Juvenal relates a horrible tale about an enemy who was torn apart and eaten.[285] Admittedly this is an example of cruel cannibalism and hence is different from the ritual offer described by Apion and Damocritus, but it nevertheless demonstrates that anti-Semitic writers did not hesitate to pass on stories about the atrocious cruelty of their enemies.

In view of the fact that only two writers relate this story, the inevitable question is where did it come from. Did Apion himself build it up around some brief item of news as basis? Do not the melodramatic features in this story, which are so typical of Apion, suggest such an answer?[286] Or does it go back to an anti-Semitic pamphlet of Apollonius Molon?[287] Or is it descended from a long pharaonic tradition that identified the despised alien with Seth, who killed Osiris and chopped him in pieces?[288] All these solutions are hypotheses. The only information supplied by the sources themselves about the origins of this story is to be found in Josephus. He says that Apion's story goes back to Greek writers, who are more concerned to uphold a sacrilegious king than to give a fair and veracious description of the rites and temple of the Jews.[289] Would a justified inference be that there were writers at the court of the Seleucids who had to lend as favourable a colour as possible to the deeds of the kings and make those of the enemies as black as possible?[290] In any case the statement of Josephus argues against the supposition that Apion thought up this story all by himself, and it also proves that such

[284] Cf. Reinach, *op. cit.*, p. 121; Lovsky, *op. cit.*, pp. 57, 63f.

[285] *Sat.* XV. 78ff, 93ff.; cf. Radin, *op. cit.*, pp. 189f.

[286] Radin, *op. cit.*, p. 189.

[287] Reinach, *op. cit.*, p. 121, note 3.

[288] Yoyotte, *op. cit.*, pp. 141f.

[289] *Ap.* ii. 89f., 97.

[290] Heinemann, *op. cit.*, pp. 30f.; cf. Tcherikover, *op. cit.*, pp. 366f.

libel was more widespread than mention by only two writers would suggest.

The charge of sexual excesses occurs only in, and not before Tacitus.[291] He describes the Jews as a nation very prone to lust (*proiectissima ad libidinem gens*). They abstain from intercourse with foreign women; yet among themselves nothing is unlawful, (*inter se nihil inlicitum*). They have a passion for begetting children (*generandi amor*).[292] This reproach recurs nowhere, though several writers mention fornication by both Jewish men and women. Demo, who is mentioned by Meleager of Gadara in a poem, is either a Jewess herself, or has a Jew as lover.[293] Ovid includes synagogues among the places where it is possible to begin very good amorous relationships.[294] These writers take it so completely for granted that such relationships occur in their own circles, that these taunts cannot be intended as a particular charge against a *proiectissima ad libidinem gens*. It is therefore questionable whether Philo is reacting to such an accusation when, in a talk with Potiphar's wife, he has Joseph say : We children of the Hebrews follow laws and customs which are especially our own.[295]

Although the charges of ritual murder and sexual promiscuity have only a narrow basis of tradition, there is another fable that occurs in many writers, and probably for the first time in Manetho : the Jews are said to be originally leprous Egyptians banished from their country.[296] This story, told in great detail by Manetho, recurs in diverse variations in several authors, even though according to Josephus, Manetho said it was just one of the fables and current reports about the Jews (τὰ μυθευόμενα καὶ λεγόμενα περὶ τῶν Ἰουδαίων). Different versions are taken from the works of other

---

[291] Heinemann, *op. cit.*, pp. 36, 41; the same in *Philons griechische und jüdische Bildung*, 1932, p. 276 : "im Sündenregister der Antisemiten taucht der Vorwurf der Unsittlichkeit gegen die Juden erst sehr spät und nur im Zusammenhang mit den unsinnigsten Fabeln auf". He refers then to the notice of Tacitus.

[292] *Hist.* V. 5.

[293] Reinach, *op. cit.*, p. 55 : *Anthol.* V. 160; cf. Juster, *op. cit.*, II, p. 212, see above p. 130.

[294] Reinach, *op. cit.*, p. 248 : *Ars Amatoria* i. 75; cf. above p. 129 and Martial above, p. 133.

[295] *De Josepho* 42; cf. Juster, *op. cit.*, II, p. 211; I. Heinemann, *Philons griechische und jüdische Bildung*, p. 276.

[296] *Ap.* i. 229-253.

writers by Josephus: Chaeremon,[297] Lysimachus,[298] and Apion.[299]

The story about the Jews as banished, leprous Egyptians is to be found in other writers than just those whose statements were preserved by Josephus. In a fragment of the writings of Diodorus Siculus he writes : When in ancient times a pestilence arose in Egypt, the common people ascribed their troubles to the working of a divine agency.[300] Pompeius Trogus states that the Egyptians obeyed the dictates of an oracle when they were plagued with skin infection and leprosy and banished from the country Moses and all the diseased, in order to put an end to the plague.[301] Tacitus writes : Most authors agree that once during a plague in Egypt which caused bodily disfigurement, King Bocchoris approached the oracle of Ammon and asked for a remedy, whereupon he was told to purge his kingdom and to transport this race into other lands, since it was hateful to the gods.[302] Apparently Tacitus knew that this history was recounted by various authors. He probably used, himself, the statements of the Alexandrian writers, particularly Lysimachus and Apion.[303] Do these two go back to Manetho, and was the story originally "a deliberate invention of Manetho himself", for which he used certain biblical data known to him (Ex. 1.12-14; 4.7)?[304] According to Josephus, Manetho's contention was different, namely that the story was one of diverse fables bandied about concerning the Jews. Whatever the case may be, this story was apparently widely known in the ancient world and was eagerly passed on.

Hence many pagan writers vented their annoyance with the strangeness of the Jewish religion not only in general terms, but also in the form of definite, concrete accusations. Fundamentally what really always annoyed them was that "sovereign self-sufficiency" of Judaism, which occupied such a special position in the ancient world, which was the only religion that "remained 'foreign', aloof, in the Roman empire, never quite ready to identify wholly with the society of the empire. Somehow Judaism remained impervious to the acids which

---

[297] *Ap.* i. 289ff.

[298] *Ap.* i. 304ff.

[299] *Ap.* ii. 15ff.; cf. above pp. 127f.

[300] Reinach, *op. cit.*, p. 14 : Diod. Sic. XL. 3. 1.

[301] Reinach, *op. cit.*, pp. 253f. : M. Junianus Justinus XXXVI. 2.

[302] *Hist.* V. 3; cf. Hospers-Jansen, *op. cit.*, pp. 119ff.

[303] Hospers-Jansen, *op. cit.*, p. 122; ed. Loeb of Josephus, Vol. I, p. 285, note d.

[304] Radin, *op. cit.*, p. 100; cf. Baron, *op. cit.*, I, pp. 194f.

ate away at every import to Rome".[305] In this seldom disowned
strangeness, emanating from the way of life and thought prescribed
by the Torah, lies the profoundest cause for the anti-Semitism of
the ancient world.

---

[305] R.L. Wilken in an article entitled : Judaism in Roman and Christian Society,
The Journal of Religion, 47 (1967), pp. 315, 314; cf. Schubert, *op. cit.*, p. 235 : "Die
jüdische Existenz allein schon ohne irgendwelche besondere Kundgebung wurde von
den Grossen der Welt als Nicht-Anerkennung und Herausforderung ihrer Absolutheits-
ansprüche verstanden. Hierin scheint mir der eigentliche Grund des *Antisemitismus*
zu liegen, gleichgültig, welche Sekundärursachen auch immer ihn auslösen und welche
konkreten Begründungen dafür gefunden werden... Der Antisemitismus ist die 'natür-
liche' Reaktion der Weltvölker auf die jüdische Existenz..."; Art. Anti-Semitism in
Encyclopaedia Judaica 3, 1971, p. 88.

CHAPTER FOUR

POLITICS

The way in which the conflicts between the Jews and non-Jews of the ancient world are described often leaves one with the impression that they were mainly of a political nature. Superficially they frequently were, but on closer study the contradistinction between this strange nation and its pagan environment almost always proves to form the background to these conflicts. The life and society of the Jews were possible only by the grace of the tolerance of the ruling authorities, but the Jews could not respond to this tolerance with the same attitude. The worship of the God of Israel and the observance of his laws could only be realised in states where the opportunity for such was given by rulers guided by a tolerance that extended to other worships as well, but the Jews who worshipped and obeyed that God were not prepared to recognise the other forms of cult and life as equal to their own. "Seul le Dieu des Juifs était farouche et insociable—la tolérance qu'on était prêt à lui accorder il ne la rendait pas".[1]

The Jews who remained true to their faith and ethics could not live in ancient society without the benefit of special privileges. Such fidelity inevitably implied going against the rules of that society, both in carrying out certain transactions and neglecting others. Privileges were therefore essential to them, and for this reason they were often hated by their fellow citizens. To say the least they roused jealousy, especially since many pagans must have felt that granting such privileges meant deferring to the incomprehensible obstinacy of a separate population group that itself showed no deference whatsoever to others. Such vexation was probably felt much more intensely by the local authorities and population than by the central government. Situations were always arising in daily intercourse with others in which the privileges granted from above to the Jews must have annoyed many people. Criticism of the policy of tolerance often

---

[1] Juster, *op. cit.*, I, p. 213; cf. Grant, *op. cit.*, p. 60 : "—paradoxically, the Roman authorities issued tolerant dispensations in favour of the intolerant Jewish God".

found expression in the lower echelons of officials and among pagan fellow citizens in a particularly antagonistic attitude towards the Jews. Bitter opposition to the Jews in word and deed was also frequently a sign of latent opposition to the authorities who had granted privileges to that people. But the people dared not attack the Roman authorities directly and openly. In the Hellenistic cities, the local officials and the population therefore often transferred their detestation of a policy that allowed the Jews the commission and omission of acts for which every other citizen was punishable to the recipients of the favours of the central government.

Under the emperors, and even before then, the Jews enjoyed diverse privileges in the Roman Empire almost without interruption. Even though, as Cicero puts it, it was a question of sacred rites at variance with the glory of the empire, the dignity of the Roman name, the customs of the ancestors,[2] the Romans, like so many others, treated them with the magnanimity (*magnanimitas*) and moderation (*mediocritas*) Josephus praised in them and which, according to him, meant their subjects were not required to violate their national laws.[3] If we are to believe Josephus,[4] the right to live according to ancestral laws and customs was, indeed, what was repeatedly granted the Jews by the Roman government. The emperors and their predecessors had confirmed this in different formulations in their decrees. The cities were compelled, if necessary, to observe these regulations. The Jews must be at liberty, and without hindrance, to observe their national customs and sacred rites (τοῖς πατρίοις ἔθεσι καὶ ἱεροῖς χρῆσθαι), to follow their native customs (χρῆσθαι τοῖς πατρίοις ἐθισμοῖς), to live in accordance with their native laws (κατὰ τοὺς πατρίους νόμους), to follow their own customs (χρῆσθαι τοῖς ἰδίοις θεσμοῖς), in accordance with the law of their fathers (κατὰ τὸν πάτριον αὐτῶν νόμον).[5] Very likely the Romans were not the first to grant such privileges to the Jews. Under the Ptolemies and the Seleucids, the Jews also enjoyed a number of privileges, though with interruptions. No political, official documents of those periods have been preserved which describe precisely such privileges, as do

---

[2] Reinach, *op. cit.*, p. 240 : *Pro Flacco* XXVIII. 69.

[3] *Ap.* ii. 73.

[4] Cf. Gutermann, *op. cit.*, pp. 108ff. and the literature mentioned by Smallwood, *op. cit.*, p. 206.

[5] *A.* XIV. 213, 227, 242; XVI. 163; still further variations : Juster, *op. cit.*, I, pp. 252, 338; *CPJ* I, p. 7, note 19.

the documents extant for the period of Roman rule. Perhaps reference
is made to such a document in the story about Ezechias, a chief
priest of the Jews who went to Egypt with Ptolemy I and then tried
to persuade a group of his friends to emigrate there by, inter alia,
reading them a statement given him by the king, apparently, stating
the conditions attached to the settlement and political status of the
Jews.[6]

There is naturally always some doubt how much value as historical
source may be ascribed to such a story. It is not surprising that,
in this case, it has not often been esteemed high : is it likely that
a chief priest of the Jews would voluntarily emigrate to Egypt ?[7]
The same holds good for the documents from the period of the Diadochi, the contents of which accord with the official decrees from
the Roman period preserved in Josephus. Antiochus III the Great
is named as a Seleucid monarch who was very favourably disposed
towards the Jews. Josephus describes in detail the favours which
the king showered on the Jews.[8] In this reference he also gives the
text of three official documents promulgated by Antiochus. Their
authenticity has likewise been frequently challenged, but, in my
opinion, various arguments can be adduced to support the postulation
that they are, on the whole, historically true.[9] If this is assumed,
then the first document, an official missive from Antiochus to Ptolemy,
then governor of Coele-Syria and Phoenicia, is in certain respects
strongly reminiscent of the later decrees of the Roman emperors.
Indeed Bickerman therefore calls it "the Seleucid charter of Jerusalem".[10] According to this document Antiochus granted the Jews
various privileges in regard of exemption from taxes and the provision
of everything needed for worship in the temple. All damages suffered
by Jerusalem during hostilities were to be repaired. The Jews were
to receive a form of government in accordance with the law of their
country (κατὰ τοὺς πατρίους νόμους).[11] Already in this document

---

[6] *Ap.* i. 189 : εἶχεν γὰρ τὴν κατοίκησιν αὐτῶν καὶ τὴν πολιτείαν γεγραμμένην.

[7] Cf. *CPJ* I, p. 7, note 18.

[8] *A.* XII. 129-153.

[9] An excellent summary of the problems connected with these documents by
R. Marcus, Loeb-ed. of Josephus. Vol. VII, pp. 743-766; cf. also Tcherikover, *op. cit.*,
pp. 82-89.

[10] Quoted by Marcus, *op. cit.*, pp. 758, 760.

[11] *A.* XII. 138-144; on the latter expression cf. Tcherikover, *op. cit.*, pp. 83f.; he
translates : "ancestral laws" and queries what these mean exactly; Marcus (Loeb-ed.)
however translates : "in accordance with the laws of their country".

from the Seleucid period, as so frequently later in Roman decrees, mention is made of these privileges being granted as reward for the fidelity of the Jews to Antiochus, a fidelity they demonstrated in practice by assisting the king to expel the Egyptian garrison quartered in the city's citadel.[12] The Jews evidently supported Antiochus in his conflict with Ptolemy Epiphanes in the years between 201 and 198 B.C.

In addition to the special privileges granted by some of the Syrian Diadochi, there were also a number of Egyptians who displayed a kindly disposition towards them. It is said of Ptolemy II that he played an important role in the realisation of the Septuagint, of Ptolemy III that he made offerings in the temple of Jerusalem. According to Josephus, under Roman rule a stream of edicts was issued by the emperors, who often refer to a predecessor, and by high Roman officials, who often called to order the local authorities of the cities in their area. In endless variations is reiterated the privilege permitting the Jews to live according to their laws and customs. All regulations that could hinder them in doing so had to be suspended.[13]

These decrees are usually not limited to generalities, but specify very concretely on which points the Jews must be shown consideration and given complete freedom. They had this freedom by virtue of the fact that Judaism was recognised as *religio licita*, especially since Caesar and Augustus. This term does not derive, however, from Roman legal terminology, but from a writing by Tertullian.[14] Roman jurisdiction spoke of *collegia licita*. For the Jews it was of extreme importance that their synagogues were recognised as *collegia*, for they consequently were entitled to their own organisation and regular congregations. Their religious service was thus guaranteed, for then they were granted the *coire, convenire*, συνέρχεσθαι, συνιέναι..[15] Their right to this was repeatedly confirmed in edicts, even though the synagogues did not comply with all the requirements demanded of *collegia* by Roman law.[16] They also consequently had the right

---

[12] *A*. XII. 138.

[13] *A*. XIV. 194. 199. 213ff., 223, 227, 235, 242, 246, 258, 260f., 263; XVI. 163, 171, 172; XIX. 283ff., 290, etc. The edicts sent out by the central government were promulgated by Caesar (*A*. book XIV), Augustus (*A*. book XVI), Claudius (*A*. book XIX).

[14] *Apologeticum* XXI. 1.

[15] Both Greek expressions occur, for instance in Philo, *Leg.* 156, 311, 313.

[16] Cf. G. La Piana, Foreign Groups in Rome during the First Centuries of the Empire, *Harv. Theol. Rev.*, 20 (1927), pp. 348-351.

to manage their own funds, which was very important with respect to the collection of the temple tax. It was therefore extremely important that, when Caesar dissolved all *collegia* except those established in days long past (*praeter antiquitus constituta*), he also excepted the Jewish synagogues from dissolution.[17] In an edict addressed to Parium it is once again recalled that, although Caesar forbade the congregation of religious bodies in the cities, he expressly made an exception for the Jews.[18] Many inscriptions evidence that in the city of Rome the Jews were also permitted to organise their communities according to the regulations of a *collegium*.[19] Josephus says that, for Augustus, the protection of the synagogues also implied that anyone who steals the sacred books or the sacred money of the Jews from the synagogues or from an ark (of the Law) shall be regarded sacrilegious, and shall be punished in accordance with the law on *sacrilegium*.[20]

Another important result of the constitutional recognition of the Jewish communities was that the Jews were able to administer justice within their own group, according to their own standards of law, and were not bound by a law that was incompatible with their own. In Alexandria they had their own πολίτευμα and their own disposition of the competencies of the various officials.[21] Already in a letter from Lucius Antonius, proquaestor and propraetor in the province of Asia in 50-49 B.C., to the authorities of the city of Sardes is reference made to a separate Jewish organisation in accordance with their native law and to a place of their own, which they are said to have had in that city from the earliest times, a place in which they decide their affairs and controversies with one another.[22]

The Jews who lived in obedience to their law could not participate in the imperial cult, this "cauchemar des Juifs",[23] at least not in the form in which it was usually practised. Now there were emperors who had no desire to enforce the worship of their own person, who

---

[17] Suet., *Gaius Julius Caesar*, XLII. 3; cf. Suet., *Augustus* XXXII. 1 : *collegia praeter antiqua et legitima dissolvit*; cf. Schürer, *op. cit.* III, p. 104; Smallwood, *op. cit.*, p. 236; H. Zucker, *Studien zur jüdischen Selbstverwaltung im Altertum*, 1936, pp. 58ff.; M.S. Ginsburg, *Rome et la Judée*, 1928, pp. 85ff.

[18] *A.* XIV. 215; cf. Guterman, *op. cit.*, pp. 131f.

[19] *CIJ* I, p. lxx, cf. LXXXII ff.; according to Dio Cassius Claudius forbade the Jews to congregate, Reinach, *op. cit.*, p. 188 : *Hist. Rom.* LX. 6.

[20] *A.* XVI. 164.

[21] Cf. Schürer, *op. cit.* III, pp. 76ff.

[22] *A.* XIV. 235.

[23] Juster, *op. cit.* I, p. 339.

were personally even very reserved in their judgment of it. Philo makes special mention of this in regard to Augustus,[24] and Suetonius says something similar of this same emperor.[25] Claudius gives his own opinion on the matter in a letter to the Alexandrians, in which he says that he declines the establishment of a high-priest and temples of himself, not wishing to be offensive to his contemporaries and in the belief that temples and the like have been set apart in all ages for the gods alone.[26] However, once an emperor expressly enjoined all his subjects to honour his person as god, the Jews were placed in a precarious position. The enormous strain placed upon them is evidenced by Philo's description of the conflict with Caligula on this point, when he and a deputation met this emperor in Rome. As soon as they saw him, they bowed low to the ground with the greatest reverence and punctiliousness and greeted him with the title "Augustus Imperator". But the emperor greeted them with a sneering grin and said : "So you are the god-haters, the people who do not believe I am a god—I, who am acknowledged as a god among all other nations by this time but am denied that title by you"? When Philo pointed out that the Jews already brought an offering three times, on his accession, on his recovery from a serious illness and in anticipation of his victory in Germany, Gaius replied : "Granted that this is true and you have offered sacrifices. But it was to another god, even if it was on my behalf. What is the good of that"? On hearing these words, a violent trembling seized the Jews, and Philo thought it a token of God's extraordinary compassion that He turned Gaius' heart to mercy.[27]

This statement shows how fully cognisant the Jews were of the fact that strict performance of the emperor cult constituted a continuing danger to them. This danger was extremely acute under Caligula who, to the consternation of the Jews, planned the erection of a

---

[24] See above p. 123 : *Leg.* 154.

[25] See above pp. 123f. : *Aug.* LII; cf. Tiberius' words in a speech in the Senate : *mortalem esse et hominum officia fungi, satisque habere si locum principem impleam...* Tacitus, *Ann.* IV. 38.

[26] *CPJ* II, p. 40, ll. 48-50; cf. A. Momigliano, *Claudius, The Emperor and his Achievement*, 1934, pp. 28f., 95[23]; V.M. Scramuzza, *The Emperor Claudius*, 1940, pp. 67ff., 246[7].

[27] *Leg.* 352-357, 366f.; cf. P.J. Sijpesteijn, The Legationes ad Gaium, *The Journal of Jewish Studies*, 15 (1964), pp. 87-96; M. Borg, A New Context for Romans XIII, *N.T.S.* Jan. 1973, pp. 210f.; see above p. 137.

statue in his honour in the temple of Jerusalem. If the privileges granted to the Jews in this respect were ignored, there was nothing left to them but a bitter, life and death struggle. The purport of those privileges, which were very strictly observed before Caligula's time, was probably accurately described by Josephus in his reaction to Apion's charge that the Jews erect no statues of emperors : This is an expression of the magnanimity and the moderation of the government of the Romans, in "being content to accept such honours as the religious and legal obligations of the donors permit them to pay".[28] The Jews did, indeed, pay homage to the emperor, but in such a form that there was no lapse from the worship of the one and only God of Israel. During the meeting between Caligula and the Jewish deputation, the emperor alluded to one of those special forms permitted the Jews : "the Jews sacrificed on behalf of the emperor, but to a different god, that is to say the offers were not made to the emperor as god, but to the God of Israel, though this could be accounted a prayer for the wellbeing of the emperor. Hence prayers and offers on behalf of governments, even foreign governments, had never been unusual".[29] In that sense Josephus could say that, twice daily, the Jews bring offers on behalf of Caesar and the Roman people, according to him at the expense of the whole Jewish community, according to Philo in any case at his own expense originally.[30]

Ordinarily the Jews were anxiously spared as regards the titles of the emperor cult and of the images testifying to that cult. As to the former, Claudius at once repaired what Caligula in his great folly and madness had misdone when he humiliated the Jews because they refused to transgress the religion of their fathers by addressing him as a god.[31] As to the latter, the Roman authorities in Palestine, for example, took care on the whole that the Jews were even spared the sight of images of the emperors.[32]

Hence it cannot be said that not a single obligation to worship the emperor was imposed on the Jews, but it can be said that the privileges were so comprehensive that they imposed no ritual acts or titles upon the Jews that were incompatible with obedience to their laws. In this respect they were thus granted a special position,

---

[28] *Ap.* ii. 73; see above p. 146.

[29] Cf. for example *Ezra* 6. 10; *Jer.* 29. 7, *1 Macc.* 7. 33, *Avot* 3.2.

[30] *Ap.* ii. 77; *B.* ii. 197; *Leg.* 157, 317.

[31] *A.* XIX. 284f.

[32] Cf. Juster, *op. cit.*, I, pp. 348ff.

one which must have been obvious and, on many occasions, very
annoying to a great number of people. In his description of the
aforesaid incident between Caligula and the Jewish deputation,
Philo was no doubt largely drawing from memory when he stated
that the pagan Alexandrian deputation gave signs of exuberant
hilarity on hearing the emperor's remark about the god-hating Jews,
called him by the titles of all the gods, threw suspicion on the civic
loyalty of the Jews and said to the emperor : "My lord, you will hate
these Jews here, and the rest of their compatriots too, even more
when you learn of their ill-will and disloyalty towards you. When
everyone else was offering sacrifices of thanksgiving for your recovery
these people alone could not bring themselves to sacrifice".[33] Such
insinuations were probably often attributed to the special position
of the Jews regarding the emperor worship. Seen from their angle,
it was not strange that the inhabitants of the Ionian Greek cities
claimed that, if the Jews were to be their fellows, they should worship
the Ionians' gods. If they did not wish to participate in the cult
of their fellow-citizens, they should be deprived of citizenship.[34] It
could also be put this way : a man who refused to worship the emperor
as god could never be a good citizen of the empire. Obviously this
was fertile ground for the seed of anti-Semitism.

The Roman authorities always ensured that the Jews were able to
live according to their law on Sabbath. Josephus several times states
that the opportunity to observe this day was explicitly granted in
the decrees.[35] When the Roman proconsul heard that the local authorities prevented this nation from observing the Sabbath, he reminded
them that the Jews were permitted to follow their customs and that
consequently they must not be prevented from celebrating the
Sabbath.[36] The same applied to their customary festivals and religious
gatherings.[37]

To enable the Jews to observe the commandments concerning the
Sabbath, special regulations had to be introduced for them to deal
with a number of concrete matters. It was forbidden, for example,
to appear in court on the Sabbath or feast days.[38] The Jews of Ionia

---

[33] *Leg.* 354, 355.

[34] *A.* XII. 125f.

[35] *A.* XIV. 242, 263.

[36] *A.* XIV. 245f.

[37] *A.* XIV. 257.

[38] Cf. *1 Macc.* 10. 34f.; Philo, *Migr. Abr.* 91; Mishnah, *Yom Tov* 5. 2, *Sanh.* 4. 1 end.

complained that the local authorities sometimes forced them to do so.[39] When Augustus issued his decree about the privileges of the Jews, it included the stipulation that on the Sabbath or the day of preparation for it they did not have to appear before the court.[40] The local authorities of Ephesus were reminded that no one had the right to enforce the Jews to do so.[41] In Dolabella's letter to the same city, the author states that Hyrcanus, the high priest and ethnarch of the Jews, has explained to him that his co-religionists cannot undertake military service because they may not bear arms or march on the days of the Sabbath.[42]

Philo, like Josephus, discusses the privileges regarding the Sabbath. If the monthly distribution of money or food in Rome fell on a Sabbath, Augustus instructed the distributors to reserve the Jews' share of the universal largesse until the next day.[43] This instance shows how the Romans had to concern themselves with the details of Judaism in order that the Jews might live according to their ancestral laws. The same concern is evidenced by the regulation that those Jews who were unwilling to use foreign oil should receive a fixed sum of money from the gymnasiarchs to pay for their own kind of oil; and when the people of Antioch proposed to revoke this privilege, Mucianus, who was then governor of Syria, maintained it.[44] All this illustrates how the central government had to risk conflicts with the local authorities on points of such detailed regulations if it wished to maintain its general policy regarding the Jewish groups.

Mention is made above of the letter of Dolabella to the city of Ephesus in which it is said, inter alia, that the Jews cannot perform any military service, because this was forbidden by their Sabbath rules. Did this mean that the Jews objected in general to military service and that on this point also they requested privileges that would enable them to live in accordance with their customs? And did they receive such privileges from the central government? Opinions vary considerably as to the answer to these questions, though it must be admitted that unanimity on fundamental points

---

[39] *A*. XVI. 27, 45.

[40] *A*. XVI. 163.

[41] *A*. XVI. 168.

[42] *A*. XIV. 226.

[43] *Leg*. 158; cf. *CPJ* I, p. LXXI.

[44] *A*. XII, 120; cf. *V*. 74; *B*. ii. 591; *Avoda Zarah* 2. 6; Loeb-ed. Josephus, Vol. VII, pp. 61, 737ff.

is growing. One can say, for example, that the contention that the Jews never performed military service under foreign rulers has now been abandoned. Certain scholars formerly drew this conclusion from the impossibility of combining military service under foreign rulers with obedience to the law, especially regarding the Sabbath rest and the purity of food. Hence they attached a much broader significance to statements about the exemption of Jews from military service and concluded Jews never served in foreign armies.[45] It has become increasingly clear that such conclusions are erroneous. The statement in the letter of Aristeas that Ptolemy had armed 30,000 of the 100,000 Jews brought from Judaea to Egypt as prisoners of war and had stationed them as garrisons in fortifications has long been common knowledge, but the historicity of this information has often been contested.[46] Nowadays, though the accuracy of the numbers may be doubted, it is not considered impossible that Ptolemy used garrisons of soldiers from different lands, including Jewish ones. Already in Herodotus' work mention is made of the building of military posts along the frontiers by the pharaohs.[47] The Aramaic papyri of Elephantine leave no doubt about Jewish soldiers occupying some of these posts during the period of Persian rule in Egypt.

The papyri have now established irrevocably that, in the period of the Ptolemies, the Jews in Egypt served in various branches of the armed forces and that they were not the only foreigners in the Ptolemaic armies. Soldiers from various countries were to be found in both the infantry and the cavalry, in the regular units and in the reserves. The Ptolemies preferred to call on these foreign mercenaries rather than on the natives, whom experience had caused them to distrust. The papyri provide many instances of Jews as soldiers, officers and sometimes even military of higher rank.[48] Hence it definitely can no longer be contended that the Jews never performed military service in foreign armies.

The situation under Roman rule was different, as can be deduced from a comparison between papyri from that period and the period of the Ptolemies. Information about Jewish soldiers is plentiful for the latter, but scarce for the former period. There is nothing to

---

[45] Cf. for example H. Willrich, *Juden und Griechen vor der Makkabäischen Erhebung*, 1895, p. 28; Schürer, *op. cit.* I, pp. 459f., II, p. 560, III, p. 115.

[46] *Letter of Aristeas* 13.

[47] *Hist.* ii. 30, 112, 154.

[48] Cf. Tcherikover, *op. cit.*, pp. 334f.; *CPJ* I, pp. 11-15, 147-178.

indicate that the Romans forbade the Jews service in their armies. Statements about Jewish soldiers in certain provinces do exist, but the papyri from Egypt say almost nothing about Jews in military service. Jews were concerned with the charge of the river(*fluminis custodia*), but it is not certain whether they were soldiers or police officials.[49] It is possible that one piece of information about a Jewish centurion in the Roman period has been preserved. A potsherd from Edfu dated 116 A.D. mentions that Aninios has to pay the Jewish tax for his slave. Was the master also a Jew? Probably he was, since non-Jewish masters would have preferred not to buy Jewish slaves, for whom a special tax had to be paid, but this is not certain.[50]

Josephus mentions that the Roman authorities exempted Jews from military service, but this was in certain regions and certain times. He cites an edict of Lucius Lentulus dated 49 B.C. The latter recruited troops in Asia, but released Jews who were Roman citizens from military service. This edict was confirmed by Dolabella in 43 B.C.[51] The reason for the exemption of Jews from Asia Minor is repeatedly given: they must be allowed to live according to their ancestral customs. In Dolabella's edict a more detailed description is given of the complications involved in their military service: they may not bear arms or march on the days of the Sabbath; nor can they obtain the native foods to which they are accustomed.[52] Josephus also mentions a decree of Caesar dealing with the raising of military troops for the Romans in Palestine. In the territories of the Jews (ἐν τοῖς ὅροις τῶν Ἰουδαίων) they may not be recruited.[53] Opinions vary considerably about this edict, especially about its interpretation and scope. Juster contests the opinion of Schürer and others who draw far-reaching conclusions from this decree as to the exemption of Jews from military service in general, in any case in Palestine, and who take it as an established fact that this regulation promulgated by Caesar also applied to the imperial age.[54] Juster rightly points out that there is no proof of this at all, whilst Josephus and Philo

---

[49] Juster, *op. cit.* II, pp. 273f. considers the first to be correct, Tcherikover, *CPJ* I, pp. 52f. the second; cf. above p. 85.

[50] *CPJ* II, pp. 135f., nr. 229: The word used here is "possibly"; *CPJ* I, p. 52 takes it to be certain that there is mention of a Jewish *centurio* in this papyrus.

[51] *A.* XIV. 228, 232, 234, 237, 240.

[52] *A.* XIV. 226.

[53] *A.* XIV. 204.

[54] Cf. Schürer, *op. cit.* I, pp. 459f.

sometimes say with regard to other points that Augustus confirmed the privileges of his predecessors. What Josephus does say is that the Ionian Jews complained in 14 B.C. that they were being forced by the Greek authorities to participate in military service and civic duties.[55] Though this statement is not very specific, it does assume that these Jews considered the possibility of exemption a matter of course. In reply to Juster's use of the statement that various writers say 4000 Jews were sent as soldiers to Sardinia as proof that the emperors did not exempt the Jews from that service, it must be noted that here it was a matter of a special punitive expedition of Tiberius, and that it says nothing about the emperor's attitude to the military service of the Jews in general.[56] Moreover, I believe Juster weakens the significance of Caesar's edict in arguing that it only deals with the question as to who had the competency to recruit auxiliary troops, the Roman authorities or the Jewish monarch. He holds that, in this decree, Caesar decided that the former could not do so directly, but that the right to recruit was reserved to the highest Jewish authority in Judaea.[57] There is nothing to indicate this in the edict.

Our conclusion must be that the papyri contain few unambiguous data concerning the service of Jews in Roman armies and that, if Josephus is to be believed, there probably once existed official documents in which the Jews were granted, as privilege, exemption from military service. It would be going too far, however, to conclude from this that "die Römer sich sogar genötigt sahen, die Juden ganz vom Kriegsdienst zu befreien",[58] or that "die Römer verzichteten darauf, die Juden überhaupt zum Waffendienst heranzuziehen".[59] The data available admit of no other conclusion than that, in certain regions of the Roman empire, this privilege was granted the Jews, in certain periods and circumstances.[60]

---

[55] *A*. XVI. 28.

[56] Jos., *A*. XVIII. 84; Tac., *Ann.* ii. 85; Suet., *Tib.* XXXVI; Juster, *op. cit.* II, p. 276; Jos. Loeb-ed., Vol. IX, pp. 60f.

[57] Juster, *op. cit.* II, pp. 272f.

[58] Schürer, *op. cit.* II, p. 560.

[59] Ed. Lohse, *op. cit.*, p. 9.

[60] Cf. Lazare, *op. cit.*, p. 32; L. Fuchs, *op. cit.*, pp. 3ff., 7f., 11f., 50f.; Hospers-Jansen, *op. cit.*, p. 43; W.C. van Unnik in *Het oudste Christendom en de antieke cultuur* I, 1951, p. 552; Heinemann, *op. cit.*, p. 13; Ginsburg, *op. cit.*, pp. 94ff.; Hopfner, *op. cit.*, pp. 27f.

The privileges concerning the temple tax were of great importance
to the Jews. Every Jew over the age of 20 had to contribute annually
half a shekel, two drachmas or two *denarii* for the temple worship.[61]
Considering every Jew in the Diaspora also paid this tax, it is understandable that the sum collected was enormous. It is also understandable, then, that this incited the avarice of all sorts of people.
Often they were just ordinary thieves, but frequently, too, it must
have been a question of "vols politiques... faits en haine des Juifs".[62]
Both Philo and Josephus frequently state that the transportation
of all this money to Jerusalem took place under the escort of heavy-
armed guards.

Various privileges were needed for the collection and transportation
of this sacred money (ἱερὰ χρήματα), which included other voluntary
contributions in addition to the temple tax. The Jewish communities
had to have special permission to export that 'sacred money', and
they had to be assured of governmental protection against attempts
on this money made by local authorities or thieves. The great weight
attached by the Jews to the regulations concerning the temple tax
is evidenced by the fact that Philo and Josephus repeatedly refer
to this matter and make frequent mention of the privileges concerning
it granted the Jews by the Roman government.[63] Since the Jewish
communities had the status of *collegia*, they had control over their
own funds and could collect local or regional contributions, which
were then sent to Jerusalem once a year. Augustus gave the Jews
explicit permission to export this sacred money : that money is
inviolable and may be sent up to Jerusalem and delivered to the
treasurers in Jerusalem.[64] According to Josephus, Augustus refers
to the time of Caesar and of the high priest Hyrcanus.[65] From this
one could conclude that the privilege had not just been recently

---

[61] *Ex.* 30. 11-15; 38. 25f.; according to *Nehem.* 10:32f. the contribution amounted
to one-third of a shekel, cf. Schürer, *op. cit.* II, pp. 314f. According to *Shekalim* 1. 3
proselytes and liberated slaves also paid the tax, but not the women and the slaves.
From the papyri of Elephantine, however, it appears that in practice the women also
paid; cf. *Mt.* 17. 24; *A.* XVIII. 312; *B.* VII. 218; Philo, *Div. haer.* 186; *Spec. leg.* i. 77.

[62] Juster, *op. cit.* I, p. 383, note 2; cf. Neusner, *op. cit.*, pp. 41ff.

[63] Philo, *Leg.* 156, 216, 291, 311, 312, 315; see also above note 61; Jos., *A.* XVI.
28, 45, 160, 163, 166, 168, 169f., 171, 172; *A.* XIV. 112 on the 800 talents of the Jews,
mentioned by Strabo, cf. Juster, *op. cit.* I, p. 379, note 1; Jos., Loeb-ed., Vol. VII,
pp. 506f., note a.

[64] *A.* XVI. 163.

[65] *A.* XIV. 162.

granted by Augustus, but previously by Caesar. Norbanus Flaccus passed on Augustus' ruling to the cities of Asia : the Jews, however numerous they may be, who have been wont, according to their ancient custom, to bring sacred monies to send up to Jerusalem, may do so without interference.[66]

Severe regulations against the theft of the sacred money of the Jews were announced in certain documents. M. Agrippa, for example, says in a decree addressed to the administration of the city of Ephesus : "If any men steal the sacred money of the Jews and take refuge in places of asylum, it is my will that they be dragged away from them and turned over to the Jews under the same law by which temple robbers are dragged away from asylums".[67] Such a regulation was indeed of far-reaching significance, for it meant that the theft of the temple money fell under the law on *sacrilegium*, that the criminal could nowhere find asylum and that he was handed over to the Jews for punishment. In his decree to the Jews of Asia, Augustus lays down similar laws, though the theft was to be accounted *sacrilegium* if committed in a synagogue and the thief was to be punished by the Roman authorities, so that his property should be confiscated to the public treasury of the Romans.[68] In this form, too, such a regulation went far to meet the request of the Jews that the sacred money be safeguarded.

These privileges probably held good up to the war of 70 A.D. During the siege of Jerusalem, Titus reminded the Jews that the Romans never impeded their extraction of tribute for God and collection of offerings, that the Jews therefore grew richer at the expense of the Romans and that they now used that money to prepare for attack.[69] A radical end was put to the lenience of the Romans after 70 A.D. Henceforth the Jews had to collect the amount of the temple tax for the cult of Jupiter Capitolinus. That was, indeed, "a cynical insult unprecedented in Jewish history".[70]

Information about this privilege is also available from non-Jewish sources. Cicero's defence of L. Valerius Flaccus, propraetor of Asia, reveals various things about the Jewish gold, *aurum Judaicum*.

---

[66] *A.* XVI. 166ff.

[67] *A.* XVI. 168.

[68] *A.* XVI. 164; cf. above pp. 148f.

[69] *B.* VI. 335.

[70] *CPJ* I, p. 82; cf. Simon, *op. cit.*, p. 126 : "une clause particulièrement vexatoire pour l'orgueil et la ferveur des Juifs".

Cicero mentions incidentally that, every year, this gold was exported from Italy and all the provinces to Jerusalem and that Flaccus had prohibited by edict the export of this gold from his province. True, Cicero does refer to a decision of the senate in 63 B.C., during his consulate, by which the gold export was forbidden, but the way he emphasises quite a different subject, namely that Flaccus did not steal the money but deposited it in his treasury, proves he knew he could achieve nothing with the former argument. Flaccus is not accused of theft, however, but of violating the special privilege of the Jews, and apparently Cicero cannot dispute this at all.[71] Flaccus is the only high Roman official who is known to have attempted to ignore this Jewish privilege, but there were probably more officials who found it difficult to favour the Jews and who let it be known. No doubt they could count on the approbation of many pagan subjects who were annoyed by this privilege and who constantly experienced that opposition to it meant being placed in the wrong by the central government, just like Flaccus.

Thus the Jews enjoyed many privileges granted by the Roman government, and there were probably all sorts of reasons for granting them to the Jews. But a special philo-Semitism must not be sought among the Romans. Their "magnanimity and moderation"[72] were no doubt due to other factors. Their far-reaching tolerance to the customs, traditions and religions emanated from a realistic policy aimed at maintaining the unity of the empire and peaceful co-existence. Such a tolerance was extraordinarily compatible with "the comprehensive piety of paganism",[73] which was widespread in the ancient world. Of course this tolerance had its limits. It must not cause trouble for the Roman government, nor be contrary to the fundamental laws of the empire.[74] If this rule were kept, the Romans were prepared to grant freedom to a certain degree. That also applied, for example, to the temple worship in Jerusalem. What Philo praised in Augustus was that he showed reverence for the Jewish traditions. He and almost all his family enriched the Temple with expensive dedications. He gave orders for regular sacrifices of holocausts to be made daily

---

[71] Reinach, *op. cit.*, pp. 237ff.: *Pro Flacco* XXVIII. 66ff.; Schürer, *op. cit* III, p. 112; Juster, *op. cit.* I, pp. 379ff.; Guterman, *op. cit.*, p. 117; Smallwood, *op. cit.*, p. 238; see above pp. 14f., 50f.

[72] Jos., *Ap.* ii. 73, see above pp. 146[3], 151[28].

[73] Smallwood, *op. cit.*, p. 240.

[74] *A.* XVI. 60; M. Avi-Yonah, *op. cit.*, pp. 43ff.

in perpetuity at his own expense, as an offering to the Most High
God.[75] Julia Augusta enriched the Temple with gold bowls. M. Vespa-
sianus Agrippa visited the Temple court every day during his stay
in Jerusalem. He adorned the Temple with all such dedications as
were permissible.[76] Josephus similarly mentions repeatedly offers and
other donations by Roman officials and also by pagans in general.[77]

This attitude of benevolent tolerance on the part of the Romans
was sometimes facilitated by a reciprocal attitude on the part of
the Jews to demonstrate clearly in return their goodwill towards
the Roman rulers. Here again Philo can be cited as witness. He
mentions all sorts of homages paid to the emperors in the synagogues
ravaged by the Alexandrian populace : gilded shields and crowns,
monuments, and inscriptions.[78] Elsewhere Philo explains that, in this
way, the Jews showed their veneration for the Augustan house in
the synagogues, and he warns : "if we have these destroyed, no place,
no method is left to us for paying this homage".[79] Archeology has
now confirmed these statements of Philo. Synagogues, or parts of
them, appear to have sometimes been dedicated to a benefactor.[80]
A few inscriptions honouring certain benefactors have been discovered.[81] Philo plainly hints that such goodwill was certainly not
demonstrated in Palestine when he describes the storm of indignation
roused among the Jews by the setting up of guilded shields in Herod's
palace in the Holy City.[82] With respect to this subject, the attitude
of the Jews in the Diaspora probably differed from that of the
Palestinian Jews. Such an incident in Jerusalem was a typical har-
binger of situations in which a radical end was put to both parties'
attitude of benevolent tolerance. Much depended on the answer to
the questions as to what the Jews thought permissible within the
limits of observance to the law and customs and what the Romans
considered a threat to the interests, the safety and the peace of their
empire.

---

[75] *Leg.* 157; see above p. 151.

[76] *Leg.* 319, 294-297.

[77] *B. V.* 562, 563; *A.* XIV. 488; *B.* . 357; ii. 412, 413.

[78] *Leg.* 133.

[79] *Flacc.* 48, 49.

[80] *CIJ* II, nrs. 1443, 1444 : Athribis; nr. 1441 : Xenephyris; nr. 1442 : Nitriae;
nr. 1440 : Shedia; nr. 1432 : Alexandria.

[81] Cf. Smallwood, *op. cit.*, p. 221.

[82] *Leg.* 299-305.

In addition to this tolerance, another factor was undoubtedly the desire to continue the policy of predecessors and not to cause unrest by suddenly and violently disrupting long-standing customs. Juster calls the Romans "conservateurs par nature et par politique".[83] It is difficult to judge whether they were so by nature, but that they were in their politics can be deduced from various data. Reference is frequently made in official decrees to what predecessors had resolved. Hence there is almost always a certain continuity in the prolongation of Jewish privileges, which was sometimes interrupted by certain emperors, but which was at once resumed on their death by their successors. This applies not only to the continuity from one Roman emperor to another, but also to the prolongation by the Romans of privileges granted the Jews by governments that ruled prior to the Roman period. When, as we have seen above, the Romans demonstrated their goodwill towards the Jews by rich donations to the temple in Jerusalem they were thereby continuing a tradition that was formerly upheld in the time of the Ptolemies and Seleucids.[84] When Philo says that, in Alexandria, Augustus confirmed the "laws" of the Jews ($\beta\epsilon\beta\alpha\iota o\hat{v}v$), this probably means that the emperor confirmed, in the same words as those of the Ptolemies, the national and religious privileges possessed by the Jews as Alexandrian *politeuma*.[85] It is even possible that the decrees of the Ptolemies and Seleucids containing favourable regulations for the Jews were themselves a continuation of an older tradition, for instance of the Persians.[86] The Romans took over existing relationships, were not passionate reformers, gladly confirmed existing legal relationships. They interfered only when economical or political relationships were prejudiced. If, for example, they considered it essential to the safety of their empire to rearrange their armies as regards the auxiliary troops of non-Romans, they never hesitated to introduce such changes.

In the third place, by granting privileges the Romans showed their gratitude for support, often military support, received from the Jews. When in 55 B.C. Gabinius restored the exiled Ptolemy Auletes to the throne, he was assisted by the Jews.[87] When Caesar

---

[83] Juster, *op. cit.* I, p. 214; cf. Grant, *op. cit.*, p. 59 : "—administrative conservatism—".

[84] *Letter of Aristeas* 40-42; *2 Macc.* 3. 2; 5. 16; *A.* XIII. 78; *Ap.* ii. 48.

[85] *Flacc.* 50.

[86] Cf. Jos., Loeb-ed., Vol. VII, pp. 746f.

[87] *A.* XIV. 99; *B.* i. 175.

was besieged in Alexandria, the Jews came to his assistance in
48-47 B.C.[88] Nicolas of Damascus alludes to this in his defence of
M. Agrippa,[89] and Augustus gratefully mentions the goodwill shown
by the Jews to the Romans in Caesar's time.[90] It cannot be said
for sure whether the Jews also lent military support to Augustus
in his struggle against Antony and Cleopatra. Josephus mentions
senatorial resolutions and letters of Caesar Augustus which contain
the expression "our services" (nostra merita), a term which is, indeed,
too vague to warrant the conclusion that military support is referred
to here, but one to which it is difficult to ascribe any concrete contents
if it did not encompass such military support.[91] Repeated mention
is made of alliances between the Jews and the Romans.[92] Caesar
calls the Jews "our friends and allies",[93] and often reference is made
to their goodwill and friendship, which were worth the fitting reward
of a grant of diverse privileges.[94]

All these statements about the good relationship between Romans
and Jews derive from Josephus and are therefore suspect of being a
little tendentious. With regard to the relationship between Caesar
and the Jews, they are, however, indirectly confirmed by the statement
of Suetonius that, on the death of Caesar, the public grief was shared
by a throng of foreigners who went about lamenting each after the
fashion of his country, above all the Jews, who even flocked to the
place where Caesar was cremated for several nights.[95] The obvious
assumption is that this exceptional display of mourning by the Jews
was partly inspired by their gratitude for the many favours Caesar
had granted them in different parts of his empire.

In the fourth place, fear of unrest among the Jews must certainly
have influenced the granting of privileges by the Romans. From
literary, and increasingly from archeological sources, it is known
that Jews lived in practically every part of the Roman empire and
in large numbers in certain regions.[96] In Egypt, for example, Philo

---

[88] A. XIV. 127-136, 193; B. i. 187-192; Ap. ii. 61.

[89] A. XVI. 52.

[90] A. XVI. 162.

[91] Ap. ii. 61; cf. Smallwood, op. cit., p. 11; CPJ I, p. 55[19].

[92] Juster, op. cit. I, pp. 215ff.; already in the time of the Maccabees, e.g. 1 Macc.
8. 17ff., 23ff.; A. XIII. 259ff., XIV. 205.

[93] A. XIV. 214, 216.

[94] Cf. for example A. XVI. 54, 60.

[95] G.J. Caesar LXXXIV. 5.

[96] Juster, op. cit. I, pp. 179ff.; J.N. Sevenster, op. cit., pp. 77ff.

reckoned there were no less than one million Jews, which probably
was equal to one-eight or one-ninth of the total population.[97] During
the imperial age in Rome they also formed a large group, and above
(p. 92) we have already seen from Cicero's defence of Flaccus that
even in his time the Jews there formed a coherent group which could
exert a certain amount of pressure if it chose.

In the course of time the Romans had learnt that the Jews were
wont to react violently if they were hampered in the observance
of their laws and customs. They also knew that, if the Jews did rebel,
they fought fanatically and that large-scale military operations and
a lenghty and bloody war were needed to restore peace and order.[98]
Sometimes the Romans felt that the violent crushing of Jewish
opposition was inevitable if the peace of the empire was to be maintained, but often they chose the alternative of peaceful agreements
with the Jews, in which the Romans went far to accommodate their
wishes. Consequently the Jews sometimes openly or covertly used
the threat of violent opposition to force accedence to certain of their
requests. Philo remarks that the nation of Jews is ready for agreement
and friendship with all like-minded nations whose intentions are
peaceful, yet it is not of the contemptible kind which surrenders
through cowardice to wrongful aggression.[99] When Caligula threatened
to desecrate the temple in Jerusalem, the legate of Syria, Petronius,
was dismayed that the emperor did not take the threat of revolt
seriously enough. Heaven forbid that the Jews everywhere should
unanimously come to the defence. That would produce an impossible
military situation. Consequently the legate was in no hurry to put
the imperial commands into execution.[100] According to Josephus,
this same legate says in a letter reprimanding the inhabitants of
Dora for erecting a statue for the emperor in a synagogue that he
and king Agrippa have no greater interest than that the Jews should
not seize any occasion, under the pretext of self-defence, to gather
in one place and proceed to desperate measures.[101] When, on the

---

[97] *Flacc.* 43; cf. Juster, *op. cit.* I, p. 209; Leipoldt, *op. cit.*, p. 32; S.G.F. Brandon,
The Fall of Jerusalem and the Christian Church, 1957, p. 221; Tcherikover doubts the
accuracy of Philo's figures, since his aim was evidently "to impress his readers by
large numbers", *CPJ* I, pp. 4, 81.
[98] On the revolts of the Jews: Juster, *op. cit.* II, pp. 182ff.
[99] *Spec. leg.* IV. 224; cf. Jos., *A.* XIII. 354.
[100] *Leg.* 208, 215.
[101] *A.* XIX. 309.

death of Caligula, Claudius puts a radical end to his predecessor's plan, he says at the close of an edict to Alexandria and Syria on behalf of the Jews that both parties should take the greatest precautions to prevent any disturbance arising after the posting of his edict.[102] Similarly in a letter to the Alexandrians known to us from the papyri, both the Alexandrians and the Jews are admonished to remain quiet now, after the serious disturbances.[103] All this shows that the Romans often looked on the Jews as a troublesome people who repeatedly threatened to disturb the peace in the empire. Josephus does not conceal that the Jews were often labelled "seditious and mostly bent on revolution", "factious and always at war", and that the Roman emperor sometimes believed he had grounds for "being suspicious of the interminable tendency of the Jews to revolution". And Tacitus says that sometimes the fact that the Jews alone had failed to surrender further increased the resentment at their behaviour.[104] Probably the Romans often hesitated between taking sharp measures and agreeing to the desires of the Jews. The granting of privileges need not necessarily have taken place under the deliberate and actual pressure of the Jews, though it could have been encouraged by the thought of the possible reactions of that people should they be denied such privileges.

Regardless of the motives behind the granting of the privileges, it need hardly be said that they were bound to raise anti-Semitic feelings in many people. Indeed, these privileges often caused difficulties between the central and the local or regional authorities. The opposition of the latter on this point often revealed a large degree of vexation and bitterness. The reason why the decrees of the Roman government have been preserved for us is usually that they were intended to correct the treatment of the Jews by the Greek cities. The entire society of a Greek *polis* was based on the assumption that everyone participated in the cult on which it was founded. The municipal authorities of a Greek city were tolerant enough to permit all sorts of religions in their city, but, understandably enough, they expected that anyone who wanted to have full citizenship should be tolerant

---

[102] *A.* XIX. 285.

[103] *CPJ* II, p. 41, ll. 73ff.

[104] Cf. *A.* XVII. 314; *B.* ii. 91; VII. 421; cf. *B.* VI. 329; Tac., *Hist.* V. 10; cf. W.H.C. Frend, *Martyrdom and Persecution in the Early Church*, 1965, p. 143 : "The Jews were regarded as at heart revolutionary, and Rome was finding it as difficult to conciliate them as Seleucids had in their day".

enough in return to participate in the worship and customs involved in citizenship. Now this was what the Jews refused to do. "The gods of Greece could easily compromise with the God of Israel, but he could not compromise with them".[105] When the Jews were encouraged in this attitude by the privileges of the Romans, this greatly annoyed the local pagan authorities and inflamed their hatred of the Jews. They, for their part, understandably thought that the Jews should not have it both ways.[106] "Why", asks Apion indignantly, "do the Jews not worship the same gods as the Alexandrians, if they are citizens of this city"?[107]

Time and again many Greek cities tried to ignore the privileges of the Jews, and time and again they had to be admonished by decrees issued or confirmed by the central government to respect the privileges of the hated Jews. The cities of Asia Minor had to be reprimanded repeatedly. One had even issued a resolution to prevent the Jews from observing their national customs and sacred rites. The Roman praetor ordered the municipal authorities to rescind this resolution at once and make it possible for the Jews to live in accordance with their native customs.[108] Something similar happened when the city of Tralles refused to recognise the privileges of the Jews,[109] and when other cities tried to make the Jews desecrate the Sabbath by summoning them to court on that day, or by trying to confiscate the sacred money and make the Jews use those funds to pay all sorts of local taxes.[110] The Greek cities naturally felt these interventions in their administration to be a negation of their autonomy. They were thus forced to take measures which they would never have freely resolved upon otherwise. The imposition from above of a line of behaviour could not but intensify the hostility to the Jewish groups in their midst.

In this respect there are grounds for devoting special attention to Alexandria, though of course there were conflicts, sometimes very bloody, between the Jews and other inhabitants of other cities and other regions. Josephus mentions, for example, that there were

---

[105] Tcherikover, *op. cit.*, p. 374.

[106] See above, p. 152.

[107] *Ap.* ii. 65.

[108] *A.* XIV. 213-216.

[109] *A.* XIV. 242.

[110] *A.* XIV. 241ff., 244ff., 256ff., 262ff.; XIX. 303ff., 286ff.; in Cyrene the main issue was the problems concerning the sacred money, *A.* XVI. 160f., 169f.

massacres in Syria which the Syrians did not always initiate out of hatred, but also to forestall the dangers menacing themselves, not only from the Jews, but also from sympathisers of the Jews, who could never be trusted.[111] According to Josephus the Jews were, indeed, sometimes the aggressors, as in Scythopolis where, however, they relied in vain on the support of their fellow-Jews inside the city.[112] Bloody massacres of Jews in Scythopolis, Ascalon, and Ptolemais were the result.[113] In Antioch an unbridled rage against the Jews broke out when they were accused of large-scale incendiarism.[114] In Seleucia Greeks and Syrians who had long been in conflict with one another agreed, as a great proof of mutual loyalty, to show enmity to the Jews. They attacked them suddenly and unexpectedly and killed more than 50,000.[115] In Caesarea the Jews revolted in 59-60 A.D. against the Syrian inhabitants because of a passionate discussion as to whom the city really had belonged since time immemorial.[116]

Josephus thus informs us that bloody conflicts burst out in various cities between the Jews and their fellow citizens. Nevertheless there is good reason to investigate further the relationships and events in Alexandria. In the first place we have more information about it than other cities. This can, of course, increase the number of questions for example regarding the chronological reconstruction of the course of events. On this point Tcherikover aptly remarks : Strangely enough, this abundance of sources is likely to complicate rather than facilitate the task of the historian.[117] This drawback is less bothersome, however, if the aim is not so much to reconstruct the chronological order, but to discover the anti-Semitic motives behind them. Then, as second peculiarity of the data on Egypt and Alexandria, is the fact that they do not derive exclusively from Jewish writings, but also from archeological, non-Jewish sources.[118]

It need hardly be said that a critical comparison of the various data gives rise to all sorts of questions. For example, can the edict of Claudius, mentioned by Josephus, be harmonised with the letter

---

[111] *B*. ii. 461ff.
[112] *B*. ii. 466ff.
[113] *B*. ii. 477.
[114] *B*. VII. 43ff.
[115] *A*. XVIII. 374ff.
[116] *B*. ii. 266ff.
[117] *CPJ* I, pp. 70f.
[118] See above pp. 17ff.

of the Alexandrians? Are they separated by a period of time and
a series of events which could account for the difference? Or does
the formulation of the edict rest on a falsification? If so, how far
does that falsification go? Is it possible to reconstruct the correct
wording?[119] One thing is certain, on a number of points the critical,
often also hostile attitude of several persons and groups towards
the Jews has become more transparent regarding their motives since
the discovery of the papyri.

An analysis of the data reveals first of all that in Egypt and
particularly in Alexandria hostility towards the Jews was intense
and of long duration. We know of several outbursts in which passions
on both sides ran high, and there are strong indications that in the
intervening period between conflicts relationships were often strained.
We know little of disturbances between 70 and 115 A.D., for example,
but there is a strong suspicion that various tensions led to conflicts
of greater or smaller magnitude in that period as well. For the events
in 66 and succeeding years Josephus is our only source, and his
neutrality was certainly less than ideal. He was an outspoken opponent
of the Jewish revolutionaries in Palestine and elsewhere and was
much concerned to let the Romans realise this as clearly as possible.
Nevertheless it is probably not untrue that an intense and bitter
conflict was waged in Alexandria in those years.[120] The passions
then inflamed could scarcely have been calmed at once and must
have smouldered long thereafter. The outbreak of the revolt of the
Jews under Trajan in 115 A.D. was so general and so furious that
one may safely assume that it was the explosion of conflict-material
that had long been accumulating. Hence there are grounds for assuming
that there was scarcely any period of peaceful relationships between
the aftermath of the 66 events and the period full of resentment
which undoubtedly preceded the events of 115 and following years.

Josephus begins his description of the 66 A.D. events in Alexandria
by saying that, since the time of Alexander, there had already existed
an "incessant strife between the native inhabitants and the Jewish

---

[119] Cf. Tcherikover, *op. cit.*, pp. 409ff., 511, note 57; *CPJ* I, pp. 70f.; L.H. Feldman,
Jos., Loeb-ed., Vol. IX. 1965, pp. 344ff.

[120] *B.* ii. 487.; cf. Frend, *op. cit.*, p. 135: "The speed at which the conflagration
of 66 spread throughout Palestine and Syria and that of A.D. 115-117 spread round
the eastern Mediterranean provinces from Mesopotamia to Cyprus and Cyrenaica
shows that there was plenty of inflammable material in these provinces".

settlers".[121] Some maintain that this statement is historically true,
others doubt it.[122] Heinemann, one of the latter, qualifies Josephus'
contention that the stream of libellous accusations against the Jews
began with the Egyptians as "reine Kombination".[123] There is no
definite proof that the Egyptian hatred of the Jews had been fomenting
ever since the Roman period. What is certain is that violent clashes
occurred between the Egyptians and the Jews during the Persian
dominion over Egypt. The Elephantine papyri state clearly that
the temple of Jahu was destroyed by Egyptian priests from the
local temple of Chnum in 410 B.C., probably with the assistance
of the Persian satrap and his son.[124] Yoyotte takes this as ground
for crediting Josephus' statement that the libel against the Jews
started with the Egyptians.[125] It must be admitted that the Egyptian
papyri do not prove that hatred of the Jews was endemic in Egypt
from early times. Possibly it was here a question of a temporary
and localised conflict of a religious nature. But the papyri do prove
that an anti-Jewish attitude manifested itself very early in Egypt.
Whether this influenced writings of Egyptian derivation depends on
the evaluation of those of Manetho. These are dealt with later. Naturally the disposition of the central government greatly influenced
the position of the Jews in Egypt. Under the Ptolemies, for example,
there was a marked difference between Ptolemy VI Philometor and
his successor Euergetes II.[126] Under the Romans, the situation under
Caesar and Augustus was quite different from that under Caligula,
Vespasian, Domitian, Hadrian.

Philo lets it be plainly known that the intense persecution of
the Jews of Alexandria during his lifetime was anything but sudden
or unexpected, but that they were the eruption of a hatred which
had long been smouldering.[127] In his description of the tumults in
that city on King Agrippa's arrival he says, inter alia, that jealousy
is part of the Egyptian nature. With respect to a Jewish king, there

---

[121] *B.* ii. 487 : ἀεὶ — ἡ στάσις πρὸς τὸ Ἰουδαικὸν τοῖς ἐπιχωρίοις.

[122] Cf. Bell. *J.u.G.*, p. 7; Heinemann, *op. cit.*, p. 6.

[123] Heinemann, *op. cit.*, p. 8.

[124] Cf. K.R. Veenhof, Balans der Elefantine-papyri, I in *Phoenix, Bulletin uitgegeven
door het Vooraziatisch-Egyptisch Genootschap Ex Oriente Lux*, 16, 1, 1970, pp. 310-327.
This article also lists the latest publications on this subject; cf. also Tcherikover,
op. cit., pp. 363, 531, note 79; Hopfner, *op. cit.*, pp. 2ff.

[125] Yoyotte, *op. cit.*, p. 135; see above pp. 48f.; *Ap.* i. 223.

[126] *CPJ* I, pp. 19ff.

[127] *Leg.* 120.

was additionally the "ancient and we might say innate hostility
to the Jews".[128] This agrees with what Josephus says about the
"incessant strife",[129] and with the intense hatred with which the
persecutors of the Jews were so possessed during the pogroms in
Alexandria that there was no stopping their inhuman atrocities.[130]
Now, as we have seen above, Philo ascribed these unbridled outbursts
of hatred mainly to the rabble of Alexandria.[131] But here his aristocratic
contempt of the plebeians is partly responsible, just as in the case
of Josephus, who often lends a very unfavourable meaning to such
words as πληθύς, πλῆθος and ὄχλος and who in no way reserves
their use for non-Jewish crowds. On the contrary, he uses them for
the revolutionary section of the Jewish nation which supported a
policy vastly different from Josephus' preference.[132] It goes without
saying, however, that these tremendous tumults would never have
happened in Alexandria if the crowds had not had the open or secret
support, or at least tacit approval, of other classes.

One gets the impression that often only the slightest provocation
was needed to discharge an ever-present, latent tension. That was
not restricted to Egypt. Once in Jerusalem an indescribable tumult
broke out under the Jews when a Roman soldier contemptuously
turned his back on the crowd near the temple, sat in an indecent
posture and made a most indecent noise.[133] In Caesarea a conflict
began with the pestering of a Greek. The Jewish synagogue adjoined
a plot of ground owned by this Greek. This site the Jews had frequently
endeavoured to purchase, offering a price far exceeding its true
value. But the Greek continued to build new constructions on that
plot, leaving the Jews only a narrow and extremely awkward passage.
A few hot-headed youths tried to put an end to these building
activities, and this marked the beginning of a violent clash. Josephus
says himself of these events that, in this instance, the ostensible
pretext for war was out of proportion to the magnitude of disasters
to which it led.[134]

---

128 *Flacc.* 29.
129 *B.* ii. 487; cf. *Ap.* i. 223; see above pp. 167f.
130 *B.* ii. 498 : — δι'ὑπερβολὴν μίσους δυσανάκλητον —.
131 Above p. 24.
132 Cf. Brüne, *op. cit.*, pp. 118f.
133 *B.* ii. 224-227.
134 *B.* ii. 285-292.

King Agrippa's visit to Alexandria thus formed the occasion in
38A .D. for the most furious pogrom of ancient times.[135] The troubles
of 66 A.D. in Alexandria began with the entrance of Jews in the
amphitheatre, where the Alexandrians deliberated on the dispatch of
a delegation to Nero. Josephus does not specify who these Jews
were or if they were Alexandrian citizens. In any case, the Alexandrians
began to insult the Jews, and then the tumult broke out in all its
fury.[136] If such relatively insignificant provocations could initiate
such dramatic events, then the mutual hatred and animosity must
have been deep-rooted and the resentment so intense that in times
of which we know little or nothing the critical point of explosion
must often have been reached or surpassed. Consequently there must
have been a prolonged hostility between the Jews and the other
inhabitants of Egypt, and of Alexandria in particular. The frequent
conflicts emanated from a permanent anti-Semitism of long standing.

Now the question is in which groups of the population must the
bitterest foes of the Jews be sought, and what were the reasons for
their opposition. Obviously a mere reference to the turbulence of
the Alexandrian rabble incited by a few villainous leaders, as described
by Philo, is not a satisfactory answer. An investigation into the
deeper reasons reveals social and political differences. Certain scholars
take these to be the prime, if not the only reason. Smallwood speaks
of "the social and political conditions in the city which were the
basic causes of the friction between the races".[137] When Heinemann
reviews the whole of the political complications between the Jews
and the world about them, he says "dass es sich in der Hauptsache
nicht um Religionskriege, sondern um Machtkämpfe handelt". As
for the events in Alexandria in particular, he observes: "Gegen
die jüdische Religion als solche hat man nichts einzuwenden (die
Hereinziehung des Kaiserkultus beweist nichts hiergegen); der Stoss
geht gegen die Rechts- und Machtstellung der Juden".[138] It is questionable whether such a contradistinction should be made between the
motives, or whether they are not closely interwoven with one another.
There is no doubt about it, the conflict in Alexandria was almost
always about politics in so far as it manifested itself openly. But
the event alluded to by Heinemann parenthetically is not so incidental

---

[135] *Flacc.* 25ff.; cf. *CPJ* I, pp. 65ff.

[136] *B.* ii. 487ff.; cf. *CPJ* I, pp. 78f.

[137] Smallwood, *op. cit.*, p. 3.

[138] Heinemann, *op. cit.*, pp. 18, 10.

as he would have us believe. What actually happened ? The enemies of
the Jews in Alexandria set fire to synagogues or destroyed them
completely in those quarters of the city where there were few Jews.
In other quarters where the Jews were very numerous however,
they could not destroy them, only desecrate them by placing portraits
of Gaius in them. In the largest and most famous synagogue, moreover,
they placed a bronze statue riding in a four-horse chariot, a very
old one which they fetched from the gymnasium, because in their
haste and the intensity of their enthusiasm they did not take the
time to make a new one.[139] The introduction of the emperor cult
into the synagogue formed part of a political game. This was a double-
edged weapon : the emperor could hardly criticise such an enthusiastic
stimulation of his cult, and simultaneously the hated Jews were struck
in the very heart of their faith, their observance of the prescripts
of the law. It also goes to show that no lengthy deliberation was
needed to decide where one could best strike at the constantly annoying, strange customs of that nation. Those Jews would find
themselves in a difficult spot. So both offensive provocations such
as those of Antiochus Epiphanes, Pilate, Caligula in Palestine and
the numerous instances of petty plaguing in all sorts of places, but
especially in Alexandria, were partly due to vexation about the
separateness of the Jews. In the latter city an additional factor was
the intense resentment roused by the political demands of the Jews
who, once they obtained constitutional privileges, placed all manner
of restrictions on the religious customs which, for everyone, were
connected with those political rights. The Greek cities, and Apion,
were annoyed by this,[140] and Claudius also gave vent to a certain
feeling of resentment against the Jews in his letter to the Alexandrians,
in which he admonishes them to be content with their position in
Alexandria and not to try to obtain even more political privileges.[141]

Claudius' letter is, without doubt, a political document as regards
purpose and contents, and as such "it evinces a high degree of common
sense".[142] With well-thought-out diplomacy, the emperor tried to
achieve his goal, namely to put an end to the conflicts in Alexandria
and thus to restore peace in that part of the Roman empire. That

---

[139] *Leg.* 134; *Flacc.* 41, 44, 53, *Leg.* 346; cf. Smallwood, *op. cit.*, p. 222.
[140] Above pp. 152, 165.
[141] *CPJ* II, p. 41, ll. 88ff.
[142] *CPJ* II, p. 38.

meant admonishing both parties. If we first read his exhortation
to the Alexandrians, we see that Claudius wished to continue the
course of conduct followed by the central Roman government before
Caligula and especially by Augustus, i.e. the Jews should have absolute
freedom of worship. The Alexandrians were not to hinder this in
any respect.[143] This inducement to show goodwill to the Jews and
to respect their cult and customs followed the pattern and even
the terminology of the decrees of the Roman emperors mentioned
by Josephus. In this letter, however, it is much more manifest that
such an admonition in no way presumed a pro-Jewish attitude on
the part of the emperors or the chancery officials who drew up the
document. The tone of the admonition to the Jews is sharper than
that to the Alexandrians, perhaps right from the opening words. To
the latter Claudius says: I conjure ($\delta\iota\alpha\mu\alpha\rho\tau\acute{\upsilon}\rho\omega\mu\alpha\iota$); to the Jews
I order ($\kappa\epsilon\lambda\epsilon\acute{\upsilon}\omega$).[144] Quite possibly "it is not a mere slip of the pen;
the Imperial Chancery was far more polite in addressing Greek civilians
than the various 'natives' in the Empire".[145] If this supposition
is correct, then the difference in the terminology of the opening
words must have irked the Jews, for thus they were classified with
groups with whom they did not wish to be identified, as we shall
see presently. His tone becomes yet more threatening and severe
when he warns the Jews that they must not try to achieve their
goal, still more privileges, by appealing to their fellow Jews of Syria
or the rural areas of Egypt, for then "I shall be forced to conceive
graver suspicions. If they (the Jews) disobey, I shall proceed against
them in every way as fomenting a common plague for the whole
world".[146] Probably what Claudius chiefly had in mind in this threat
was the possible political consequences of Jewish disobedience of
his orders: such opposition by the Jews in Alexandria could become
the centre of Jewish revolt throughout the entire empire. But the
very fact that Claudius represented the Jews as possible spreaders
of a sort of plague throughout the world demonstrates that his sympathy was not for the Jews primarily or as a matter of course. On the
contrary, such a remark is particularly in keeping with the emotionally-
charged aversion to that ever-restless nation which, because of its

---

[143] Ll. 82ff., *CPJ* II, p. 43; see above p. 95.

[144] ll. 82 and 89.

[145] *CPJ* II, p. 49.

[146] ll. 96ff.; Momigliano, *op. cit.*, p. 34 considers these words to contain "a tone
of the utmost violence against the Jews".

peculiarities, could never peacefully assimilate with the society of other peoples and which had to be subdued, with difficulty, by threats.

This sharp pronouncement of Claudius would have to receive even more emphasis if it were established that he addressed himself especially to the Jews in another passage of that letter. When dealing with the responsibility for the disturbances and rioting, or rather to speak the truth the war against the Jews, about which the delegates of the Alexandrians had just held a passionate and circumstantial speech, he formulates his decision thus : I have not wished to make an exact inquiry, but I harbour within me a store of immutable indignation against those who renewed the conflict. I merely say that unless you stop this destructive and obstinate mutual enmity, I shall be forced to show what a benevolent ruler can be when he is turned to righteous indignation.[147] Immediately thereafter follow passages directed separately to the Alexandrians and the Jews, parts of which have already been quoted. Who is meant by "those who renewed the conflict" ? The difference of opinion about the answer to this question is evident from the divergent translations. Hunt translates, for example, the words κατὰ τῶν πάλειν ἀρξαμένων by "against whichever party renews the conflict".[148] The alteration of ἀρξαμένων into ἀρξομένων is a hypothesis that is clearly inspired by the wish to simplify the text and context along certain lines and is quite arbitrary. If it were certain that the future tense is used here, the meaning of the text would be that Claudius turns down a new inquiry into the causes of the conflict, as desired by the Alexandrians. He considers the matter closed. Beware he who reopens it. In this case, these words contain a warning addressed by Claudius to both parties. Tcherikover, who translates "those who renewed the conflict", rightly accentuates the aorist. He believes that Claudius here sharply turns against the Jews who, as Josephus says, began the attack in 41 and so renewed the conflict of 38. This would then mean that the emperor says in this passage that he harbours an "immutable indignation" against the Jews. The aorist does, indeed, argue in favour of this explanation, or in any case for the supposition that Claudius has in mind something that happened in the past. The question is, however, whether the aorist has not here the meaning

---

[147] ll. 73-82
[148] A.S. Hunt and C.C. Edgar, *Select Papyri* II, 1956, p. 85; Grant, *op. cit.*, p. 135.

of the future tense. I believe there are strong indications of this in
the context. In this section of the letter, Claudius states that he
does not want any new inquiry into the responsibility for the disturbances. No matter who was guilty, the matter must now be over
and done with for good. His immutable indignation (ὀργὴ ἀμετα-
μέλητος) will turn against whichever party begins again. If the
parties do not end the hostilities completely, they will experience
what it means when a benevolent ruler loses his patience. Only after
saying this does he begin to admonish each separate party, first
the Alexandrians and then the Jews. Hence the context so strongly
supports the interpretation of the disputed passage as "against whatever party renews the conflict", that the aorist must here be assumed
to have the significance of the future tense. Hence l. 78 ceases to
be evidence of Claudius' attitude to the Jews. Even without it, from
ll. 98ff. it is sufficiently evident that this emperor was anything
but philo-Semitic.[149]

Confirmation of this is given by Claudius' warning to the Jews
"not to intrude themselves in the games presided over by the *gym-
nasiarchoi* and the *kosmetai*, since they enjoy what is their own,
and in a city which is not their own they possess an abundance of
all good things".[150] Claudius' meaning is obvious: the Jews already
have so many privileges. They must not go on trying to obtain more,
such as full citizenship of Alexandria, for which participation in
the education of the gymnasium and hence enrolment in the list
of *epheboi* was necessary.[151] The question whether the Jews had
civic rights in Alexandria cannot be discussed at length here.[152]
Since the discovery of several papyri, including the letter of Claudius,
it would seem to me impossible that all Jews possessed civic rights
in Alexandria. The very way in which, earlier on in this letter, Claudius
guarantees the citizenship of those who were registered as *epheboi*

---

[149] Cf. *CPJ* II, p. 48, commentary l. 78.

[150] ll. 92ff.; cf. above p. 171.

[151] Cf. *CPJ* I, pp. 38f.

[152] On this subject see for example H.I. Bell, *Jews and Christians in Egypt*, 1924,
pp. 11ff.; *J.u.G.*, pp. 11ff.; M. Engers, Der Brief des Kaisers Claudius an die Alexandriner, *Klio* 20 (1926), pp. 168-178, especially pp. 173ff.; Momigliano, *op. cit.*, pp. 30f.,
96[25]; Scramuzza, *op. cit.*, pp. 74ff.; H. Box, *Philonis Alexandrini In Flaccum*, 1939,
pp. xxviii ff.; Smallwood, *op. cit.*, pp. 6ff.; Tcherikover, *op. cit.*, pp. 309ff., 409ff.;
CPJ I, pp. 39ff., 69ff., II, pp. 46f.; L.H. Feldman, *Josephus*, Vol. IX, pp. 344ff., 583ff.;
A. Schalit, *König Herodes*, 1969, pp. 38f.; A.D. Nock, *Essays on Religion and the
Ancient World* II, 1972, pp. 960-962; L. Fuchs, *op. cit.*, pp. 79-105.

up to the time of his rule[153] and warns the Jews against attempts to penetrate these circles renders impossible the supposition that the Jews possessed that citizenship. Moreover, the fact that the Alexandrians and Jews were addressed separately proves that the former were not spoken to as inhabitants of Alexandria, for the Jews were that too, but as citizens of that city. Hence the author did not place the Jews in the same category, unlike the edict of Claudius mentioned by Josephus.[154] The weightiest argument for the view that Claudius assumed that the Jews did not have civic rights in Alexandria lies in the expression "a city which is not their own" (ἐν ἀλλοτρίᾳ πόλει, l. 95). If the emperor had looked on the Jews as full citizens, he would never have phrased it so. True, they have been inhabitants of Alexandria for many years (ἐκ πολλῶν χρόνων l. 84), but, since they do not possess complete citizenship, it remains a ἀλλοτρία πόλις for them.

Apparently many Jews tried to obtain Alexandrian citizenship. They probably looked upon it as a token of higher political and social status. Most likely they were often prepared to be less faithful to their ancestral customs in return for such a desirable status symbol. Complete participation in the civic and cultural life of the city also implied involvement in religious ceremonies that were not, or scarcely, compatible with the observance of the commandments of their laws. Even the athletic training of the *epheboi*, part of the Greek *paideia* and considered the introduction to the receipt of civic rights, demanded a "departing from the native customs", with which Josephus accused Herod when this monarch undertook the organisation of such games : "Through foreign practices he gradually corrupted the ancient way of life, which had hitherto been inviolable".[155] Participation in such religious and cultural manifestations need not always have meant complete defection from Judaism as in the case of some renegades. Many must have tried to remain as faithful as possible to their religion and to avoid diverse obligations incumbent in the possession of citizenship. But then the annoyance of the others must have been all the greater. On the other hand, the open or latent opposition of the Greek citizens of Alexandria to the wishes of the Jews in this respect must have been felt as a humiliating discrimination by the

---

[153] ll. 53ff.
[154] *A*. XIX. 280ff.
[155] *A*. XV. 267ff.; cf. *2 Macc*. 4. 9-15.

Jews. Josephus was annoyed at Apion's surprise about the fact that the Jews were called Alexandrians.[156]

The papyri contain clear indications that the Alexandrians looked on the attempts of the Jews to obtain the citizenship of that city as an impertinent intrusion into circles where they did not belong. The irritation felt by both sides is discernible in the simple deletion in a papyrus from 5/4 B.C., in which a Jew called Helenus petitions the prefect of Egypt. In the opening words of this document he called himself Ἀλεξανδρεύς, Alexandrian, but either he or the scribe changed this to Ἰουδαῖος τῶν ἀπὸ Ἀλεξανδρείας, a Jew of Alexandria. Some consider this merely a more precise description of Helenus' civic status.[157] I believe it more plausible, however, that he had to admit, or the scribe pointed out to him with the precision of a civil servant, that the fact that Helenus' father was a citizen of Alexandria did not automatically make him one too. He was therefore forced "to designate himself by the humble and civically insignificant title of 'Jew of Alexandria' ".[158]

A document with almost certainly an anti-Semitic tint due to a political conflict is the so-called "Boule papyrus" dating from the time of Claudius, or more probably of Augustus. Since Jews are not mentioned by name in it, this is rather uncertain, but a few passages are definitely directed against them, though perhaps not exclusively.[159] In this document a personage of Alexandria, speaking on behalf of a group of other citizens, requests the emperor to set up or to reintroduce a city council. If he agrees, it is promised that the council "will see to it that none of those who are liable to enrolment for the poll-tax diminish the revenue by being listed in the public records along with the *epheboi* for each year; and it will take care that the pure(?) citizen body of Alexandria is not corrupted by men who are uncultured and uneducated (ἄθρεπτοι καὶ ἀνάγωγοι)".[160] The obvious assumption is that these 'uncultured and uneducated people' who threatened to defile the elite group of Alexandrian citizens were really all non-Greeks. It is also possible that the expression refers particularly to the Jews, since it is not known that the Egyptians,

---

[156] *Ap.* ii. 38.

[157] Cf. for example Juster, *op. cit.* II, pp. 9f. and others mentioned by Tcherikover, *CPJ* II, p. 30.

[158] Tcherikover, *Hell. Civ.*, p. 312; Scramuzza, *op. cit.*, p. 253[37]; Hopfner, *op. cit.*, p. 37.

[159] *CPJ* II, pp. 25ff.

[160] ll. 1-6, *CPJ* II, p. 28.

the other non-Greek group, frequently attempted to acquire civic rights. If this is so, then these words contain a great contempt of the Jews which must have grievously offended most of them, especially those who deliberately wished to share the culture of their surroundings. In a few scornful words they were here bundled together with the simplest and most backward people of the country.

Ever since 24-23 B.C. the Jews had had cause for such vexation. In that year Augustus introduced the *laographia*, a poll-tax. Every Egyptian between 14 and 60 years of age had to pay this tax, but the possessors of civic rights, i.e. Romans and citizens of Greek cities, were exempted from payment. That is why some Jews made determined efforts to acquire citizenship. Hence it is not surprising that, in this papyrus, mention is made of people who want to be enlisted in the register of *epheboi*, for that meant opening the door to citizenship. And it is certainly not coincidental that, in the papyrus containing the deleted words "an Alexandrian", this λαογραφία is thrice mentioned. By acquiring citizenship they tried to avoid paying this poll-tax, probably not so much for financial reasons, but because it was looked on as "a mark of extreme political and cultural degradation".[161] It placed them in the same category as the Egyptian peasants, those primitive souls who were exploited in so many ways. Such a tax regulation could not fail to be a constant grievance to many Jews. It made them feel humiliated, degraded, and its introduction probably caused them to bear malice towards the Roman government. Now the papyri manifestly evidence the degree of irritation in the inter-relationship caused by all this and the various ways in which the Jews were thwarted in this matter. Needless to say the introduction of the famous *fiscus Judaicus* by Vespasian offended the Jews to an even greater degree. This measure was aimed especially against them, and the payment of this didrachme for Jupiter Capitolinus replaced the temple tax.

From papyri of a much later date it appears that such embitterment was long-lived. The *Acts of the Alexandrian Martyrs* were probably written in the second and third centuries A.D., but it is also quite possible that they are based on older documents.[162] They contain

---

[161] *CPJ* I, p. 61; cf. V.A. Tcherikover, The Decline of the Jewish Diaspora in Egypt in the Roman Period, *The Journal of Jewish Studies* 14 (1963), p. 9; L. Fuchs, *op. cit.*, p. 108; Musurillo, *op. cit.*, p. 139.

[162] Cf. *CPJ* II, pp. 55ff.

accounts, albeit fragmentary, of discussions between prominent anti-
Semitic figures known to us from other sources and Flaccus, Caligula,
Claudius, Trajan, Hadrian, Commodus. One might say that these
works are primarily a fierce attack on the Roman emperors and
that anti-Semitism is only a secondary motif.[163] Nevertheless it is
very revealing that the writer takes for granted that it is a damning
charge when he mentions a relationship between the emperors and
the Jews for which the Alexandrian leaders reproach their dialogists
in trenchant words. Themes sometimes then recur which also appear
in papyri from the first century B.C. and in the letter of Claudius
to the Alexandrians, parts of which are cited above. When Isidorus
and Lampon, leaders of the Greeks in Alexandria, stood before
Claudius, Agrippa was also present. To him Isidorus says : "To you,
Agrippa, I wish to retort in connection with the points you bring
up about the Jews. I accuse them of wishing to stir up the entire
world... We must consider every detail in order to judge the whole
people. They are not of the same nature as the Alexandrians, but
live after the fashion of the Egyptians. Are they not on a level with
those who pay poll-tax ? Agrippa : The Egyptians have had taxes
levied on them by their rulers... But no one has imposed tributes
on the Jews".[164] The expression "to stir up the whole world" is
reminiscent of "fomenting a common plague for the whole world"
in Claudius' letter. The observation, evidently intended as an insult,
that the Jews culturally belong with the Egyptians, whom the Alexandrians consider far beneath them, is strongly reminiscent of the
Boule-papyrus, also in the association of this charge with the taxation
question. The same fiercely abusive tone can be heard in another
of these papyri in which Isidorus says to Claudius when he stands
up for his friend Agrippa : "My Lord Caesar, what do you care for
a twopenny-halfpenny Jew like Agrippa ? ; to which Claudius indignantly replies : What ? You are the most violent of men..."[165] When
Claudius taunts Isidorus with his dubious parentage and calls him
"the son of a girl-musician", the Alexandrian, proud of his city,
counter-attacks with : "I am neither a slave nor a girl-musician's

---

[163] Rostovtzeff says of these Acts that they "reflect the political opposition of
the Alexandrians to the Roman government and that they used the prosecutions of
the leaders of the Jewish 'pogroms' as a pretext for expressing their anti-Roman spirit",
op. cit., p. 587; cf. Musurillo, op. cit., pp. 259-266.

[164] CPJ II, pp. 78f., ll. 20ff.

[165] CPJ II, p. 76, see commentary on l. 18 on p. 77.

son, but gymnasiarch of the glorious city of Alexandria. But you are the cast-off son of the Jewess Salome ![166] In a conversation between Trajan and Hermaiskos, the latter bitterly charges the emperor and his wife Plotina with biased conduct and with the fact that the emperor's council "is filled with impious Jews".[167]

All these fierce tirades against the Jews form part of a sharp polemical attack on the Roman emperors. Evidently one of the ways to cast reflection on them in the eyes of the readers was for the author to describe them as men who were on good terms with the Jews. The description of these scenes was prompted by a matter-of-course anti-Semitism which could also be utilised to foster bitter hatred of the Roman authorities. Numerous fragments of this literature have been found, and this could mean that such writings were very popular in broad circles of Alexandria. Here, once more, is plain testimony of how strong political, social, cultural and religious motives were for a very long time interwoven in Alexandrian anti-Semitism. In the background is ever and again the hatred of those ἀνόσιοι Ἰουδαῖοι,[168] that separate nation that is despised and is continually and with vexation being reminded of the place where it really belongs.[169]

---

[166] *CPJ* II, p. 80, ll. 7ff., see commentary on p. 81.

[167] *CPJ* II, p. 83, Col. II, ll. 26ff.; cf. above p. 99.

[168] Cf. above pp. 99ff.

[169] Cf. W. Holsten, Art. *Antisemitismus* in *R.G.G.* ³I, p. 456 : "In der *Antike* hat zweifellos die religiöse Besonderheit der Juden den grössten Anstoss erregt. Sicherlich hat diese religiöse Besonderheit auch das politische und wirtschaftliche Verhalten geprägt und sicherlich hat das Bewusstsein von dieser Besonderheit sich auch als Stolz und Hochmut gegenüber den Nichtjuden auswirken können".

CHAPTER FIVE

DIVERSITY OF OPINIONS REGARDING JEWRY

In the preceding pages pronouncements of an anti-Semitic nature have been cited from literary and archeological sources, from varying periods and places. The danger of presenting a biased picture is therefore real. Such a compilation of all the anti-Semitic statements could enhance the impression that the entire ancient world, at all times and in all places, was strongly opposed to the Jews. If, however, the traces of anti-Semitism in certain countries, regions and cities are described separately and in chronological order, then it would be quite apparent that, in certain periods and certain places, anti-Semitism did not play anything like such an important role as suggested by the compilation of data from all periods and all places. Only in this way can the concept of eternal anti-Semitism, so fiercely contested by Isaac, be created.[1]

It must be borne in mind that the expressions of anti-Semitism in word and deed discussed above are limited in time and place. Regarding time, they derive mainly from the two centuries before and the two centuries after Christ. The latter period is a limitation of time selected by the present author. This does not apply to the former period. Does this mean that hardly any traces of anti-Semitism are to be found in the ancient world before then, and that consequently there is absolutely no question of eternal anti-Semitism ? Some scholars believe that anti-Semitism developed relatively late in the ancient world. Reference is made above to Heinemann's contention that, in all probability, there was no question of a 'Judenhetze' before 88 B.C.[2] Nor of anti-Semitism in a different form ? It is remarkable that elsewhere Heinemann mentions the middle of the second century as the point in time before which we have no indications of unfriendly

---

[1] See above pp. 5ff.; with reference to the localisation it is said in the article *Anti-Semitism* in *Encyclopaedia Judaica* : "Prejudice against Jews appeared in antiquity almost exclusively in those countries which later became part of the Roman Empire" (*Enc. Jud.* 3, 1971, p. 87). The hatred for the Babylonian Jewry was never great. (Cf. Jos., *Ap.* i. 71).

[2] Heinemann, *op. cit.*, p. 19, above p. 6; cf. *CPJ* I, p. 25.

measures against the Jews. Evidently he is referring to the persecution under Antiochus Epiphanes, which is characterised in a rather over-friendly way by the term "unfriendly measures".[3] Is it true that, before the time of Antiochus Epiphanes, "geht der gebildete Hellene an die Juden aus weltanschaulichem Interesse heran"?[4] Can one really say that, prior to that time, the ancient authors only wrote about the Jews, because they were interested in their view of life, and that they reported on it in a neutral, and positively non-hostile way?

Statements to this effect recur again and again. As point in time when Judaism became a problem for the outside world and anti-Semitism was born, Bousset says "mindestens seit Beginn des ersten vorchristlichen Jahrhunderts".[5] Parkes believes that before the period of Alexander the Great the Jews escaped the attention of the outside world.[6] Poliakov is of the same opinion and concludes that the Greek travellers, who were curious enough, apparently found nothing special to say about this little nation of Judaea.[7] Hengel believes that the anti-Semitic movement began in the second or first century before Christ.[8]

If we distinguish between anti-Semitism in deed and in word, then the commencement of the former must certainly be dated in the second century B.C., the time of Antiochus Epiphanes. The outbreak of hatred and persecution of the Jews under this monarch very probably had a political background. Both the Jewish accounts of these events, and also the way in which diverse pagan writers mention Antiochus' action[9] plainly indicate that a fierce hostility towards the Jews became manifest at that time. Was this actually the first outbreak of anti-Semitism in deed? Definitely not, according to biblical sources. The Book of *Esther* is often assumed to be relatively young and to project in a fictitious story back to a much earlier period the feelings and relationships of its contemporary period, the second century B.C. There are good grounds for this hypothesis. Even so, the book is important for an assessment of the relationships

---

[3] Heinemann, *op. cit.*, pp. 6, 32.

[4] Heinemann, *op. cit.*, p. 32.

[5] Bousset, *op. cit.*, p. 87.

[6] Parkes, *op. cit.*, p. 14.

[7] Poliakov, *op. cit.*, p. 19.

[8] Hengel, *op. cit.*, pp. 464, 469.

[9] See above pp. 98f.

between Jews and non-Jews in the period of the author, but it has no validity as testimonial of the plan for a pogrom *before* the time of Antiochus Epiphanes.[10]

It is questionable, in my opinion, whether the statements about this matter in the beginning of *Exodus* must be denied any significance whatsoever. Isaac emphasises the fact that this book was likewise written long after the events it describes. If this is used as argument against its historicity, it must be noted that the same applies to many literary sources from the ancient world, Jewish and non-Jewish, which are used, be it critically, for historiography. Isaac personally believes the essence of the data in *Exodus* to be probable : the sojourn of Israelite tribes in Egypt, the severe regime under which they lived and their flight under Moses. According to him, however, such facts constitute an exceptional feature in the history of Egypt. Israel was truly not the only recipient of such treatment. There prevailed in Egypt a strong dislike of all Asians, of all intruders who were attracted by the riches of that country.[11] Data of Egyptian derivation can, indeed, confirm this. Even so, it is still remarkable that, of all the Asians, the Jews are specifically mentioned and that we now know from the Elephantine papyri of a violent conflict between Jews and Egyptians in the fifth century B.C. One may contend that this conflict was limited in time and locale and was of a religious nature,[12] but these papyri show, nevertheless, that even in that period the Jews were identified as a very peculiar people among the Asians and that the hostility towards them focussed on a cult which distinguished them from all other Eastern peoples. Consequently this happening may be accounted valid testimony of a hostile attitude towards the Jews in particular which found expression in deeds a long time before Antiochus Epiphanes.[13]

With regard to anti-Semitism in word it is undoubtedly true that the pagan reports on the Jews are not permeated with a hostile attitude right from the beginning. Admittedly various writers manifest an interest in the way of life and thinking of the Jews which may, at times, be termed neutral-objective, and at others clearly imbued with a certain sympathy for Jewish conceptions. As people who

---

[10] Cf. Isaac, *op. cit.*, pp. 47f.

[11] Isaac, *op. cit.*, pp. 40f.; cf. Yoyotte, *op. cit.*, pp. 135ff.; see above pp. 48f.

[12] See above p. 168.

[13] Leipoldt calls these papyri "den ältesten urkundlichen Beleg" for anti-Semitism, Art. *Antisemitismus* in *Reallexikon für Antike und Christentum*, Bd. I, 1950, p. 469.

practise circumcision, Herodotus mentions the Syrians of Palestine. Some have doubted whether his reference here is to the Jews.[14] To my mind he does, indeed, speak of them, but he simply confines himself to mentioning a few noteworthy features of this nation. There is nothing to prove he was particularly interested in it.[15] There are writers from the centuries before Christ who discuss the Jews at greater length and also their conceptions. As indicated above, some of them record with approval the Jews' repudiation of image-worship.[16] Frequently the Jews are praised as good philosophers. Megasthenes, who was employed as historiographer by Seleucus I in the fourth and the beginning of the third century B.C., was sent by this monarch as diplomat to India. The book he wrote about that country has not been preserved, but Clemens of Alexandria has handed down this observation made by him about the Jews : Everything recorded by the wise men of ancient times about nature is to be found also among the philosophers outside Greece, part among the Brahmans in India, part in Syria among the people known as the Jews.[17] Theophrastus, a pupil of Aristoteles who died in 287 B.C., decribes how the Jews sacrifice and says : Their system is the following : they do not eat of the sacrificial flesh, but burn it at night, after they have poured a great deal of honey and wine upon it. The sacrifice they seek to complete rather rapidly so that the All-Seer may not become a witness of pollution. Throughout the entire time, inasmuch as they are philosophers by race ($ἅτε$ $φιλόσοφοι$ $τὸ$ $γένος$ $ὄντες$), they discuss the nature of the Deity among themselves, and spend the night in observing the stars, looking up at them and invoking them as divine in their prayers.[18] Such an observation may not testify to a thorough study of what the Jews really thought, but it is plain that the ideas ascribed to them are judged favourably. Clearchus of Soli, a contemporary of Theophrastus and similarly a pupil of Aristoteles, says that his master once met a Jew and reported of him : the man was a Jew of Coele-Syria. These people are descended from the Indian philosophers. The philosophers, they say, are in India called Calani, in Syria by the territorial name of Jews; for the district they inhabit is known as Judaea. Their city has a remark-

---

[14] Reinach, *op. cit.*, p. 2, note 1; Radin, *op. cit.*, pp. 80f.

[15] Cf. Isaac, *op. cit.*, pp. 51f.; see above p. 47.

[16] See above pp. 119ff.

[17] Reinach, *op. cit.*, p. 13 : quotation Clem. Alex., *Stromat.* I. 15.

[18] Reinach, *op. cit.*, p. 8 : quotation Porphyry, $Περὶ$ $ἀποχῆς$ $ἐμψύχων$ ii. 26.

ably odd name : they call it Hierusalame. Now this man, who was
entertained by a large circle of friends and was on his way down from
the interior to the coast not only spoke Greek, but had the soul of a
Greek (Ἑλληνικὸς ἦν οὐ τῇ διαλέκτῳ μόνον, ἀλλὰ καὶ τῇ ψυχῇ). During my stay in Asia, he visited the same places as I did and came to
converse with me and some other scholars, to test our learning. But
as one who had been intimate with many cultivated persons, it was
rather he who imparted to us something of his own.[19] Most scholars
have strong doubts about the veracity of this story.[20] But even if
it were pure imagination, it would still demonstrate that Clearchus
did not hesitate to tell a story in which a Jew is described in very
favourable terms. Since the judgments of Megasthenes, Theophrastus
and Clearchus, probably mutually independent, largely give approximately the same picture of the Jews, it may indeed be said of these
testimonials : We may find in them accordingly such knowledge of
the Jews as at about 300 B.C. had reached educated Greeks.[21] Proof
that this tradition was long continued is to be found in the pronouncement of Hermippos of Smyrna, probably from the second half of
the third century B.C. In his biography of Pythagoras he records a
few rules of conduct and tenets of the philosopher and then says
of him : practising and repeating these precepts he was imitating
and appropriating the doctrines of the Jews and Thracians. Josephus,
who mentions this, adds : In fact, it is actually said that that great
man introduced many points of Jewish law into his philosophy.[22]

So we see that there were diverse statements made by non-Jewish
writers of that time which pass favourable judgment on the Jews.
Does this imply that the literature from before the second century B.C.
contains not a trace of anti-Semitism ? In my view, no. Mention must
first be made of Manetho, the Egyptian priest under Ptolemy I who,
in the first half of the third century B.C., wrote a book on the history
of Egypt. Josephus twice quotes from it at length.[23] According to
his first quotation Manetho describes an invasion of the Hycsos,
called in the beginning a people of ignoble origin from the east (ἐκ
τῶν πρὸς ἀνατολὴν μερῶν ἄνθρωποι τὸ γένος ἄσημοι).[24] That nation

---

[19] Jos, Ap. i. 179-181.

[20] Tcherikover, op. cit., pp. 287-359; Hengel, op. cit., pp. 467ff.

[21] Radin, op. cit., p. 86.

[22] Ap. i. 164f.; cf. Böhl, op. cit., pp. 475f.

[23] Ap. i. 73ff., 227ff.

[24] Ap. i. 75.

ruled over Egypt with an iron hand. Having overpowered the chiefs, they then savagely burnt the cities, razed the temples of the gods to the ground and treated the whole native population with the utmost cruelty, massacring some, and carrying off the wives and children of others into slavery.[25] The kings of these so-called shepherds ruled over Egypt for 511 years. Then the Egyptians revolted against them. The invaders were driven forcibly from the country. They fled to Syria, and on their way they founded the city of Jerusalem in the land of Judaea.[26]

The second fragment contains the well-known story about the exodus of a host of soldiers from Egypt which recurs in diverse versions in later writers. King Amenophis, who dearly wished to see the gods, was foretold that this would happen "if he purged the entire country of lepers and other polluted persons".[27] The king had them assembled and put to work as slaves in quarries. Later they were given the city Avaris as their own territory. Their numbers increased to 80,000. They revolted against the king under the leadership of a priest of Heliopolis called Osarsiph, whom they themselves had chosen as leader. "They swore to obey all his orders".[28] Osarsiph fortified Avaris and sent a delegation to the shepherds who had been driven from Egypt and were living in Jerusalem. He asked them to organise an expedition against Egypt together with him and his followers. They acceded to this request, and 200,000 of them came to Osarsiph's assistance. King Amenophis fled to Ethiopia and remained there during the 13 years when the lepers ruled Egypt. Meanwhile the Solymites came down with the polluted Egyptians and treated the inhabitants in so sacrilegious a manner that the regime of the shepherds seemed like a golden age to those who now beheld the impieties of their present enemies. Not only did they set cities and villages on fire, not only did they pillage the temples and mutilate the images of the gods, but, not content with that, they habitually used the very sanctuaries as kitchens for roasting the venerated sacred animals, and forced the priests and prophets to slaughter them and cut their throats, and then turned them out naked.[29] Finally, however, King Amenophis marched against the

---

[25] *Ap.* i. 76.

[26] *Ap.* i. 84ff.

[27] *Ap.* i. 233.

[28] *Ap.* i. 238f.; see above p. 90.

[29] *Ap.* i. 248f.

lepers with a great army, defeated them and pursued them "to the frontiers of Syria".[30]

There is a great divergence of opinion about the significance of these fragments from the work of Manetho quoted by Josephus. It is patently obvious from the aforesaid quotations that both stories paint a very unfavourable picture of the nations and groups described, both as regards origins and conduct. But it is doubtful whether Manetho included the Jews in those nations and groups. Josephus assumes this unmistakably,[31] and if this were so, one could say there is intense anti-Semitism in Manetho. Many deny such most positively. Reinach comments on the first story : "rien n'indique que les Hycsos doivent être confondus avec les Hébreux", and adds "on verra par le fragment suivant que Manéthon ne faisait pas cette assimilation".[32] Isaac believes that "le simple exposé des faits démontre que cette réputation (d'antisémite) n'est pas justifiée".[33] Heinemann states it with great assurance : Dass Manethon Antisemit war, ist durch die neuere Josephuskritik widerlegt.—In Wahrheit hat dieser (Manetho) nie von Juden geredet; weder die Juden noch die Antisemiten haben ihm einen Satz zugeschrieben in dem diese Volksbezeichnung stand. He agrees with Willrich's contention "dass Manethon kein Gegner der Juden gewesen ist; wenn die Juden seine Hyksos, die Antisemiten seine Aussätzigen mit dem jüdischem Volk gleichsetzen, so ist er an beiden unschuldig".[34]

In my view there are no grounds for denying so categorically any trace of anti-Semitism in Manetho. From the extensive publications on these fragments from Manetho's work it is possible, to say the least, to find arguments in support of a different opinion.[35]

It is very difficult indeed to determine exactly what Manetho wrote himself and what he meant. Sometimes it is even difficult to distinguish between Manetho's own words and Josephus' personal view.[36] Moreover the possibility of later interpolations must be taken into account. According to Bousset, for example, the statement in the second story identifying the Jews with the lepers once driven

---

[30] *Ap.* i. 251; cf. above pp. 142f.

[31] *Ap.* i. 74, 228.

[32] Reinach, *op. cit.*, p. 26[1].

[33] Isaac, *op. cit.*, p. 61.

[34] Heinemann, *op. cit.*, pp. 6, 27.

[35] Other works in Schürer, *op. cit.* III, pp. 529-531; cf. also Böhl, *op. cit.*, pp. 382ff.

[36] Radin, *op. cit.*, p. 99; Tcherikover, *op. cit.*, p. 361.

out of Egypt is definitely an interpolation.[37] Isaac places great
emphasis on the lengthy period of time, about two and a half centuries,
between the publication of Manetho's work and that of Josephus
and on the possibility that, during that time, various alterations
were made in Manetho's work "d'après des apologies juives et des
pamphlets antisémites d'époque postérieure".[38] Naturally account must
be taken of such a possibility. The difficulty, however, lies in determining where such interpolations were made. Laqueur and after
him Heinemann believe, for instance, that the following passage,
mentioned by Josephus, was inserted later : It is said that the priest
who gave them a constitution and a code of laws was a native of
Heliopolis, named Osarsiph after the Heliopolitan god Osiris, and
that when he went over to this people he changed his name and was
called Moses.[39] If these words were, indeed, inserted later by an
anti-Semitic writer, then, according to Laqueur, the identification
of Osarsiph with Moses and of the Jews with the lepers would be
invalid. Partly for this reason Heinemann also believes that what
Manetho originally said had nothing to do with the Jews. A story
which memorised persecution under the monotheistic Amenhotep IV
is supposed to have been associated later with a statement about
the invasion of the Hycsos and still later with stories about the Jews.

For such a construction, however, it is not sufficient to declare
one text an interpolation. It is quite probable that, in these stories,
Manetho had the Jews in mind even when they are not mentioned
specifically. Since the lepers and the Hycsos are repeatedly associated
with Jerusalem, it is natural to assume that the Jews are being
referred to, and when mention is made of Solymites or Jerusalemites,
everyone who read Manetho's works must have thought of the Jews.
I believe, therefore, that what Manetho wrote about the Hycsos
and the lepers was most likely aimed at the Jews. It is from such
people that the Jews are descended. The horrible things told about
the Hycsos and those lepers therefore also apply to them.[40]

Furthermore, the way in which, according to Josephus, Manetho
speaks of the sources of his stories does not argue against his having
drawn data from them when compiling his book. At the conclusion

---

[37] Bousset, *op. cit.*, p. 71.

[38] Isaac, *op. cit.*, p. 60.

[39] *Ap.* i. 250; Tcherikover, *op. cit.*, p. 326; Heinemann, *op. cit.*, p. 27.

[40] Jerusalem *Ap.* i. 90, 94, 228, 230, 241, 262f., 270, 271ff., 275, 282, 290; Solymites
i. 248, Jerusalemites i. 264; cf. Tcherikover, *op. cit.*, pp. 362f.

of the first large fragment from Manetho Josephus says : His additional statements, which he derived not from the Egyptian records, but, as he admits himself, from fables of unknown authorship (ἐκ τῶν ἀδεσπότως μυθολογουμένων), I shall refute in detail later on and show the improbability of these lying stories.[41] Similar expressions are to be found in the second fragment : fables and current reports about the Jews (τὰ μυθευόμενα καὶ λεγόμενα περὶ τῶν Ἰουδαίων), unauthenticated legends.[42] Isaac finds it difficult to believe that Manetho would have included such data in his history of Egypt. To my mind, however, Manetho could quite possibly, as anti-Semite, have used sources of such dubious nature and passed on with pleasure "Egyptian gossip about the Jews".[43] This is more plausible than the later interpolation of such passages by an anti-Semite, who would not have admitted so frankly that he had used dubious sources for his observations on the Jews.

Even though these fragments from Manetho's work are surrounded by problems and all too positive conclusions must be avoided, I believe that this Egyptian priest was very likely an anti-Semite. In this respect he probably followed an older, oral or written tradition, which was continued after him by other non-Jewish writers.[44] His version of the exodus from Egypt, evidently intended to gainsay the not very flattering biblical-Jewish account, continued to be influential in all sorts of ways right up to Tacitus. Other anti-Semitic themes, which were later frequently heard, are also heard in Manetho. This being true, the inference is that already in the first half of the third century B.C. there was an anti-Semitic attitude.

Possibly one must go even further back in time for anti-Semitic pronouncements, back to the time when Hecataeus of Abdera wrote Αἰγυπτιακά (about 300 B.C.), a work in which he proclaimed in a more popular form than Manetho that Egypt was the source of all culture. From fragments that have been handed down to us it is quite plain that, on the whole, he was sympathetically disposed towards the Jews. It was noted above that he approved of the Jews' repudiation of the image-cult and sympathised with them on other points.[45]

---

[41] *Ap.* i. 105; cf. Radin, *op. cit.*, p. 100.

[42] *Ap.* i. 229, 287.

[43] *Ap.* i. 251.

[44] Cf. Lazare, *op. cit.*, p. 27; Radin, *op. cit.*, pp. 99ff.; Parkes, *op. cit.*, p. 15; Yoyotte, *op. cit.*, p. 135; Hengel, *op. cit.*, pp. 339, 464[1], 473, 475[28], 486[60].

[45] Pp. 89f., 121; cf. Schalit, *op. cit.*, p. 748 : "Was wir bei Hekataios lesen, ist

Still he lets it be known that he is aware of the peculiar character of the Jewish people, of their self-imposed segregation midst the other nations.[46] When he accuses the Jews of $\dot{\alpha}\pi\alpha\nu\theta\rho\omega\pi\dot{\iota}\alpha$ and $\mu\iota\sigma o\xi\epsilon\nu\dot{\iota}\alpha$, he gives vent to an annoyance with their separateness which he feels called upon to mention as a matter of course. Therefore he could hardly have been the first to observe with indignation this seclusion from mankind and hatred of aliens. Perhaps he knew from experience or from others that the Jews always isolated themselves from their fellow men and never ate at the same table as pagans. In any case he is not the last one to note the peculiar way of life of the Jews. The accusation around which anti-Semitic polemics later concentrated can already be clearly discerned in Hecataeus. It can rightly be pointed out that, for the rest, Hecataeus comments very amicably on the Jews and shows understanding for the incipience of their separateness, but here the terminology is no longer that of a "strictly scientific statement".[47] The words $\dot{\alpha}\pi\alpha\nu\theta\rho\omega\pi\dot{\iota}\alpha$ and $\mu\iota\sigma o\xi\epsilon\nu\dot{\iota}\alpha$ contain a serious charge. True, this attitude on the part of the Jews is "weniger aus Hass als aus der Erinnerung an die eigene $\xi\epsilon\nu\eta\lambda\alpha\sigma\dot{\iota}\alpha$, also aus Misstrauen erklärt".[48] It is doubtful, however, whether one may go as far as Isaac, who calls this passage an "allusion très nette au séparatisme des Juifs, toutefois sans parti pris critique, au contraire avec le souci de comprendre et d'expliquer".[49] As it is, clear choice of position is implied in the heavily charged words themselves.[50] One must therefore, at least, speak of "a hint of anti-Semitism" in Hecataeus.[51] In any case, this Jewish way of living

---

keine gehässige Schilderung, sondern eine aus ethnographischer Neugierde und ehrlicher Verwunderung geborene Darstellung des interessanten Barbarenvolkes der Juden"; Nock, *op. cit.*, II, pp. 864ff.

[46] Reinach, *op. cit.*, pp. 19, 17 : Diod. Sic. XL. 3; see above p. 90 .

[47] Heinemann, *op. cit.*, p. 37 : Die einzigen streng wissenschaftlichen Berichte über sie (die Juden) stammen von Hekataios und Poseidonius.

[48] Heinemann, *op. cit.*, pp. 32, 42.

[49] Isaac, *op. cit.*, p. 59; cf. H. Willrich, *Hekataios von Abdera und die jüdischen Literaten*, 1900, of which pp. 86-111 are included in the collection *Zur Josephus-Forschung*, 1973, herausgeg. von A. Schalit: "Hekataios braucht einige der Ausdrücke, welche wir bei den späteren Judenfeinden finden ($\xi\epsilon\nu\eta\lambda\alpha\sigma\dot{\iota}\alpha$, $\mu\iota\sigma\dot{o}\xi\epsilon\nu os$), aber er zeigt durchaus keine Antipathie gegen das Volk...", p. 4.

[50] Tcherikover, *op. cit.*, p. 367 : $\mu\iota\sigma o\xi\epsilon\nu\dot{\iota}\alpha$ meaning hatred of mankind, loathing of strangers; cf. Radin, *op. cit.*, pp. 182ff. : "inhospitality, lack of feeling of common humanity, a term which for Greeks and Romans embodied a number of conceptions not suggested by the word to modern ears".

[51] Tcherikover, *op. cit.*, p. 360.

was "schon dem frühesten Bericht-erstatter Hekataios aufgefallen und
wurde später eine der Hauptursachen des antiken Antisemitismus".[52]
This writer does, indeed, hereby introduce a theme that was to go
on resounding in all keys in the anti-Semitic polemics. His testimonial
may therefore be taken as a clear indication that the anti-Semitic criticism of the Jewish way of living was already current in Egypt at
the end of the fourth century B.C.

Obviously it is difficult to determine with absolute certainty the
spreading of anti-Semitism in the ancient world. Rightly it is said
that there were several centres of conflict, primarily the cities, and
especially those with a numerous Jewish group in their population,
such as Alexandria, Antioch and Rome.[53] The sources contain sufficient
evidence, however, that outbursts of anti-Semitism were certainly
not confined to those cities. In his defence of Flaccus, Cicero mentions
incidentally that clashes had occurred in various cities in Asia Minor.[54]
The decrees of the Roman authorities also reveal that friction between
Jews and non-Jews had been recurring frequently in the cities of
Asia Minor. Josephus informs us about conflicts in Palestine and
the cities surrounding it. Apart from the centres of conflict about
which we are somewhat better informed, therefore, there were many
other cities where anti-Semitism found expression, more or less violently, in word and deed.

It has now become evident from the papyri that one must not
assume that hostility towards the Jews was limited to the cities.
Needless to say information about the relationships in rural areas
is much scarcer than about urban ones. So it is all the more pregnant
that it is not lacking and that it sometimes suddenly, in different
periods, emerges. Hence it appears, for example, that in Egypt there
was also tension between the Jews and the people about them outside
the cities. In a letter from the first half of the first century B.C.,
the writer says to the addressee : You know that they loathe the
Jews (οἶδας γὰρ ὥτι βδελύσσονται ᾿Ιουδαίους). This was probably a
Jew writing to another Jew about a priest of Tebtunis, an Egyptian.
He warns his fellow nationalist : when dealing with the priest remember
that they hate (us) Jews. If this is true, this papyrus could then
truly be denoted "the first known example of anti-Semitic feeling

---

[52] Hengel, *op. cit.*, p. 549.

[53] Heinemann, *op. cit.*, pp. 5ff., 33, 35, 37; Simon, *op. cit.*, p. 244.

[54] See above pp. 14f.

in the daily life of Hellenistic Egypt".[55] In that case, then, the existence of such feelings can undoubtedly be antedated much further back in time. The writer was possibly speaking from the bitter experience of many Jews and assumed his co-religionist was only too well acquainted with such animosity towards them.

Similarly the businessman Sarapion, who wrote the letter to his agent in Alexandria in 41 A.D. which contains that warning against the Jews, probably lived in a rural area of Egypt. As we saw above, various interpretations can be given to his words : like everyone else, do you too beware of the Jews. One thing is clear, however, Sarapion thought he had to warn Herakleides emphatically about the Jews at that moment.[56]

The papyri that have been preserved from the time of the revolt of the Jews under Trajan (115-117 A.D.) testify in several ways to an intense hatred for the Jews, not only in Alexandria, but also in different parts of the country.[57]

If suddenly and incidentally testimonials of anti-Semitic feelings frequently occur in rural areas, which were normally not important enough for writers to pay much attention to, we can be assured that anti-Semitism was widespread there as well.

To concentrate only on the anti-Semitic words and deeds of ancient times would be to form a completely distorted picture of the place of Judaism in the ancient world. This has already appeared above from the quotations of the observations of non-Jewish writers who commented favourably on Judaism. More significant in this respect are the numerous statements about the strong attraction which Judaism exercised on many pagans. Needless to say a writer like Josephus mentions this with satisfaction and a certain degree of pride. After stating that the Greek philosophers "in their conduct and philosophy were Moses' disciples, holding similar views about God, and adoring the simple life and friendly communion between man and man", he goes on to say : But that is not all. The masses have long since shown a keen desire to adopt our religious observances; and there is not one city, Greek or barbarian, nor a single nation, to which our custom of abstaining from work on the seventh day has not spread, and where the fasts and the lighting of lamps and

---

[55] *CPJ* I, p. 256.

[56] *CPJ* II, pp. 33ff., see above pp. 33ff.

[57] See above pp. 16ff., 28f., 167; *CPJ* II, pp. 225-260.

many of our prohibitions in the matter of food are not observed. Moreover, they attempt to imitate our unanimity, our endurance under persecution on behalf of our laws. The greatest miracle of all is that our Law holds out no seductive bait of sensual pleasure, but has exercised this influence through its own inherent merits; and, as God permeates the universe, so the Law has found its way among all mankind.[58] Opinions may differ as to whether Josephus is referring here to an imitation of Jewish customs by pagans within the structure of their own religion and way of life, or to the adoption of the customs of the Jews and the acceptance of the Jewish way of life in various respects. Josephus speaks of a $\mu\iota\mu\epsilon\hat{\iota}\sigma\theta\alpha\iota$, and in this passage he does not say in so many words that he is referring to proselytes or God-fearers, though elsewhere he shows he is acquainted with those terms. Nevertheless his use of certain expressions in this passage renders it feasible that he was also thinking of these groups. The way he speaks of the Sabbath and the prescripts about food, but especially about the lighting of the lamps, suggests that in the imitation he includes the adoption of Jewish customs by pagans.[59]

Whatever the case may be, there is evidence elsewhere that Josephus knew of proselytes and God-fearers. He mentions individual conversions to Judaism. He describes at length the conversion of members of the royal house of Adiabene.[60] He relates how a dastardly Jew betrayed in a scandalous manner in Rome Fulvia, a woman of high rank who had become a Jewish proselyte.[61] He says of Poppaea, wife of Nero, that she was a worshipper of God and that she stood up for the Jews.[62] Of Azizus, king of Emesa, he says that he "had consented to be circumcised".[63]

Not only individuals, but also groups were more or less susceptible to influence by Judaism. According to Josephus there was really no great gulf separating the Greeks and the Jews : From the Greeks we are severed more by our geographical position than by our institutions, with the result that we neither hate nor envy them. On the contrary

---

[58] *Ap.* ii. 281-284.

[59] Schürer, *op. cit.* III, p. 166[49]; opposed by Munck, *op. cit.*, p. 264.

[60] *A.* XX. 24-53; cf. Neusner, *op. cit.*, pp. 58-67.

[61] *A.* XVIII. 81f.

[62] *A.* XX. 195; cf. *V.* 16; Feldman comments : the term $\theta\epsilon o\sigma\epsilon\beta\eta s$ does not necessarily identify Poppaea as a sympathizer in the technical sense, Loeb-ed., Vol. IX, pp. 242f.; Leon, *op. cit.*, pp. 251f.; Juster, *op. cit.* I, p. 256.

[63] *A.* XX. 139.

many of them have agreed to adopt our laws. In fairness he feels
compelled to add at once : of whom some have remained faithful,
while others, lacking the necessary endurance, have again seceded.[64]
Josephus states that the Jewish colony in Antioch increased steadily
in numbers. Moreover they were constantly attracting to their religious
ceremonies multitudes of Greeks, and these they had in some measure
incorporated with themselves.[65] At the beginning of the Jewish revolt
of 66-67 A.D., the inhabitants were determined to massacre the Jews
in their midst. They considered that the execution of their plan
would present no difficulty whatsoever; their only fear was of their
own wives who, with few exceptions, had all become converts to
the Jewish religion, and so their efforts were mainly directed to
keeping the secret from them.[66] Wholesale massacres were wrought
among the Jews in Syria. The perpetrators of these atrocities were
never quite at ease about their own fate. They passed their days
in blood, their nights, yet more dreadful, in terror. For, though
believing that they had rid themselves of the Jews, still each city
had its Judaisers ($iov\delta\alpha i\zeta ov\tau\epsilon s$), who aroused suspicion; and while
they shrunk from killing offhand this equivocal element in their
midst, they feared these neutrals as much as pronounced aliens.[67]

Josephus emphasises that non-Jews who adopted the customs of
the Jews were always welcome among this people. Moses, already,
devoted a great deal of attention to an "equitable treatment of
aliens", and his aim was not just "to secure our own customs from
corruption", but also "to throw them open ungrudgingly to any who
elect to share them. To all who desire to come and live under the
same laws with us, he gives a gracious welcome".[68] The Jews are not
like the Spartans who drive aliens out of their country. We, on the
contrary, while we have no desire to emulate the customs of others,
yet gladly welcome any who wish to share our own.[69]

Philo, too, often speaks of the proselytes and always with great
warmth and complete understanding for the difficult position in
which their election of Judaism placed them. Philo uses the expression
$\pi\rho o\sigma\eta\lambda\upsilon\tau os$, with which the LXX usually translates the biblical

---

[64] *Ap.* ii. 123.
[65] *B.* VII. 45.
[66] *B.* ii. 559f.
[67] *B.* ii. 463.
[68] *Ap.* ii. 209f.
[69] *Ap.* ii. 261.

גֵּר, almost always not for the alien who has entered the Jewish country, but the non-Jew who has entered the Jewish religion, who has become converted to Judaism.[70] Consequently he repeatedly applies to the latter group texts which refer to the former in the Bible. He is deeply conscious that proselytes have made a difficult, definite choice that radically affects their lives. They have forsaken the ancestral customs in which they were bred, customs packed with false inventions and vanity, they have crossed over to piety in whole-hearted love of simplicity and truth.[71] As a result they are left standing alone in their own surroundings. They have left their country, their kinsfolk and their friends for the sake of virtue and religion. Let them not be denied another citizenship or other ties of family and friendship, and let them find places of shelter standing ready for refugees to the camp of piety. For the most effectual love-charm, the charm which binds indissolubly the goodwill which makes us one, is to honour the one God.[72] Like all oppressed persons who stand defenceless in society, may they, too, count on the special care and attention of God. This God commands his people to look on precisely these proselytes, who have turned their kinsfolk into mortal enemies, as friends and kinsfolk, because they have shown the godliness of heart, which above all leads to friendship and affinity. All possible help must be offered them in bodily and mental matters.[73] Philo must not have found this a difficult task, for he believed in the wonderful evolution of a life abounding in all possible virtues for the proselytes after their conversion.[74]

The writings of Josephus and Philo therefore contain many and varied statements about proselytes and give the impression that the authors often came into contact with them in their own circles and knew that these converts to Judaism were to be found everywhere. Now one might think that, being Jewish writers, they were exaggerating about this matter, but their statements are often indirectly and on many points confirmed by information given by non-Jewish writers. Their ridicule, but especially their vexation and indignation plainly reveal that they, too, were regularly being confronted by

---

[70] Philo also uses other words for this; cf. K.G. Kuhn, Art. προσήλυτος, *Th.W.N.T.* VI, p. 732.

[71] *Spec. leg.* i. 309; cf. *Spec. leg.* i. 51; *Virt.* 219.

[72] *Spec. leg.* i. 52.

[73] *Spec. leg.* IV. 178; *Virt.* 179, 102ff.

[74] *Virt.* 182.

the phenomena of proselytism. Mention is made above[75] of a satire
of Horace in which bantering words camouflage his vexation with
his friend Fuscus, who was unable to discuss business with him
because of his observance of "the thirtieth Sabbath" : Why, man,
would you want to offend the circumcised Jews ? Elsewhere the poet
Horace writes to Maecenas that if he will not allow him to write
a certain sort of poetry, he will be joined by a large band of fellow
poets who, "like the Jews, will force you to come into our crowd".[76]
Tacitus expresses his horror that so many have turned to Judaism.
He is convinced that only inferior persons can come to this : diverse
customs of the Jews, base and abominable, owe their persistence
to their depravity. For the worst rascals among other peoples, renoun-
cing their ancestral religions, always kept sending tribute and contributions to Jerusalem... those who are converted to their ways follow
the same practice, and the earliest lesson they receive is to despise
the gods, to disown their country, and to regard their parents,
children, and brothers as of little account.[77] We have already seen
how Juvenal, Seneca and Rutilius Namatianus were terribly annoyed
by the large number of Roman proselytes.[78] One can picture, therefore,
how the non-Jews shrank from cutting themselves off from their
country, kinsfolk and friends, and why Philo praised this quality in
them. This illustrates the degree of loneliness, the contempt of acquain-
tances that lay in store for those who were converted to Judaism
and how reflection was cast on their new way of life. To these bitter
complaints about conversion to Judaism can be added observations
made by Tibullus, Ovid, and Persius, whose sarcasm alludes to the
attention paid to Jewish customs in certain circles of Roman society,
as well as Suetonius' comment that the grammarian Diogenes, who
used to lecture every Sabbath at Rhodos, would not admit Tiberius
where he came to hear him on a different day.[79]

Throughout several centuries, and even after 70 A.D., numerous
testimonials thus confirm the impression one receives from Jewish

---

[75] P. 129, Reinach, *op. cit.*, p. 246 : *Sat.* i. 9. 60ff.

[76] Reinach, *op. cit.*, p. 244 : *Sat.* i. 4. 138ff.

[77] *Hist.* V. 5.

[78] Above pp. 53ff.

[79] Reinach, *op. cit.*, pp. 247, 248, 264; Tib., *Eleg.* i. 3. 17f., Ov., *Ars amat.* i. 75, 415;
Pers., *Sat.* V. 176ff.; Suet., *Tib.* XXXII; Rolfe's comment on this : "The designation
of the seventh day of the week (Saturday) by the Jewish term 'Sabbath' seems to have
been common"; cf. *Aug.* LXXVI. 2.

reports that, in the ancient world, proselytes or at least persons who were more or less attracted to the Jewish faith and way of life were anything but scarce. Further proof of this is inherent in the severe measures taken against Judaism by several emperors, often with the specific intention of combatting proselytism. Romans who became proselytes were all to be classified as persons who undermined the state religion and disrupted family life, since they endangered the authority of the pater familias by a decisive choice. Even when the authorities were willing to grant special privileges to the Jews themselves, they looked upon proselytism as a menace to unity, as a disruption of a harmonious and tolerant society within the Roman empire. There are indications that certain reports about Jews being expelled from Rome should be viewed from this angle. Valerius Maximus, a contemporary of Tiberius, says that in 139 B.C. Hispalus, the *praetor peregrinus* banned from Rome the Jews "who had attempted to contaminate Roman beliefs by foisting upon them the worship of Jupiter Sabazios". The same edict affected the Chaldaeans who had to leave Rome and Italy within 10 days, because they had confused irresolute and foolish souls with their deceptive and mendacious astrological speculations.[80] According to Josephus, when the scandals surrounding Fulvia, mentioned above, assumed grave proportions, Tiberius ordered the whole Jewish community to leave Rome. This step may have been taken to keep possible proselytes from being influenced by the Jews. The comments on this event of 19 A.D. made by Tacitus and Suetonius report that the measures taken against the Jews were also applied to adherents of Egyptian worship. Evidently a check was placed on all too large an expansion of alien worship and customs, and grounds for taking action against them were not unwelcome.[81] It is possible that Claudius' prohibition of Jewish meetings, mentioned by Dio Cassius, was inspired by anxiety for too great an expansion of Jewish influence.[82]

---

[80] Reinach, *op. cit.*, pp. 258f. : Julius Paris, *Epitome* i. 3. 3; cf. Schürer, *op. cit.* III, p. 59; Radin, *op. cit.*, p. 255; Hengel, *op. cit.*, pp. 478ff.

[81] Jos. *A.* XVIII. 81ff.; Tac., *Ann.* ii. 85; Suet., *Tib.* XXXVI; cf. Radin, *op. cit.*, pp. 304ff.; E.M. Smallwood, Some Notes on the Jews under Tiberius, *Latomus* 1956, pp. 319ff.; Feldman, *Josephus*, Loeb-ed., Vol. IX, pp. 59-61; R. Syme, *Tacitus*, 1958 Vol. II, p. 468; D.R. Dudley, *The World of Tacitus*, 1968, pp. 194f.; also see above pp. 56, 156.

[82] Cf. Schürer, *op. cit.* III, p. 62; a possible connection with the statements about the expulsion of the Jews by Claudius in 49 A.D. in Suet., *Claudius* XXV and *Acts* 18. 2 is also discussed here.

Whereas these measures indicate incidental intervention, general laws were laid down by succeeding emperors which concentrated on hindering proselytism. The introduction of the *fiscus Judaicus* by Vespasian must have dealt a serious blow to the recruiting of proselytes, not only because the converts to Judaism now had to pay two drachmas a year, but also because they now were subject to a ruling that was extremely offensive to Judaism and was undoubtedly felt as such. Matters became even more vexatious when this tax began to be rigourously levied, as under Domitian.[83] Dio Cassius reports that, apart from Flavius Clemens and Flavia Domitilla, many others were sentenced under this emperor for having allowed themselves to be converted to the customs of the Jews. Some were put to death, others had their fortunes confiscated.[84] Nerva mitigated these practices somewhat. The *fiscus Judaicus* was not abolished, but the emperor no longer allowed anyone to inform against people for $\dot{a}\sigma\acute{e}\beta\epsilon\iota a$ or living according to Jewish customs.[85] The fact that this emperor put an end to informing is commemmorated in the legend of a coin dating from the time of Nerva : *Fisci Judaici calumnia sublata.*[86] A shattering blow to the continuance of Judaism and often too of proselytism was dealt by the measures taken by several emperors, beginning with Hadrian's prohibition of circumcision. Naturally it affected others who practised this custom as well. It was not directed specifically against the Jews, but could not fail to affect the Jews and those who wished to be converted to Judaism.[87] A remarkable thing is that Hadrian's successor, Antoninus Pius, once more and expressly permitted the circumcision of Jews, but he continued to prohibit the circumcision of all not Jewish-born. Here the measure was deliberately aimed against proselytism. Septimius Severus threatened to impose severe penalties on proselytes.[88]

---

[83] Suet., *Domit.* XII; cf. above p. 135.

[84] Reinach, *op. cit.*, pp. 195f. : Xiphil., *Epitome* LXVII. 14; cf. above p. 119.

[85] Reinach, *op. cit.*, p. 196 : Xiphil., *Epitome* LXVIII. 1f.

[86] Cf. Schürer, *op. cit.*, III, p. 118, note 67; Radin, *op. cit.*, p. 334.

[87] Reinach, *op. cit.*, p. 343 : "*Hist. Aug., Hadrianus* XIV; Spartianus is the only author who states this. Sometimes little value is ascribed to the reliability of the *Hist. Aug.*, of which the biography of Spartianus is part. In my opinion there are no conclusive grounds for doubting the truth of this statement; cf. Reinach, *op. cit.*, p. 343, note 2; Schürer, *op. cit.* I, pp. 674-679, III, p. 118; Radin, *op. cit.*, pp. 344ff.

[88] Reinach, *op. cit.*, p. 346 : *Hist. Aug., Severus* XVII : *Judaeos fieri sub gravi poena vetuit*; cf. above p. 135.

These imperial measures are further proof that Jewish proselytism constituted a problem for the Roman authorities that was serious enough to warrant full attention. The often energetic attempts to check the spread of proselytism suggest that the number of those who sympathised with Judaism were not slight. Just how large these numbers were is extremely difficult to establish. There is unanimity of opinion on this point.[89] A distinction must be made between the real proselytes who were circumcised and lived strictly according to the law and the φοβούμενοι τὸν θεόν or σεβόμενοι τὸν θεόν, the God-fearers who sympathised with Judaism and observed some of the Jewish customs. The hypothesis that there were two sorts of proselytes, that the term 'proselytes of the gate' was used by the rabbis to denote partial proselytes, has been abandoned on the whole.[90] The dividing line separated the full proselytes and the sympathisers, though Juvenal's outburst, for example, proves that frequently sympathy led to complete conversion.[91] The natural assumption is that there were many more sympathisers than true proselytes. The Roman authors often allude to the former. Josephus states that the vast wealth of the temple did not derive merely from the gifts of the Jews from all over the inhabited world, but also from those who worshipped God (σεβόμενοι τὸν θεόν).[92] This group is frequently mentioned in the Acts of the Apostles,[93] in one passage of which the group is said to have included eminent women.[94] A statement of Josephus, referred to above, also reveals that in Damascus very many women had become converts to the Jewish religion, though evidently not their husbands.[95] From the number of proselytes named

---

[89] For example Schürer, *op. cit.* III, pp. 175f.; Moore, *op. cit.* I, p. 348; Simon, *op. cit.*, p. 324.

[90] Schürer, *op. cit.* III, pp. 177ff.; Juster, *op. cit.* I, p. 275; Moore, *op. cit.* I, pp. 326, 340f.; Leon, *op. cit.*, p. 253; Kuhn, *op. cit.*, p. 731, note 31; for the Godfearers see further: K. Lake, *The Beginnings of Christianity*, Part I, Vol. V, 1933, pp. 84-96; B.J. Bamberger, *Proselytism in the Talmudic Period*, 1939, pp. 135ff., 289; W.G. Braude, *Jewish Proselyting in the First Five Centuries of the Common Era*, 1940, pp. 137f.; Lifshitz, *op. cit.*, pp. 77- 84; Grant, *op. cit.*, p. 61.

[91] Reinach, *op. cit.*, p. 292 : *Sat.* XIV. 96ff.

[92] *A.* XIV. 110.

[93] *Acts* 10:2, 22; 13. 16, 26, 43, 50; 16. 14; 17. 4, 17; 18. 7; once the expression σεβόμενοι προσήλυτοι *Acts* 13. 43; on this point see F.F. Bruce, *The Book of Acts*, 1954, p. 280; E. Haenchen, *Die Apostelgeschichte*, 1959, p. 355, note 5.

[94] *Acts* 17. 4, 12.

[95] Above p. 193; *B.* ii. 560.

in the Jewish catacombs of Rome it has been deduced that women in particular were attracted to Judaism, for of eight inscriptions found there which concern proselytes, six refer to women.[96] A contributing factor could be the fact that women, on the whole, were attracted by eastern religions, though it must be assumed that the female, like the male proselytes realised that Judaism occupied a very special position among the eastern religions and that it differed essentially from the others. The convert to Judaism sought something entirely different from the focal aspects of the eastern religions. Consequently I believe it incorrect to identify the attraction exercised by Judaism on women with that by other alien religions.[97] A more feasible explanation for the majority of proselytes being women is that it was easier for them than for men. After all only the men had to undergo circumcision.[98]

Furthermore the data from the Roman catacombs are too scarce to admit far-reaching conclusions. The same applies to any conclusions drawn from these data regarding the number of proselytes in general. Of the 554 inscriptions in the Roman catacombs listed by Frey, 8 make mention of a proselyte.[99] Leon says : We may safely conclude, on the basis of both literary and epigraphic sources, that the Roman Jews welcomed proselytes and that the Jewish community had a fair number of them.[100] That there were a fair number of them can be inferred from the literary, not the epigraphic sources. It must be admitted of the latter that "c'est fort peu", though one might add that great caution must be used in arguing ex silentio in this case, since the numerical ratio could be purely coincidental and could be refuted by later findings.[101]

---

[96] *CIJ* I, p. LXIII; cf. Leon, *op. cit.*, p. 256.

[97] Leon, *op. cit.*, p. 256. In his comments on the inscriptions in the catacombs of Rome, which mention more female than male proselytes, he refers to a pronouncement of Cumont, who, however discusses the cults of Isis and Cybele, F. Cumont, *Les religions orientales dans le paganisme romain*, 1929, p. 40; cf. Kuhn, *op. cit.*, p. 731; J. Munck, *Paulus und die Heilsgeschichte*, 1954, pp. 264f.; P. Dalbert, *Die Theologie der Hellenistisch-Jüdischen Missionsliteratur unter Ausschluss von Philo und Josephus*, 1954, p. 24: "Auch das Judentum zog nun seine Vorteile aus dieser Orient-Freundlichkeit"; Ch, Guignebert, *Le monde juif vers le temps de Jésus*, 1935, pp. 298f.

[98] Cf. Leon, *op. cit.*, p. 256; Simon, *op. cit.*, p. 330; Kuhn, *op. cit.*, p. 734; Moore, *op. cit.* I, p. 326.

[99] *CIJ* I, p. LXIII here the numbers are mentioned, which agree with those in Leon, *op. cit.*

[100] Leon, *op. cit.*, p. 256.

[101] Simon, *op. cit.*, p. 330.

Proof can also be found in the inscriptions in the catacombs that the Jews distinguished clearly between proselytes and sympathisers of Judaism who demonstrated this by observing certain of the Jewish customs. According to the inscriptions, only the proselytes were buried in the same place as the Jews. Only they were held to be Jews, not the others. The few who were buried along with the Jews therefore had made a choice which radically affected their whole way of living. Three rites made a man a full proselyte : circumcision, immersion in water (baptism) and the presentation of an offering in the temple.[102] The first must have been, "physiquement pénible et, pour un païen de l'époque, moralement humiliante".[103] The second symbolised the impurity of the non-Jew which had to be washed away before he could be fully admitted to Judaism. The third, which of course was only performed during the existence of the temple, was necessary because, as R. Eliazer b. Jacob puts it, a proselyte's atonement is yet incomplete until the blood (of his offering) has been tossed for him (against the base of the Altar).[104] Once the proselyte had definitely decided for Judaism and thereafter lived according to the prescripts of the law, he was isolated from his surroundings. He broke with his family and friends, as is evidenced by the words of Philo cited above. Se convertir au judaïsme, c'est rompre avec le monde : telle est du moins l'impression qu'en ont les contemporains.[105] A proselyte became "a naturalised citizen of a new religious commonwealth in which he is on full equality of rights and duties with born Jews".[106] C'était là pour un Romain une sorte d'émigration à l'intérieur : il était agrégé à un peuple chez lequel les pratiques religieuses étaient indissolublement liées au sentiment national.[107]

---

[102] On these three see : Schürer, *op. cit.* III, pp. 181ff.; Moore, *op. cit.*, I, pp. 331ff.; Str. Bill. I, pp. 106ff.; Kuhn, *op. cit.*, pp. 738f.; K. Lake, *op. cit.*, Part I, Vol. V, 1933, pp. 77ff.; Bamberger, *op. cit.*, pp. 42ff.; Braude, *op. cit.*, pp. 74ff.; *Enc. Jud.* 13, 1971, pp. 1183f.

[103] Simon, *op. cit.*, p. 486; Lerle, *op. cit.*, pp. 43ff. describes how painful and how dangerous circumcision was.

[104] *Keritot* 2. 1.

[105] Simon, *op. cit.*, p. 327.

[106] Moore, *op. cit.* I, p. 328.

[107] Frey, *CIJ* I, p. LXIII; cf. Frend, *op. cit.*, p. 211 : "There was an awareness that conversion to Judaism meant conversion to a way of life completely alien to that of Greco-Roman civilisation... It entailed rejection of all previous family ties, and, incidentally, contributions to the Jewish war-chest".

If one attempts to form a picture of what complete conversion to Judaism involved, one is astonished that so many took this step. In the ancient world itself this astonishment was always accompanied by vexation in the pagans, but even the Jews seemed to have looked on that conversion as something unnatural, as expressed, for example, in the parable of the stag who, untrue to his nature, remained in the neighbourhood of a herd of small livestock.[108] Perhaps with the amazement of gratitude, however, the rabbis did not hesitate to pass on the tradition that several of their pre-eminent leaders were proselytes or descended from them, such as Shemaiah, Avtalion, Aquila, the translator of the Bible, Meir, Akiva and two of his famous pupils.[109]

What inspired people to sympathise with, or be converted to Judaism? Did the Jews bend their efforts to this end, did they make propaganda, or was the attractive power of the Jewish faith and Jewish way of life something inherent? The former assumption is the more usual one, and it is taken almost for granted that the large number of proselytes and God-fearers was the result of energetic propaganda. Schürer repeatedly uses the term "Jewish propaganda" and gives what he believes to be a detailed description of it.[110] Juster says Judaism had a "besoin de se faire valoir, d'acquérir des adeptes pour sa foi", and speaks of an "ardeur prosélytique", of a "fougue prosélytique", of the "propagande juive", which made the number of semi and full proselytes greatly increase.[111]

---

[108] *Num. R.*, c. 8; cf. Lerle, *op. cit.*, pp. 13f.; Klausner, *op. cit.*, p. 50.

[109] Moore, *op. cit.* I, p. 347; Simon, *op. cit.*, p. 325; cf. Kuhn, *op. cit.*, p. 735 : "Simon, son of Gioras, the man who played an important role in the revolt of 70 A.D., mentioned several times by Josephus, known to Tacitus", *Hist.* V. 12; Bamberger, *op. cit.*, pp. 221ff., 238, 282; Art. *Proselytes, Encyclopaedia Judaica*, 13, 1971, pp. 1185f.

[110] Cf. for example Schürer, *op. cit.* III, pp. 150ff., 155ff., 162ff., 553ff.

[111] Juster, *op. cit.* I, pp. 253, 274, 277; Kuhn speaks of "eine lebhafte jüdische Mission" within the Diaspora, *op. cit.*, p. 731; Heinemann of "die Wirkung der jüdischen Propaganda", *op. cit.* p. 38; Lerle strongly emphasises the "Proselytengewinnung" of the Jews. They "versäumten keine Gelegenheit, um für ihre Religion zu werben", *op. cit.*, pp. 12ff.; cf. N. Bentwich, *Hellenism*, 1919, p. 142 : "For two hundred years and more, from the time of the Maccabees till the loss of national independence the Jews were preeminently a missionary people". From about 200 A.D., however, "the fear of disintegration and denationalization led to the gradual withdrawal of the Jewish people into itself and to the diminution of the proselytising which had been in the main the work of Hellenistic Jewry... But it must not be thought that the (missionary) activity ceased; the Haggadah of Tannaim and Amoraim is full of beautiful thoughts about proselytes..." (p. 298); similarly all sorts of commentaries on Jewish writings

There is no longer any communis opinio on this point nowadays. It was Munck in particular who argued that Judaism has never been a religion that engaged in missionary work. Naturally he does not deny that, in all ages, it was possible for non-Jews to be admitted to Judaism and that this often happened out of a general interest in eastern religions, "aber hierbei ist nicht von dem Ergebnis einer Mission die Rede. Das Judentum hat weder irgendeine Missionstheorie besessen, noch den Ruf dazu gefühlt, die Heiden in das auserwählte Volk aufzunehmen".[112] Munck is well aware that on this point he contradicts what many accept as established conceptions. Particularly he contests Schürer's argumentation. The issue then has to be the interpretation of concrete facts, but one might first consider whether it is plausible that the many proselytes and God-fearers known to us were won over exclusively by the recruiting power of Judaism itself, without the Jews having actively or deliberately exercised any influence to this end. When proselytes gradually or suddenly turned completely to Judaism, did they do this quite independently right from the first moment when they became aware of the faith and life of the Jews down to that final irrevocable moment of decision? Not, in my view, particularly likely.

Obviously, however, such reasoning is not a valid argument of proof. The question is whether any concrete information about missionary activity can be found. In the first place it must be admitted that the Jewish sources, specifically the rabbinical, contain hardly any manifest indications of organised missionary activities among the Jews. When Judaism and the earliest form of Christianity are compared in this regard, the difference is remarkable.[113] There is nothing in

---

assume that the Jews engaged in propaganda, for example, L. Cohn, *Die Werke Philos von Alexandria in deutscher Übersetzung*, II, 1910, p. 364, note 1; L.H. Feldman, *Josephus*, Vol. IX, p. 58 note a speaks of "the Jewish zeal for proselytism"; cf. also Guignebert, *op. cit.*, pp. 287ff., 295ff; J. Jeremias, *Jesu Verheissung an die Völker*, 1956, pp. 9-16.

[112] Munck, *op. cit.*, p. 259; similarly in *NTS* 1960, p. 115: "Judaism, which has never been a missionary religion". Practically no one agreed with Munck. Nock, however, seems to be quite impressed by Munck's argumentation. In a review on the book of H.J. Schoeps, *Paulus*, in which a connection is made between propaganda and pagan missions and Jewish piety, he points out that Munck "makes it clear that we should be cautious in inferring widespread efforts by Jews to convert Gentiles", *op. cit.* II, p. 929.

[113] Juster, for example, when speaking of "la propaganda juive", of "l'activité des missionnaires", immediately adds: "dont l'histoire nous reste d'ailleurs presque inconnue", *op. cit.* I, p. 254; cf. Moore, *op. cit.* I, pp. 323f.; K. Lake, *op. cit.*, Part. I, Vol. V, 1933, pp. 74f.: "There is no evidence at all that missionaries were ever sent out in the modern or Christian sense"; Braude, *op. cit.*, pp. 8, 38.

the sources to show that the Jews sent out individuals or groups
to act as missionaries among the pagans. This does not necessarily
preclude a certain amount of Jewish propaganda. The Jews lived in
smaller or larger groups in all parts of the Roman empire, both in
the towns and in the country. Many of them were acquainted with the
language and culture of their region and through their professions
and business were frequently in contact with non-Jews. Every Jew
does not have to be looked on as a fervent propagandist in order to
support the hypothesis that many could have attracted attention
through their own way of living. They could also have endeavoured
to win others to their way, and often successfully with all sorts of
people who were not so inwardly bound to the traditional religious
rites and customs, or who felt rather uncertain of themselves midst
the motley life of an ancient city. A powerful recruiting activity
could very easily have evolved then, without there being any question
of a missionary theory or of a systematic despatch of people to recruite
proselytes. A more feasible supposition is spontaneous campaigns of
individual Jews who felt such a compulsion in diverse relationships.

Indications of this type of missionary work on the part of Jews
are not lacking. Perhaps the allusion to this work made by certain
authors are most eloquent simply because they are expressed incidentally in quite a different context. The earliest, and I believe very
important, testimonial is to be found in a passage in Horace, cited
above, in which the poet alludes to the insistent conduct of Jews
towards people they want to include in their circle.[114] This is, indeed,
a "simple allusion à un prosélytisme trop insistant",[115] but of great
significance precisely because of its simplicity. This author from the
first century A.D. hereby reveals a familiarity with the conduct
of Jews in public or in all sorts of personal relationships. Apparently
he has had plenty of opportunity to observe "la rage de prosélytisme
qui distinguait alors les Juifs"[116] and assumes his readers are also
acquainted with it. Hence many scholars properly devote close attention to these verses in Horace. This is one of the earliest and most
important testimonials, if not the earliest and most important, of
deliberate, premeditated activities of Jews in this field.[117] Munck

---

[114] Reinach, *op. cit.*, p. 244 : *Sat.* I. 4. 142f.; see above pp. 129, 195.

[115] Isaac, *op. cit.*, p. 113.

[116] Reinach, *op. cit.*, pp. 244f.

[117] Cf. Leon, *op. cit.*, p. 250 : "That the Jews in Rome itself were energetic proselytisers
as early as the time of Augustus is clearly indicated by a well-known passage in the

should not, therefore, have ignored this observation, whilst Schürer, his opponent in polemics, does mention it.

The aforesaid statement of Valerius Maximus also clearly refers to attempts by the Jews to corrupt Roman morals by their exceptional activity (*Romanos inficere mores conati erant*).[118] Perhaps the reference is to members of the delegation sent by the Maccabean Simon to Rome in 140-139.[119] The verb *imbuere*, used by Tacitus in his previously quoted pronouncement on those who adopted the Jewish way of life, indicates deliberate Jewish activity. The translations sometimes rightly interpret this word *imbuere* as referring to education. Tacitus frequently uses it for "to teach".[120] Often this testimonial of Tacitus is therefore, also rightly, laid alongside of Horace's as proof of "the Jewish zeal for proselytism".[121] If all three pronouncements about Jewish recruiting activities taken from Roman authors of different periods are laid side by side, then it becomes more feasible that, behind the statements of other Roman authors about more or less far-reaching sympathy felt by many in their circles for Judaism, one might assume annoyance with proselytising even though not expressed explicitly by such as Seneca, Martial and Juvenal.

In this way, information from quite a different source is no longer so isolated, and it becomes more likely that it is based on historical fact. First, Josephus' statements. We have already seen how he praises the powerful attraction of Judaism. On a few occasions he explains the reasons for the large number of converts. Directly connected with the above, mention must first be made of Claudius' edict, referred to by Josephus. The emperor decrees that the Jews must everywhere be given the opportunity to observe the customs of their fathers without let or hindrance and continues : I enjoin upon them also by these presents to avail themselves of this kindness in

---

Satires of Horace" (I. 4. 140-143); Lerle, *op. cit.* p. 14 says in reference to this passage : "Die jüdische Aktivität in der Proselytenwerbung war so auffallend, dass sie bei Römern sprichwörtlich wurde"; cf. also Klausner, *op. cit.*, p. 49; Hospers-Jansen, *op. cit.*, p. 50; Schürer, *op. cit.* III, p. 164; Simon, *op. cit.*, p. 329; Hopfner, *op. cit.*, pp. 63ff.

[118] Reinach, *op. cit.*, p. 259 : Julius Paris, *Epitome* i. 3. 3; see above p. 196.

[119] Reinach, *op. cit.*, p. 259, note 3; Schürer, *op. cit.* III, p. 58; Juster, *op. cit.* I, p. 259, II, pp. 169f.; Lerle, *op. cit.*, p. 14, note 29.

[120] *Hist.* V. 5; see above p. 195; Reinach, *op. cit.*, p. 307 translates : "La première instruction qu'on leur donne..."; also Isaac, *op. cit.*, p. 118.

[121] Feldman, *Josephus*, Vol. IX, p. 58, note a; cf. Lerle, *op. cit.*, p. 14 : "Nach einer Notiz bei Valerius Maximus versuchte eine jüdische Gesandtschaft in Rom in so aufdringlicher Weise religiöse Propaganda zu treiben, dass sie ausgewiesen wurde".

a more reasonable spirit, and not to set at nought the beliefs about the gods held by other peoples (μὴ τὰς τῶν ἄλλων ἐθνῶν δεισιδαιμονίας ἐξουθενίζειν), but to keep their own laws.[122] If these words are historically true,[123] I believe it might be inferred that Claudius was also annoyed by Jewish propaganda that cast reflection on other religions. Since his aim was to restore peace and quiet in Alexandria, he thought it necessary to warn the Jews to cease their activities which caused unrest.

In one passage Josephus explicitly mentions the activities of a Jew who persuaded a very prominent proselyte to take the decisive step. Izates strongly sympathised with Judaism; he ardently desired to be converted to Judaism, completely, by circumcision. But his mother Helena feared the reactions of his subjects to such a step. She gained the support of the Jewish merchant Ananias, who nevertheless had started a recruiting campaign at the court. He "visited the king's wives and taught them to worship God after the manner of the Jewish tradition". As a result he was noticed by Izates, "whom he (Ananias) similarly won over with the co-operation of the women". Izates' mother had likewise been instructed by another Jew and had been brought over to their laws. But when Helena began to fear that if Izates became a full proselyte through circumcision, this would cause serious trouble in the realm, Ananias agreed with her. Then, however, another Jew named Eleazar, who came from Galilee and who had a reputation for being extremely strict when it came to the ancestral laws, urged him to carry out the rite.[124] Strangely enough Munck deals with this lengthy passage in Josephus in just one sentence: Und als einen besonderen Triumph für den jüdischen Bekehrungseifer führt Schürer den Übertritt des Königshauses von Adiabene zum Judentum an.[125] Schürer does indeed use these words.[126] No wonder, for here several Jews are named who attempted, in word and deed, to convert non-Jews and were successful. Moreover we are given a glimpse of the way it happened: propagandists were

---

[122] *A.* XIX. 290.

[123] Tcherikover, *op. cit.*, p. 413 says of these words specifically "not to behave with contempt toward the gods of other peoples", that they "evidence the trustworthiness of the document".

[124] *A.* XX. 34f., 38ff., 43.

[125] Munck, *op. cit.*, p. 264.

[126] Schürer, *op. cit.* III, p. 169; cf. Str.-Bill. I, p. 926; Bamberger, *op. cit.*, pp. 225ff., 278.

not systematically chosen and given a certain message, but merchants or other itinerant Jews personally took the initiative. Nothing was organised. In his zeal for Judaism the one went further than the other. But there can be no doubt whatsoever that this was recruiting activity. And if, in this regard, Munck stresses that this flocking of "Greeks" to Judaism can very easily be explained as part of a general interest in oriental religions and that neither Jewish missionary activity nor zeal to win proselytes need be presumed, then he contradicts the statement of Josephus, who considers the event so important that he frequently, and evidently with some pride, refers to the members of the royal house of Adiabene and the tokens of their disposition towards Judaism in other passages as well as in the lengthy one in *Ant.* XX.[127]

There is most likely another reference to recruiting activity in the above cited statement of Josephus about the Jewish colony in Antioch : they were constantly attracting to their religious ceremonies multitudes of Greeks, and these they had in some measure incorporated with themselves.[128] These words could be interpreted as testimonial of the inherent attraction of the Jews' religious ceremonies : by celebrating these ceremonies the Jews naturally attracted many of their community. But the verb προσάγω presupposes an activity of the subject, sometimes literally, sometimes figuratively.[129] For the medium used here, Liddell and Scott give the meanings "bring or draw to oneself, attach to oneself, bring over to one's side". The German translation "heranziehen" also points clearly in this direction.[130]

The New Testament also contains two passages of importance for our subject. The first is *Mt.* 23.15 : Woe to you, scribes and Pharisees, hypocrites ! for you traverse sea and land to make a single proselyte, and when he becomes a proselyte, you make him twice as much a child of hell as yourselves. Munck's comment is that this text is

---

[127] *B.* ii. 520, IV. 567, V. 55, 119, 147, 252f., VI. 355, 356; for the source of these stories : A. Schalit, Eine aramäische Quelle in den Jüdischen Altertümern, in the collection *Zur Josephus-Forschung*, 1973, pp. 394ff.

[128] *B.* VII. 45; see above p. 193.

[129] Cf. the use of this verb in the N.T. : *Mt.* 18. 24; *Luc.* 9. 41; *Acts* 16. 20; *1 Pt.* 3. 18. The last text in particular can be of importance for the interpretation of the passage in Jos.; cf. E.G. Selwyn, *The First Epistle of St. Peter*, 1946, p. 196.

[130] For example Schürer, *op. cit.* III, p. 167; Klausner, *op. cit.*, p. 51; Munck, *op. cit.*, p. 264.

one of the obscure passages in *Mt.* 23.[131] True, certain problems
are attached to the exegesis of these words. In the first place the
question is whether they were spoken by Jesus himself, or were
ascribed to him by the later congregation. That is difficult to say
with absolute certainty. In my view there is not a single conclusive
argument against the former alternative, and the criterion set by
those who say they were not the words of Jesus is often subjective.
Kümmel recognises this danger, but believes that verse 13 can be
said with some considerable certainty to be compatible with the
preaching of Jesus in the original form. Still, he queries whether
verse 15, with its "Verteufelung" of the opponents, might not belong
to those parts of *Mt.* 23 which must be interpreted as "irrtümliche
Verzeichnung der Wirklichkeit ,als Verrat an Jesu Gebot der Feindes-
liebe und als Aufgeben des Glaubens". But do not such verses as
13 and 23, as above, and 27 pose problems when tested against this
criterion?[132] The choice is significant for our subject, since it helps
determine the period in which this statement was made.

Was it directed against the missionary zeal of the Pharisees, or
against the fact that they make of a proselyte twice as much a child
of hell as themselves? The latter, in my opinion. What, then, do these
words signify? In what way do the proselytes become even worse
children of hell than the Pharisees? Probably because, in this missionary zeal, they place their faith even more surely in the excellence
of the observance of the commandments.

Admittedly there are problems, but this text is not obscure as
regards the answer to our question. C'est en tout cas un éloquent
hommage à l'esprit prosélytique des rabbins, either in the time of
Jesus, or in the time of the earliest congregation.[133] And it will not
do to minimise the significance of these words by attributing them
to a political manoeuvre in the family history of Herod.[134] Too much

---

[131] Munck, *op. cit.*, p. 260.

[132] W.G. Kümmel, *Die Weherufe über die Schriftgelehrten und Pharisäer* (*Matthäus 23, 13-36*) in the collection published by W.P. Eckert, N.P. Levinson and M. Stöhr, *Antijudaismus im Neuen Testament?*, 1967, pp. 144-147.

[133] Simon, *op. cit.*, p. 329; he calls the verse "suffisamment clair", p. 483; Klausner, *op. cit.*, p. 49 also speaks of "diesen klaren und entschiedenen Worten"; cf. Art. Prose-lytes, *Encycl. Judaica*, vol. 13, 1971, p. 1183; W.C. van Unnik, De ἀφθονία van God in de oudchristelijke literatuur, *Mededelingen der Kon. Ned. Akad. van Wet., Afd. Letterkunde, Nieuwe Reeks, Deel 36*, No. 2, 1973, pp. 27f.

[134] Munck, *op. cit.*, p. 261; cf. Simon, *op. cit.*, p. 483.

is said in general about the missionary activities of the Pharisees
to warrant that. The passage is not aimed against that, but against
the doctrine and the way of life of the perpetrators of this activity,
who therefore bring to ruin the proselytes they make. The reference
to the sometimes very poor results of this activity illustrates how
passionately it was carried out. Everything possible was done to
win one single person if necessary.[135]

Seen in this light, this text is an important testimonial about
the fervent recruiting of proselytes by the Pharisees in Palestine
in the first century A.D. That means it was not merely practised
in the Diaspora, but also from Palestine. It has been said that this
testimonial stands completely alone and can hardly be accurate and,
indeed, there is hardly anything else to support it. One statement
made by Josephus in his lengthy description of the conversion of
several members of the royal house of Adiabene could, however, serve
well as an illustration of this verse : Eleazar who came from Galilee
and who had a reputation for being extremely strict when it came
to the ancestral laws ($\pi\acute{a}\nu\nu$ $\pi\epsilon\rho\grave{\iota}$ $\tau\grave{a}$ $\pi\acute{a}\tau\rho\iota\alpha$ $\delta\omega\kappa\hat{\omega}\nu$ $\dot{a}\kappa\rho\iota\beta\acute{\eta}s$).[136] Here
again the person in question is a Palestinian Jew who strictly observes
the commandments, who, after a long journey, makes a proselyte
of an eminent personage. The second text of the New Testament
that is of importance is *Rom.* 2.17-21. Obviously Paul is alluding
here to the strong self-confidence of a Jew, who knew the law, in his
community. Such an instructor ($\pi\alpha\iota\delta\epsilon\upsilon\tau\acute{\eta}s$) and teacher ($\delta\iota\delta\acute{a}\sigma\kappa\alpha\lambda\sigma s$)
was highly conscious that he had something to offer others. He brought
light to those who walked in darkness, he could lead the blind, and
guide along the right path the foolish and the babes, for he possessed,
in the law, the embodiment of everything which man sought regarding
knowledge and truth in the ancient world. If he were convinced
of that, he must also have been aware of a special mission. It must
have meant a great deal to him to pass on to others what he possessed
in the law.

On the one hand, these words of Paul mark the profoundest motives
which inspired the Jews in their zeal to pass on the best of what they
had, and on the other hand the ostensible arrogance which the pagans
must have discerned in the pretentions of these instructors and

---

[135] See further on this text within the framework of our subject : Juster, *op. cit.* I,
p. 254; Mommsen, *op. cit.*, p. 492; Schürer, *op. cit.*III, p. 163; Str.-Bill. I, pp. 924ff.;
Lovsky, *op. cit.*, p. 27; Bamberger, *op. cit.*, pp. 267-273.

[136] *A.* XX. 43, see above p. 205.

teachers who felt called upon to convert the uninstructed pagans. Diverse Jewish writings contain testimonials of the vocation to pass on to the pagans the riches and the assurance of the law. The *Wisdom of Solomon* speaks of Israel as the nation of those through whom the imperishable light of the law was to be given to the world.[137] The *Sibylline Oracles* look forward to the time when the nation of the Mighty God shall be again powerful, that nation which shall be to all mortals the guide of life.[138] Note how lyrical Josephus becomes when he concludes his second book against Apion with an eulogy on the Jewish laws addressed to Epaphroditus, a devoted lover of truth, to whom he dedicates his work. What a wealth of exceedingly beautiful thoughts has been passed on to others by the Jews through those laws.[139] Philo likewise reveals on many occasions that he is filled with the magnificence of the law. To this he testifies, not only to keep Jews in danger of renegading faithful to the law, but also to convince the pagans of the virtue, the constancy, the inner richness of a life according to that law. This holds good for many Jewish writings from before and after that time. They try to hold on to the Jews by pointing out to them what they possess, but also, more or less explicitly, to attract pagans to Judaism by informing them of the exceptional worth of a life lived according to the law. In many Jewish-Hellenistic writings there is definitely a trend that is not only inwardly preservative, but also outwardly proselytising.[140]

There are few explicit pronouncements on missionary activity in the rabbinical writings. They are not entirely lacking, however, for the winning of proselytes is mentioned as meritorious work. R. Eleazar said : if one brings a proselyte (to God) it is as though he created him.[141] An exhortation to recruit proselytes can be discerned in the

---

137 *Wisdom of Solomon* 18. 4.

138 *Sib. Or.* 3. 194f.; cf. *Enoch* 105. 1.

139 *Ap.* ii. 291-296.

140 In my opinion Munck is incorrect in saying that "diese jüdische Literatur ihr Ziel innerhalb der eigenen religiösen Gemeinschaft hat", *op. cit.*, p. 262. Here he carries on a controversy against Schürer, *op. cit.*III, pp. 554ff. On the other hand Simon, *op. cit.*, p. 484 is correct in saying : "Il est arbitraire de postuler que la littérature judéo-alexandrine est nécessairement destinée à une catégorie unique de lecteurs Juifs ou païens et d'opter, sans autre preuve, pour une destination juive..." Cf. Lerle, *op. cit.*, p. 13 : "Die schriftstellerisch tätigen Juden haben eine Literatur hervorgebracht, deren missionarische Tendenz ausser Zweifel steht"; see also G.N. Box, *Judaism in the Greek Period*, 1932, pp. 56-76.

141 *Gen. R.* 84. 4, *Midrash Rabbah*, Genesis, translated by H. Freedman, II, 1939,

words of the Rabbis : Let the left (weaker) hand repulse but the right
hand always invite back; not as Elisha, who thrust Gehazi away
with both hands.[142] Here missionary activity is not spoken of in
so many words, but it is presumed, and various other statements
in the Talmud and the Midrashim could also be so construed to mean
that proselytes were often won by the deliberate efforts of Jews.

This is not the place to deal at length with what the rabbis said
about proselytes,[143] nor is it essential, strictly speaking, to the present
subject as a whole, since there is general agreement as to what the
rabbis thought about them. Needless to say there is no unanimity
in the Talmud as to the opinion about proselytes. No fixed doctrine
is laid down on this subject. It contains divergent opinions of rabbis
from different periods which cannot be arranged in a given schema.
The opinions were influenced by all sorts of factors of time, place,
circumstances.[144]

Somewhere Moore says : Speaking generally, the tone of utterances
about proselytes is friendly, though not unduly enthusiastic.[145] Unfavourable utterances do, indeed, occur, but only seldom. One such
is the oft-quoted statement of R. Ḥelbo from the latter part of the
third century A.D. : Proselytes are as hard [to endure] for Israel as

---

p. 771; cf. *Yev.* 48b : R. Jose said : "one who has become a proselyte is like a child
newly born".

[142] *Sanh.* 107b; *Sot.* 47a.

[143] For further information on this point see Moore, *op. cit.* I, pp. 323-353; S. Bialo-
blocki, *Die Beziehungen des Judentums zu Proselyten und Proselytismus*, 1930; B.J. Bamberger, *Proselytism in the Talmudic Period*, 1939; W.G. Braude, *Jewish Proselyting
in the First Five Centuries of the Common Era*, 1940; M. Avi-Yonah, *op. cit.*, pp. 81-83;
K. Schubert, *op. cit.*, pp. 193-247, especially pp. 216ff.

[144] Werner, *op. cit.*, pp. 180ff. correctly points out again and again that the views
expressed in the Talmud naturally differ very often on this point : "Man kann den
Talmud nicht wie ein systematisch aufgebautes Rechtskorpus oder wie eine Dogmatik
zitieren, sondern man muss alle Stellungnahmen der freien Diskussion mit anführen".
Rightly, too, he therefore reproaches the collaborators on the series *Forschungen zur
Judenfrage*, e.g. K.G. Kuhn and G. Kittel, that they used "ein selektives Auswahl-
prinzip" and hence gave a very distorted picture of the *Spätjudentum* in order thus
to strengthen with ostensibly scientific arguments the national-socialistic prejudices
concerning Jewry (see especially pp. 180-183, 190-193). On the other hand, however,
one must of course admit that "there is strong evidence in rabbinic sources that some
authorities were opposed to the concept of conversion and proselytes. Those scholars
who ignore or obliterate such evidence cannot be justified", Art. Proselytes in *Encycl.
Judaica*, 13, 1971, p. 1185.

[145] Moore, *op. cit.* I, p. 342; Bamberger calls this "a decided understatement",
op. cit., p. 169.

a sore.[146] This rabbi could have been enchanted with a witty pun on the root of the Hebrew verb. סחם and, therefore, did not intend that his words should be as venomous as they sound.[147] Such an unfavourable opinion was not unique. In the days of the Messiah, no more proselytes were admitted, for when the war of Gog and Magog will come... each one of them will remove the precepts from himself and go on his way.[148] Because of their sins, the proselytes reduce the necessary merit of Israel and thus they delay the advent of the Messiah.[149] Ever and again such unfavourable or sceptical presumptions prove to derive from apparently bad experience with the motives for conversion to Judaism and from a profound distrust of the constancy of the proselytes. It was all too well known that proselytes were not always inspired by pure motives. R. Nehemiah taught : Both a man who became a proselyte for the sake of a woman and a woman who became a proselyte for the sake of a man, and similarly, a man who became a proselyte for the sake of a royal board or for the sake of joining Solomon's servants, are no proper prose-lytes.—Neither lion-proselytes (see 2 *Kings* 17.24.41), nor dream-proselytes (a dream commanded them to become Jews), nor the proselytes of Mordecai and Esther (*Esth.* 8.17) are proper proselytes unless they become converted at the present time (i.e. in the dire days after the war of Hadrian).[150] R. Ḥiyya said : Do not have any

---

[146] *Yev.* 47b; *Kid.* 70b, and also in various other places.

[147] Str.-Bill. I, p. 930; Moore, *op. cit.* I, pp. 346f.; Kuhn, *op. cit.*, p. 738; Simon, *op. cit.*, p. 318; Bamberger notes : "R. Ḥelbo's saying is the opinion of an individual and a most atypical one. He was not the only scholar who was hostile to converts, but such were very few" (*op. cit.*, p. 164)—"he was in no sense expressing a general opinion" (p. 287). This writer points out that, as opposed to the very large number of pronouncements made by the rabbis which evidence a friendly attitude towards the proselytes, there are only a very few that are unfavourable, *op. cit.*, pp. 143ff., 161ff., 274ff., 286; see further on the statement of Ḥelbo, Braude, *op. cit.*, pp. 42ff., 47f.

[148] *Av. Zar.* 3b; *Yev.* 24b.

[149] *Nid.* 13b.

[150] *Yev.* 24b; cf. *TJ. Kid.* 65b; Moore, *op. cit.* I, pp. 336ff.; *Enc. Jud.* 13, 1971, p. 1186. Epictetus is probably alluding to a feigned conversion to Judaism when he holds up in warning to his fellow Stoics a man "halting between two faiths", of whom it must be said : "He is not a Jew, he is only acting the part", *Diatr.* ii. 9. 19-21. Some believe that here Epictetus is referring to people who pretended to become Christians in order to obtain all sorts of advantages, see for example W.A. Oldfather, *Epictetus, Discourses*, Vol. I, 1961, pp. XXVI, 272f. I believe it more probable that here Epictetus is alluding to feigned conversions to Judaism. The expression παραβαπτισταί, counterfeit baptists, is in my opinion not a conclusive argument against this, cf. Th. Zahn, *Der*

faith in a proselyte until 24 generations have passed because the inherent evil is still within him.[151] R. Eliezar's experience with proselytes had probably often been bad, for he says : A proselyte has a strong inclination to evil.[152] Nonetheless he maintained : When a person comes to you in sincerity to be converted, do not reject him, but on the contrary encourage him.[153] Enforced mass conversions such as that of the Idumaeans under John Hyrcanus, of the Ituraeans under Aristobulos and probably also of the nation of Adiabene under Izates could hardly have produced steadfast professors. It is not surprising, therefore, that the rabbis sometimes set high standards to avoid rash conversions. That did not always help, for frequently the proselytes turned renegade, and the rabbis sometimes commented bitterly on this. As we have already noted, Josephus was acquainted with persons "lacking the necessary endurance".[154]

Although there is no lack of critical comments about proselytes in the rabbinical writings, it is all the more remarkable that in general "the tone of utterances about proselytes is friendly".[155] Repeatedly they are said to be welcome in the Jewish nation. Josephus says so explicitly, as noted above.[156] In the rabbinical writings occur frequent exhortations to understand and appreciate the weaknesses of proselytes, to remember they have cut themselves off from their old surroundings and therefore to show them special attention and love in their new ones. The powerful motive for the Jews' love for proselytes was held to be the special love of the God of Israel for all who joined that nation. God's love is graphically expressed in

---

Stoiker Epiktet und sein Verhältnis zum Christentum, 1894; K. Kuiper, *Epictetus en de Christelijke moraal, Verslagen en Mededelingen der Kon. Akad. van Wetenschappen, Afd. Letterkunde, vierde reeks, zevende deel*, jrg. 1906, pp. 370-405; A. Bonhöffer, *Epiktet und das Neue Testament*, 1911, pp. 41f., 72f., 273; D.S. Sharp, *Epictetus and the New Testament*, 1914, p. 134; D.C. Hesseling, *De Kolleges van Epictetus*, 1931, p. 140; J. Souilhé, *Epictète, Entretiens*, 1948, pp. LXIIIf.; Frend, *op. cit.*, p. 213; Hopfner, *op. cit.*, p. 66; McEleney, *op. cit.*, p. 332.

[151] *Mid. Ruth Zuta* on 1. 12.

[152] *BM* 59b.

[153] *Mekh. Amalek* 3.

[154] *Ap.* ii. 123, see above p. 193 ; see on the strict requirements Simon, *op. cit.*, pp. 321f; on the complaints about apostasy Moore, *op. cit.* I, pp. 341f., 346ff.; Klausner, *op. cit.*, pp. 59ff.; Simon, *op. cit.*, p. 319; Bamberger, *op. cit.*, pp. 165ff.

[155] Praiseworthy comments on the proselytes are frequent, e.g. *Tanḥ. Lekh Lekhah* 6; *Num. R.* 8. 9; *Mid. Ps.* 146. 8.

[156] *Ap.* ii. 209f., 261; see above p. 193.

a late homiletical Midrash in the parable of the stag that returned each evening with a herd of the king's small livestock to its stall, and which the king therefore loved deeply.[157] The rules of conduct laid down by the law for the stranger are frequently declared to be particularly applicable (e.g. *Ex.* 22.1; 23.9; *Deut.* 10.19). One must love a proselyte, despite his natural depravity.—Now who is greater— he who loves the king or he whom the king loves? One must say— he whom the king loves, as the verse says : and He loves the stranger (the proselyte).—The proselytes are dear to God, for our father Abraham was not circumcised till he was 99 years old. If he had been circumcised at 20 or 30 a man could have become a proselyte only at a lower age than 20 or 30; therefore God postponed it in his case till he arrived at the age of 99, in order not to bolt the door in the face of proselytes to come.[158]

It is inferred from *Lev.* 19.34 that no one must harm a proselyte. You shall not say to him : Yesterday you were an idolater and now you have come beneath the wings of the Shekinah. As the native born is one who takes upon him all the commandments of the law, so the proselyte is one who takes upon him all the commandments of the law. This is again followed by the exhortation to place oneself in the feelings of a proselyte. For the Israelites, who were strangers in Egypt, that could not have been difficult.[159]

The proselyte is often said to come under the wings of the Shekinah. This expression is strongly reminiscent of the oft-repeated words of the psalms, "shelter in the shadow of God's wings", which belongs to the life of the pious, or is ardently desired by him.[160] But if it is said of someone who converts a proselyte that he brings him under the wings of the Shekinah, the reference was probably to the words of Boaz to Ruth about the God of Israel, under whose wings she came to shelter.[161] Ruth's case was proof for the rabbis that God gladly accepts a person who wishes to approach him and that, if Israel

---

[157] *Num. R.* c. 8, *Midrash Rabbah*, Numbers, translated by Judah J. Slotki, I, 1939, pp. 204f.; cf. Bamberger, *op. cit.*, p. 155; see above p. 201.

[158] From *Mekh. Nezikim (Mishpatim)* 18; cf. *BM* 58b, 59b; *Gen. R.* 46, init.; cf. Bamberger, *op. cit.*, pp. 149ff., 154ff.

[159] *Sifra* on *Lev.* 19. 34.

[160] *Ps.* 57. 2; cf. *Ps.* 17. 8; 36. 8; 61. 5; 91. 4.

[161] *Ruth* 2. 12, *Ruth R.* in loc.

does his will, He also admits the righteous of the pagan world to his people.[162]

The rabbis' attitude to proselytes was, of course, not uniform. The one was more critically inclined towards them than the other. Different standards were set for them. In this respect, the difference between the schools of Hillel and Shammai is well-known. That the former was more friendly towards proselytes than the latter is evidenced by the words quoted about it in the Mishnah: Be of the disciples of Aaron, loving peace and pursuing peace, loving mankind and bringing them nigh to the Law. Further evidence is contained in the different answer to someone's request: Make me a proselyte, on condition that you teach me the whole Torah while I stand on one foot. Shammai repulsed him with the builder's cubit which was in his hand. Hillel said: What is hateful to you do not to your neighbour: that is the whole Torah, while the rest is the commentary thereof; go and learn it.[163]

Taking the data on proselytism as a whole, they prove to be drawn from so many different sources, so many different periods, that they provide a clear picture of the missionary activity of Judaism and of the continued preoccupation of Jewish and pagan writers with proselytism in practice and in thought throughout the ages. Naturally it was stronger in the one region or period than in the other, but the testimonials from the first century B.C. and the first two centuries A.D. are plain enough to warrant the assumption that the recruiting of proselytes and, in any case, the conversion of rather large numbers of them was never interrupted in those times. Some draw a sharp distinction between the periods before and after 70 A.D. Strack-Billerbeck, for example, assumes in his commentary on Mt-23.15 that after 70 the synagogue was not very actively engaged in recruiting converts. It persevered in passivity. The internal construction of the Jewish communities was difficult enough without attracting strangers to them. This, however, does not necessarily decide the question about the historical accuracy of Mt. 23.15. This verse deals with the pre-70 period, and even though the rabbinical writings do not provide such definite evidence about proselytising in that

---

[162] Cf. Str.-Bill., I, pp. 20f., 928i; Simon, *op. cit.*, pp. 319f.; D. Daube, *The New Testament and Rabbinic Judaism*, 1956, pp. 131f., 135f.; Bamberger, *op. cit.*, pp. 195-199; Braude, *op. cit.*, pp. 49ff.

[163] *Avot* 1. 12; *Shabb.* 31a; cf. Daube, *op. cit.*, pp. 108ff., 115; Bamberger, *op. cit.*, pp. 278, 280.

period, the propaganda literature of Jewish Hellenistic derivation speaks enough about Jewish missionary activity. Its success is demonstrated not only by the utterances of Josephus, but also by those of Seneca and Dio Cassius.[164] If, however, Seneca and Dio Cassius are put forward as witnesses to the existence of proselytism before 70, with equal justification the statements of Juvenal and Tacitus can be cited to demonstrate that the winning of proselytes was not abandoned after 70. The fierce attacks of Juvenal prove that proselytes were not unique in his time and circles. When he reproaches these circumcised persons that they despise Roman law, but learn and observe and revere Israel's code and all from the sacred volume of Moses, Juvenal's words reveal that he knew about the instruction that preceded conversion. In particular the *ediscere*, which means to learn thoroughly or by heart, suggests this. The events of 70 evidently did not deter certain Jews from winning proselytes, nor many pagans in Rome from taking the decisive step.[165] Even the war of 132-135 did not constitute a serious deterrent in this respect, as is evidenced by the aforesaid ruling of Antoninus Pius, which certainly was aimed against proselytism and hence was apparently necessary even after 135 A.D.[166]

Consequently it is an established fact that, about the beginning in the Christian era, there were many proselytes and God-fearers, of part won over by the inner strength of the faith and life of the Jews, in part, too, persuaded by deliberate recruiting. On the one hand this proves that Judaism was very attractive to many, and on the other that proselytism must often have accentuated sharply the relationship between Jews and non-Jews. The way in which the Jews passed judgment on other religions or on the depravity of the pagan society in writings, in words and deeds and taught their opinions to others must have greatly irritated the pagans. Tacitus' tirade about the *contemnere deos, exuere patriam, parentes, liberos, fratres vilia habere*, which was implanted in these *transgressi in morem eorum*,[167] is clear enough in this respect and probably reproduces

---

[164] Str.-Bill. I, pp. 924-926; cf. J. Schniewind, *Das Evangelium nach Matthäus*, ⁹1960, p. 231 on *Mt.* 23. 15 : "seit der Zerstörung Jerusalems ist ein Wandel des Urteils (about the proselytes) eingetreten".

[165] Reinach, *op. cit.*, p. 292; see above pp. 194f. and also p. 204 on *imbuere* in Tacitus.

[166] Cf. Simon, *op. cit.*, pp. 316f., 326f., 60f.; Bamberger, *op. cit.*, pp. 31, 40f., 143, 275ff., 279, 283ff., 291, 297f.; Braude, *op. cit.*, p. 38, see above p. 135.

[167] *Hist.* V. 5.

very well what many non-Jews thought. They saw nothing but an expression of unbounded arrogance in the conduct of the Jews. The way the Jews expressed themselves must often have confirmed the pagans in their opinions. When Jews sharply gave utterance to their contempt of the pagan faith and way of life, this must often have been taken personally to heart. And when the rabbis allotted the proselytes a very bad position in their classification of people and presumed their "natural depravity", this sounded like a contempt for the pagans which must have offended them excessively.[168] It is not always easy to say when an honest, passionate consciousness of having something valuable to offer, which should be passed on if at all possible, transforms into personal aggressiveness. The readiness to use the latter qualification depends on the degree of understanding felt for the former. This applies not only to an opinion about proselytism in the ancient world, but also about it today.[169] One who cannot appreciate the profoundest motives for the winning of proselytes will readily find serious charges to be levelled against the fanatical, arrogant Jews, who were always a threat to the peaceful tolerance of society. One who endeavours to view the background to that exclusiveness so offensive to outsiders will hesitate to make such charges. Nevertheless, one will still be able to admit that "eine der Ursachen für die unzähligen Konflikte des Alltagslebens lag in der Aktivität der Proselyten-werbung".[170]

The data on proselytism and pagan reaction to it prove irrevocably, however, that Judaism had a great power of attraction for many. Obviously this does not mean that they all made a definitive choice

---

[168] Cf. Moore, *op. cit.*, pp. 335, 343; Hellenistic-Jewish writings such as *The Letter of Aristeas, The Sibylline Oracles, The Wisdom of Solomon* often reveal a strong Jewish consciousness when they compare the moral life of the Jews and the pagans; cf. Dalbert, *op. cit.*, pp. 23, 137, 140, 142, 143; Bamberger, *op. cit.*, p. 64; Braude, *op. cit.*, pp. 108f.

[169] Bludau speaks of "der aggressive wie polemische Charakter" of Judaism, *op. cit.*, p. 48, of "der mitunter etwas aufdringliche Bekehrungseifer der Juden", p. 52, on the clashes in Alexandria : "Wir werden sagen können, dass das Kapital von Hass, das die Juden sich durch ihr Verhalten aufgespeichert hatten, damals reichliche Zinsen getragen hat", p. 79; Lazare speaks of "un orgueil immense" in the Jews, *op. cit.*, p. 9, of "l'indomptable et tenace patriotisme d'Israël", p. 15.

[170] Lerle, *op. cit.*, p. 23; cf. A. Schlatter, *Die Theologie des Judentums nach dem Bericht des Josefus*, 1932, of which pp. 237-251 are included in the collection *Zur Josephus-Forschung*, herausgeg. von A. Schalit, 1973, pp. 190-204; p. 203 : "Der grosse Erfolg der jüdischen Missionsarbeit war nicht der wirksamste Grund, der den Antisemitismus hervortrieb; doch ist auch er an seiner mächtigen und dauernden Ausbreitung wesentlich beteiligt".

and thereafter remained true to it. Many renegaded, as we have
seen above. Besides, there must have been a great diversity in the
interest shown in Judaism. Sometimes it was probably only a passing
thought on the observance of one single Jewish custom. Somewhere
Philo says that a festival was celebrated every year on the island
Pharos to commemorate the creation of the Septuagint and that
this festive gathering was not only attended by the Jews, but also
by a great crowd of non-Jews. According to him, everyone crossed to
the island to glorify the place where this translation first shed its
light.[171] It is also quite possible that many of these non-Jews did not
know why the festival was held, but just wanted a pleasant outing.

The Sabbath was particularly suited for adoption as the only
custom. No doubt some were deeply impressed by the way the Jews
lived on that day and by their services in the synagogue. It appears
from diverse literary works of supporters and opponents that the
Sabbath was a special day for many non-Jews.[172] But this did not
imply that they were converts to Judaism. It may be inferred from
many papyri that there were many pagan observers of the Sabbath,
people who adopted the Jewish customs of the Sabbath but, for
the rest, went on living and believing as pagans.[173] In this case the
tie with Judaism was very thin. On the other hand, proselytes who
made their choice in the time of Hadrian, when joining the Jewish
nation brought no advantages and only meant danger, were accounted
the only true proselytes by the rabbis.[174] Between such extremes
lay a vast range of gradations in interest and motives. Still, it is
certain that among the pagans who so often fiercely attacked the
Jews there were also many who, for varying reasons, felt attracted
to Judaism. Many were impressed by the great age of Judaism, by
its proclamation of one God, by the exceptional standard of life
and society in accordance with the Jewish laws, by the fixed line
in their way of thinking and living, by their courage in life and in
death. It may be apologetical exaggeration on the part of Philo,
but he could just be right in his proud contention that one can say
of the Jewish laws what cannot be said of any other institution:
they attract and win the attention of all, of barbarians, of Greeks,

---

[171] *Mos.* ii. 41.

[172] *Ap.* ii. 282; *Mos.* ii. 21; Suet., *Tib.* XXXII; the informations in Horace, Ovidius,
Seneca, see above pp. 124ff.

[173] *CPJ* III, pp. 52ff.; I, pp. 94ff.

[174] Cf. Moore, *op. cit.* I, p. 337.

of dwellers on the mainland and islands, of nations of the east and
the west, of Europe and Asia, of the whole inhabited world from
end to end.[175]

It was necessary to discuss proselytism at some length. If a certain
amount of attention is devoted to it, the impression that a fervent
anti-Semitism prevailed in the ancient world is eradicated. Apparently
Judaism repelled many, but greatly fascinated others. "Animosité
haineuse d'une part, sympathie admirative de l'autre, ce sont les
deux réactions entre lesquelles oscille l'opinion païenne à l'égard du
judaïsme".[176]

Moreover this proselytism reconfirms the observation that racial
theories had no influence whatsoever on the choice for or against
Israel. Once a person acquired a sympathy for this nation, racial
prejudices in no way prevented him from joining Israel or from sharing
its isolation in the ancient world. If one recognised the true motives
behind the "auto-ségrégation"[177] of Judaism and agreed with their
truth, there was no longer any reason for anti-Semitism. The deepest
reason for pagan anti-Semitism lay in the offense caused by the
strangeness of the Jews in ancient society. Those who emigrated
to this strangeness lost their anti-Semitic feelings. But they had
to prepare themselves against the ridicule, hatred and contempt
aimed against the separateness of the Jews that were now about
to be turned equally against them, for now they had become part
of that *sceleratissima gens*.[178]

---

[175] *Mos.* ii. 17, 20.
[176] Simon, *op. cit.*, p. 244.
[177] Simon, *op. cit.*, p. 493.
[178] Seneca, Reinach, *op. cit.*, p. 263 : Augustinus, *De Civ. Dei* VI. 11.

BIBLIOGRAPHY

Anderson, J.G.C., *Cornelii Taciti de origine et situ Germanorum*, 1938.

Anti-Semitism, Art. in *Encyclopaedia Judaica*, 3, 1971, pp. 87ff.

Antisemitismus, Art. in *Reallexikon für Antike und Christentum*, Bd. I, 1950, pp. 469ff.
(J. Leipoldt).

Applebaum, S., Cyrenensia Judaica, *The Journal of Jewish Studies*, 13 (1962), pp. 31-43.

Avi-Yonah, M., *Geschichte der Juden im Zeitalter des Talmud*, 1962.

Bamberger, B.J., *Proselytism in the Talmudic Period*, 1939.

Baron, S.W., *A social and religious history of the Jews*, Vol. I, ⁴1962, II, ⁴1962.

Barth, M., *Jesus, Paulus und die Juden*, 1967.

Behm, J., Art. νῆστις in G. Kittel, *Theologisches Wörterbuch zum Neuen Testament*
(*Th. W.N.T.*), Bd. IV, 1942, pp. 925-935.

Bell, H.I., *Jews and Christians in Egypt*, 1924.

——, *Juden und Griechen im römischen Alexandreia*, ²1927.

Beltrami, A., *L. Annaei Senecae ad Lucilium Epistulae Morales*, II, 1949.

Bentwich, N., *Hellenism*, 1919 (in the Series *Movements in Judaism*).

Bergmann, J., *Jüdische Apologetik im neutestamentlichen Zeitalter*, 1908.

Bertholet, A., *Die Stellung der Israeliten und der Juden zu den Fremden*, 1896.

Bevan, E.R., *A History of Egypt under the Ptolemaic Dynasty*, 1927.

Biablocki, S., *Die Beziehungen des Judentums zu Proselyten und Proselytismus*, 1930.

Bickermann, E., Ritualmord und Eselskult, *Monatsschrift für Geschichte und Wissenschaft des Judentums* 71 (1927), pp. 171ff., 255ff.

Bludau, A., *Juden und Judenverfolgungen im alten Alexandria*, 1906.

Böhl, F.M.Th., Die Juden im Urteil der griechischen und römischen Schriftsteller,
Theologisch Tijdschrift, 48 (1914), pp. 371ff., 473ff.

Bolkestein, H., Het "anti-semietisme" in de oudheid, *De socialistische gids*, 21 (1936),
pp. 152ff.

Bonhöffer, A., *Epiktet und das Neue Testament*, 1911.

Bonsirven, J., *Le judaïsme palestinien au temps de Jésus-Christ*, 1935.

Bo Reicke, *Neutestamentliche Zeitgeschichte*, 1965.

Bousset, W., *Die Religion des Judentums im neutestamentlichen Zeitalter*, ²1906.

Box, G.H., *Judaism in the Greek Period*, 1932.

Box, H., *Philonis Alexandrini In Flaccum*, 1939.

Braude, W.G., *Jewish Proselyting in the First Five Centuries of the Common Era*, 1940.

Bruce, F.F., *The Book of Acts*, 1954.

Brüne, B., *Flavius Josephus und seine Schriften in ihrem Verhältnis zum Judentume,
zur griechisch-römischen Welt und zum Christentume*, 1969.

Burr, V., *Tiberius Iulius Alexander*, 1955.

Burton, A., *Diodorus Siculus, Book I, A Commentary*, 1972.

Cohn, L., *Die Werke Philos von Alexandria in deutscher Übersetzung*, I, 1909.

Dalbert, P., *Die Theologie der Hellenistisch-Jüdischen Missionsliteratur unter Ausschluss
von Philo und Josephus*, 1954.

Daube, D., *The New Testament and Rabbinic Judaism*, 1956.

Deissmann, A., *Licht vom Osten*, ⁴1923.

Delaunay, F., *Philon d'Alexandrie. Écrits historiques*, 1867.

Delling, G., *Studien zum Neuen Testament und zum hellenistischen Judentum*, 1970.

Dittenberger, W., *Orientis Graeci Inscriptiones selectae*. Bd. I, II, 1903-1905 (= *OGIS*).

Drachmann, A.B., *Atheism in Pagan Antiquity*, 1922.

Drexler, H., Untersuchungen zu Josephus und zur Geschichte des jüdischen Aufstandes, *Klio* 19 (1925), pp. 277-312.

Dudley, D.R., *The World of Tacitus*, 1968.

Engers, M., Der Brief des Kaisers Claudius an die Alexandriner, *Klio* 20 (1926), pp. 168 -178.

Feldman, L.H., *Josephus, Jewish Antiquities, Books XVIII-XX*, Loeb Classical Library, Vol. IX, 1965.

——, *Studies in Judaica. Scholarship on Philo and Josephus (1937-1962)*, n.d.

Fischer E./Kittel, G., *Das antike Weltjudentum*, 1943.

Foakes Jackson, F.J., *Josephus and the Jews*, 1930.

Freese, J.H., Suetonius, *History of Twelve Caesars*, 1930.

Frend, W.H.C., *Martyrdom and Persecution in the Early Church*, 1965.

Frey, J.B., *Corpus Inscriptionum Judaicarum* (= *CIJ*), I, 1936.

Friedländer, M., *Das Judentum in der vorchristlichen griechischen Welt*, 1897.

Fuchs, L., *Die Juden Ägyptens in ptolemäischer und römischer Zeit*, 1924.

Ginsburg, M.S., *Rome et Judée*, 1928.

Goodenough, E.R., *The Politics of Philo Judaeus*, 1967.

Grant, M., *The Jews in the Roman World*, 1973.

Green, P., *Juvenal, The Sixteen Satires*, 1967.

Guignebert, Ch., *Le monde Juif vers le temps de Jésus*, 1935.

Guterman, S.L., *Religious Toleration and Persecution in Ancient Rome*, 1951.

Guttmann, M., *Das Judentum und seine Umwelt*, 1927.

Hare, D.R.A., *The Theme of Jewish Persecution of Christians in the Gospel according to St Matthew*, 1967.

Harnack, A., *Der Vorwurf des Atheismus in den drei ersten Jahrhunderten, Texte und Untersuchungen*, Bd. 28, 1905.

Haenchen, F., *Die Apostelgeschichte*, 1959.

Heinemann, I., Art. *Antisemitismus* in *Paulys Real-Encyclopädie der classischen Altertums-wissenschaft*, Supplementband V, 1931, pp. 3-43.

——, *Philons griechische und jüdische Bildung*, 1932.

Heinisch, P., *Griechentum und Judentum im letzten Jahrhundert vor Christus*, 1908.

Hengel, M., *Judentum und Hellenismus*, 1969.

Hennecke, E.-Schneemelcher, W., *Neutestamentliche Apokryphen in deutscher Übersetzung*, II, ³1964.

Herzfeld, L., *Handelsgeschichte der Juden des Altertums*, ²1894.

Hesseling, D.C., *De Kolleges van Epictetus*, 1931.

Highet, G., *Juvenal the Satirist*, 1954.

Holsten, W., Art. *Antisemitismus* in *Religion in Geschichte und Gegenwart*³, I, 1957, pp. 456-459.

Hopfner, Th., *Die Judenfrage bei Griechen und Römern*, 1943.

Hospers-Jansen, A.M.A., *Tacitus over de Joden*, 1949.

Humphreis, R., *The Satires of Juvenal*, 1958.

Hunt, A.S., and Edgar, C.C., *Select Papyri*, I, 1952.

Jacob, B., Art. *Antisemitismus* in *Encyclopaedia Judaica*, II, 1928, pp. 958-972.

Jacoby, A., Der angebliche Eselskult der Juden und Christen, *Archiv für Religions-wissenschaft*, 25 (1927), pp. 265ff.

Jeremias, J., *Jesu Verheissung an die Völker*, 1956.

Juster, J., *Les Juifs dans l'empire romain*, I, II, 1914.

Klausner, J., *Von Jesus zu Paulus*, 1950.

Kuhn, K.G., Art. προσήλυτος in G. Kittel-G. Friedrich, *Theologisches Wörterbuch zum Neuen Testament (Th.W.N.T.)*, Bd. VI, 1959, pp. 727-745.

Kuiper, K., Epictetus en de christelijke moraal, *Verslagen en Mededelingen der Koninklijke Akademie van Wetenschappen, Afd. Letterkunde, vierde reeks, zevende deel,* jrg. 1906, pp. 370-405.

Kümmel, W.G., *Die Weherufe über die Schriftgelehrten und Pharisäer (Matthäus 23, 13-36)* in *Antijudaismus im Neuen Testament? Exegetische und systematische Beiträge*, Heraus gegeben von W.P. Eckert, N.P. Levinson und M. Stöhr, 1967.

Lake, K., *The Beginnings of Christianity*, Part I, Vol. V. 1933.

Laqueur, R., *Der jüdische Historiker Flavius Josephus*, 1920.

Lazare, B., *L'Antisémitisme, Son histoire et ses causes*, 1894.

Leipoldt, J., *Antisemitismus in der alten Welt*, 1933.

Leon, H.J., *The Jews of ancient Rome*, 1960.

Lerle, E., *Proselytenwerbung und Urchristentum*, 1960.

Lifshitz, B., Du nouveau sur les "sympathisants", *Journal for the Study of Judaism*, 1 (1970), pp. 77-84.

Lohse, E., Art. σάββατον in G. Kittel-G. Friedrich, *Theologisches Wörterbuch zum Neuen Testament (Th.W.N.T.)*, Bd. VII, 1964, pp. 1-35.

Lovsky, F., *Antisémitisme et mystère d'Israel*, 1955.

Maier, P.L., Sejanus, Pilate and the Date of the Crucifixion, *Church History*, 37 (1968), pp. 3-13.

Masqueray, P., *Xénophon, Anabase*, I, 1952.

Mauersberger, A., *Tacitus, Germania*, n.d.

McEleney, N.J., Conversion, Circumcision and the Law, *New Testament Studies*, April 1974, pp. 319-341.

Meyer, J.W., *Publius Cornelius Tacitus, Historien*, 1958.

Mitteis, L., und Wilcken, U., *Grundzüge und Chrestomathie der Papyruskunde*, I, 2, 1912.

Momigliano, A., *Claudius, The Emperor and his Achievement*, 1934.

Mommsen, Th., *Römische Geschichte*, V, ⁴1894.

Foot Moore, G., *Judaism*, I, II, 1927.

Munck, J., *Paulus und die Heilsgeschichte*, 1954.

Musurillo, H.A., *The Acts of the Pagan Martyrs*, 1954.

Neusner, J., *A History of the Jews in Babylonia. The Parthian Period*, 1965.

Nock, A.D., *Essays on Religion and the Ancient World*, Selected and edited by Z. Stewart, I, II, 1972.

Parkes, J., *The Conflict of the Church and the Synagogue*, 1934.

——, *The Foundations of Judaism and Christianity*, 1960.

Phillips Barker, E., *Seneca's Letters to Lucilius*, 1932.

Piana, G.la, Foreign Groups in Rome during the First Centuries of the Empire, *Harvard Theological Review*, 20 (1927), pp. 183-403.

Poliakov, L., *Histoire de l'antisémitisme*, 1955.

Radin, M., *The Jews among the Greeks and Romans*, 1915.

Reinach, Th., *Textes d'auteurs grecs et romains relatifs au judaisme*, 1895 (reprint 1963).

Rostovtzeff, M., *The Social and Economic History of the Roman Empire*, ²1957.

Safrai, S. and M. Stern in co-operation with D. Flusser and W.C. van Unnik, *The Jewish People in the First Century*, Vol. One of *Compendia Rerum Iudaicarum ad Novum Testamentum*, 1974.

Schalit, A., *König Herodes. Der Mann und sein Werk*, 1969.

——, *Eine aramäische Quelle in den jüdischen Altertümern*, in *Zur Josephus-Forschung*, 1973, pp. 394ff.

Schlatter, A., *Die Theologie des Judentums nach dem Bericht des Josephus*, 1932.

Schreckenberg, H., *Bibliographie zu Flavius Josephus*, 1968.

Schubert, K., *Das Selbstverständnis des Judentums in der rabbinischen Theologie*, *Judaica*, 12 (1956), pp. 193-247.

Schürer, E., *Geschichte des jüdischen Volkes im Zeitalter Jesu Christi*, I, ⁴1901, II, ⁴1907, III, ⁴1909.

Scramuzza, V.M., *The Emperor Claudius*, 1940.

Seaver, J.E., *Persecution of the Jews in the Roman Empire (300-438)*, 1952.

Selwyn, E.G., *The First Epistle of St. Peter*, 1946.

Sevenster, J.N., *Do you know Greek? How much Greek could the First Jewish Christians have known?*, 1968.

Sharp, D.S., *Epictetus and the New Testament*, 1914.

Sherwin White, A.N., *Racial Prejudice in Imperial Rome*, 1967.

Simon, M., *Verus Israel*, ²1964.

Sizoo, A., *Reizen en trekken in de oudheid*, 1962.

Smallwood, E.M., Some Notes on the Jews under Tiberius, *Latomus*, 15 (1956), pp. 314-329.

——, *Philonis Alexandrini Legatio ad Gaium*, 1961.

——, *Documents illustrating the principates of Nerva Trajan and Hadrian*, 1966.

Souilhé, J., *Epictète, Entretiens*, 1948.

Stähelin, F., *Der Antisemitismus des Altertums*, 1905.

Stauffer, E., Art. ἄθεος in G. Kittel, *Theologisches Wörterbuch zum Neuen Testament (Th.W.N.T.)*, Bd. III, 1938, pp. 120-122.

Stern, M., Strabo's Remarks on the Jews (summarised by Mervyn Lewis), *Immanuel*, 1 (1972), pp. 42-44.

Strack, H.L., und Billerbeck, P., *Kommentar zum Neuen Testament aus Talmud und Midrasch*, 1922ff.

Syme, R., *Tacitus*, 1958.

Sijpesteijn, P.J., The Legationes ad Gaium, *The Journal of Jewish Studies*, 15 (1964), pp. 87-96.

Tcherikover, V.A., *Hellenistic Civilization and the Jews*, 1961.

——, The Decline of the Jewish Diaspora in Egypt in the Roman Period, *The Journal of Jewish Studies*, 14 (1963), pp. 1-32.

——, and A. Fuks, *Corpus Papyrorum Judaicarum (CPJ)*, I, 1957, II, 1960, III, 1964.

Thiaucourt, C., Ce que Tacite dit des Juifs, *Revue des études juives*, 19 (1889), pp. 56ff.

Thoma, C., Die Weltanschauung des Josephus Flavius, *Kairos, Neue Folge*, 11 (1969), pp. 39ff.

Travers Herford, R., *Das Pharisäische Judentum*, 1913.

van Unnik, W.C., *Het Jodendom in de verstrooiing*, in J.H. Waszink, W.C. van Unnik, Ch. de Beus, *Het oudste Christendom en de antieke cultuur*, I, 1951, pp. 537ff.

——, De ἀφθονία van God in de oudchristelijke literatuur, *Mededelingen der Koninklijke*

Nederlandse Akademie van Wetenschappen, Afd. Letterkunde, Nieuwe Reeks, Deel 36,
No. 2, 1973, pp. 19ff.

Werner, F., Das Judentumsbild der Spätjudentumsforschung im Dritten Reich, Dargestellt anhand der "Forschungen zur Judenfrage", Bd. I-VIII, *Kairos, Neue
Folge,* 13 (1971), pp. 161ff.

Wessely, C., Das Ghetto von Apollinopolis Magna, *Studien zur Paläographie und Papyruskunde,* 13 (1913), pp. 8ff.

Wilcken, U., Zum alexandrinischen Antisemitismus, *Abhandlungen der philologisch-
historischen Klasse der königl. Sächsischen Gesellschaft der Wissenschaften,* 27 (1909),
pp. 781-839.

Wilken, R.L., Judaism in Roman and Christian Society, *The Journal of Religion,* 47
(1967), pp. 314ff.

Willrich, H., *Juden und Griechen,* 1895.

——, Hekataios von Abdera und die jüdischen Literaten, Chapter three of *Judaica,
Forschungen zur hellenistisch-jüdischen Geschichte und Litteratur,* 1900.

Wolff, M., Het oordeel der Helleensch-Romeinsche schrijvers over oorsprong, naam en
viering van den sabbath, *Theologisch Tijdschrift,* 44 (1910), pp. 162ff.

Yoyotte, J., L'Égypte ancienne et les origines de l'antijudaïsme, *Revue de l'histoire
des religions,* 147 (1963), pp. 133ff.

Zahn, Th., *Der Stoiker Epiktet und sein Verhältnis zum Christentum,* 1894.

Zucker, H., *Studien zur jüdischen Selbstverwaltung im Altertum,* 1936.

TRANSLATIONS USED

The translations used are from The Loeb Classical Library, except where otherwise indicated.

Cicero

In Catilinam I-IV, Pro Murena, Pro Sulla, Pro Flacco. Translated by L.E. Lord, 1964.

Pro Milone, In Pisonem, Pro Scauro, Pro Fonteio, Pro Rabirio Postumo, Pro Marcello, Pro Ligario, Pro Rege Deiotaro. Translated by N.H. Watts, 1958.

De Natura Deorum, Academica. Translated by H. Rackham, 1960.

Dio Cassius

Roman History. Translated by E. Cary, 1954.

Diodorus of Sicily

Diodorus of Sicily, Vol. XII, Translated by F.R. Walton, 1967.

Horace

Satires, Epistles, Ars Poetica. Translated by H.R. Fairclough, 1961.

Josephus

Vol. I, The Life-Against Apion. Translated by H.St.J. Thackeray, 1961.

Vol. II, The Jewish War, Books I-III. Translated by H.St.J. Thackeray, 1961.

Vol. III, The Jewish War, Books IV-VII. Translated by H.St.J. Thackeray, 1961.

Vol. IV, Jewish Antiquities, Books I-IV. Translated by H.St.J. Thackeray, 1961.

Vol. V, Jewish Antiquities, Books V-VIII. Translated by H.St.J. Thackeray and R. Marcus, 1958.

Vol. VI, Jewish Antiquities, Books IX-XI. Translated by R. Marcus, 1958.

Vol. VII, Jewish Antiquities, Books XII-XIV. Translated by R. Marcus, 1961.

Vol. VIII, Jewish Antiquities, Books XV-XVII. Translated by R. Marcus and A. Wikgren, 1963.

Vol. IX, Jewish Antiquities, Books XVIII-XX. Translated by L.A. Feldman, 1965.

Juvenal

Juvenal and Persius. Translated by G.G. Ramsey, 1969.

Macrobius

The Saturnalia. Translated by P. Vaughan Davies, 1969.

Martial

Epigrams. Translated by W.C.A. Ker, 1961.

Petronius

Petronius. Translated by M. Heseltine, 1930.

Philo

Vol. I, *On the Creation-Allegorical Interpretation*, Books I-III.
Translated by F.H. Colson and G.H. Whitaker, 1949.

Vol. II, *On the Cherubim-The Sacrifices of Abel and Cain-The Worse Attacks the Better-The Posterity and Exile of Cain*. Translated by F.H. Colson and G.H. Whitaker, 1950.

Vol. III, *The Unchangeableness of God-On Husbandry-Noah's Work as a Planter-On Drunkenness-On Sobriety*. Translated by F.H. Colson and G.H. Whitaker, 1954.

Vol. IV, *The Confusion of Tongues-The Migration of Abraham-Who is the Heir of Divine Things?-The Preliminary Studies*. Translated by F.H. Colson and G.H. Whitaker, 1949.

Vol. V, *On Flight and Finding-On the Change of Names-On Dreams* I and II. Translated by F.H. Colson and G.H. Whitaker, 1949.

Vol. VI, *On Abraham-On Joseph-Moses* I and II. Translated by F.H. Colson, 1950.

Vol. VII, *The Decalogue-The Special Laws* I-III. Translated by F.H. Colson, 1950.

Vol. VIII, *The Special Laws IV-On Virtues-On Rewards and Punishments*. Translated by F.H. Colson, 1954.

Vol. IX, *That Every Honest Man is Free-On the Contemplation of Life-On the Eternity of the World-Against Flaccus-Apology for the Jews-On Providence*. Translated by F.H. Colson, 1954.

Only for the *Legatio ad Gaium* have I used the translation of E.M. Smallwood instead of The Loeb Classical Library (see Bibliography).

Philostratus

Life of Apollonius of Tyana. Translated by F.C. Conybeare, 1927.

Plato

Eutyphro, Apology, Crito, Phaedo, Phaedrus. Translated by H.N. Fowler, 1966.

Pliny

Natural History, Vol. IV. Translated by H. Rackham, 1952.

Plutarch

The Parallel Lives. Translated by B. Perrin, 1967.

Morialia, Vol. II. Translated by F.C. Babbitt, 1962; Vol. VIII. Translated by P.A. Clement, 1969.

Seneca

Ad Lucilium Epistulae Morales. Translated by L.M. Gummere, 1953.

The quotations from Seneca by Augustine: *The City of God against the Pagans*. Translated by W.M. Green, Vol. II, 1963.

Strabo

Geography. Translated by H.L. Jones, Vol. VII, 1961.

Suetonius
   The Lives of the Caesars. Translated by J.C. Rolfe, Vol. I, 1970; Vol. II, 1959.

Tertullian
   Apology, De Spectaculis. Translated by T.R. Glover, 1953.

Tacitus
   Agricola and *Germania.* Translated by M. Hutton, 1970.
   Histories. Translated by C.H. Moore, 1962.
   Annals. Translated by J. Jackson, 1962-'63.

   The quotations from *Jubilees* and *The Sibylline Oracles* are from R.H. Charles, *The Apocrypha and Pseudepigrapha of the Old Testament*, Vol. II, 1913.
   The quotations from 1 and 2 *Maccabees* and *The Wisdom of Solomon* are from *The Apocrypha of the Old Testament, Revised Standard Version*, 1957.
   The quotations from the *Mishnah* are from H. Danby, *The Mishnah*, 1933.

   The quotations from the *Babylonian Talmud* are from Rabbi Dr I. Epstein. *The Babylonian Talmud.*

INDEX OF QUOTATIONS

DATE DUE

HIGHSMITH   # 45220